AIDS and the Church

Also by the same authors

AIDS: A Manual for Pastoral Care
by Ronald H. Sunderland and Earl E. Shelp

A Biblical Basis for Ministry
edited by Earl E. Shelp and Ronald H. Sunderland

AIDS and the Church

The Second Decade

Earl E. Shelp
and
Ronald H. Sunderland

Westminster/John Knox Press
Louisville, Kentucky

Book design by Kristen Dietrich

Published by Westminster/John Knox Press
Louisville, Kentucky

This book is printed on acid-free paper that meets the American National Standards Institute Z39.48 standard. ♾

PRINTED IN THE UNITED STATES OF AMERICA

9 8 7 6 5 4 3 2 1

Library of Congress Cataloging-in-Publication Data

Shelp, Earl E., 1947–
AIDS and the church : the second decade / Earl E. Shelp and Ronald H. Sunderland.
p. cm.
Includes bibliographical references.
ISBN 0-664-25202-8

1. AIDS (Disease)—Patients—United States—Pastoral counseling of. 2. AIDS (Disease)—Religious aspects—Christianity.
I. Sunderland, Ronald, 1929– . II. Title.
BV4460.7.S54 1992
261.8'321969792—dc20 91-39062

To the growing number of colleagues throughout the church with whom we share ministry to people touched by HIV/AIDS, and who share with us their theological insights on that ministry as it opens new vistas of faith and discipleship to God's people.

Contents

Preface

The shadow of HIV/AIDS grows longer. As we embark upon the second decade of experience with this public health crisis in the United States and around the world, it seems appropriate to review the course to date and anticipate what lies ahead. We have attempted to perform this task for a religious audience in this revised and expanded edition of *AIDS and the Church.* Much has happened since 1986, when the original manuscript was written. Some of the scientific, medical, epidemiological, psychosocial, economic, and religious changes are reported in the following chapters. As the original text was revised, we were not surprised by the changes required in the historical introduction (Chapter 1) and in the medical/scientific information, which here appears in two chapters (Chapters 2 and 3) instead of the original one. We were surprised, however, that comparatively few revisions seemed indicated in the biblical and theological chapters (4 and 5). The chapter on ministry also has been expanded (Chapter 6). Chapter 7 is a new discussion of HIV/AIDS outside the United States, particularly in the developing world. The final chapter is an expansion of the original "Concluding Reflections." In each chapter we have sought to include information and perspectives that should be helpful to God's people as we confront familiar and new challenges occasioned by an evolving HIV/AIDS epidemic.

Much has changed in our lives since 1986. Our scholarly and pastoral interests have centered on HIV/AIDS. Most of our time is committed to learning about HIV/AIDS, developing specialized AIDS ministries, and reporting on our work in journal articles and books. The work is compelling. What we are learning about HIV disease as a chronic, debilitating disease appears to have implications for ministry to people touched by other chronic, debilitating diseases like, for example, Alzheimer's disease, stroke, cancer, and mental or physical impairments of both adults and children. HIV/AIDS has become a prism for us through which we try to understand finitude and faith.

We have noted elsewhere that the diagnosis of Jay Jones with AIDS in early 1985 drew us into this arena. Jay lived with AIDS from April 1985 to June 1989. We miss him. He was an insightful and valued colleague and friend. We never thought at the beginning that HIV/AIDS would so preoccupy us or command our attention for so long. We speak of HIV/AIDS metaphorically in terms of an astronomical black hole: it grasps and magnetically draws into itself all that comes within reach. The magnetic pull is the lives of the people being touched directly by HIV/AIDS and the complexity of the issues illuminated by this multifaceted crisis. We are dedicated to continue our efforts to learn about HIV/AIDS and to interpret our experiences for others.

Our readers have honored us with invitations to participate in workshops and symposia across the country. We have learned through these excursions that God's people in small towns and large cities are discovering for themselves what faith and discipleship require of them in the midst of this crisis. These hosts and workshop participants have taught us more than we have taught them. They have inspired us. We thank God for their commitment and creativity. We are pleased that the congregation-based AIDS Care Team ministry that we pioneered in Houston has been a model for similar programs in communities large and small. As long as people with AIDS invite us and the dedicated lay people who serve with us into their homes, we will continue to learn and share our lessons with others.

We hope that a second revision of this text will not be required, but there is no reason to think that the crisis will not be worse five or even ten years from now. Of course, we pray that the unexpected and unforeseen will occur—a vaccine or cure will be found and made available to people throughout the world. We even would celebrate the development of therapies that would permit people to live normally for a long time. At present, however, these developments are too distant to be anticipated. Thus, we may again put pen to paper during the second decade of HIV/AIDS to offer an interim assessment of developments and the evolving challenges the epidemic presents to the people of God.

So many people have contributed to our understanding of HIV/AIDS and its significance to the church that it is impossible to acknowledge our debt to them all. Some are not even known by name. We have learned of them by second-person testimony. Nevertheless, we thank them all for their contribution to our work. Our lives have been enriched by their charity toward us. This volume, accordingly, represents a collaborative effort to interpret Christian identity and mission in a world with HIV/AIDS.

1

The Evolving HIV/AIDS Crisis

From the vantage point of ten years of experience, it may be difficult to recall the earliest days of the HIV/AIDS epidemic. News reports of "fast lane" gay men being stricken and succumbing to devastating diseases tended to be dismissed as random events or curiosities for physicians. It was almost impossible in those days to imagine or foresee that these reports were heralding an important chapter in the history of infectious diseases. It is equally important from a faith and moral perspective that relatively few people seemed concerned about the first untimely deaths.

Much has changed since 1981, when what would be named acquired immune deficiency syndrome (AIDS) was first described in the United States. The retroviruses that render a human host susceptible to a variety of conditions now associated with AIDS have been identified, named (human immunodeficiency viruses: HIV-1 and HIV-2), and increasingly understood. The human behaviors by which HIV can be transmitted from person to person have been established. Information and educational campaigns to avoid and reduce a person's risk for infection have made "condom" a household word. The most significant change of all, however, is the relentlessly steadily growing number of people whose lives are being affected by AIDS.

When the first edition of this book was being written in 1986, we thought it important to introduce people with AIDS through the story of Robert, who died soon after the original manuscript was completed. We considered it important then for members of religious communities to know people, even if by proxy, whose lives were being transformed by a retrovirus. We were so committed to this strategy as a means for God's people to overcome stereotypes and negative attitudes about people with HIV disease that we devoted our first book on the subject to it.[1]

To continue that approach in this volume now seems artificial. The stories of people living with HIV/AIDS have become commonplace in the print and visual media. The landmark announcement of Rock Hudson's diagnosis and subsequent death in 1985 opened a floodgate of journalistic and public interest in the effects of this epidemic on the lives of the famous and the humble. Published accounts have helped the public to acknowledge, even if belatedly, that HIV/AIDS is affecting people from all walks of life. The most powerful means by which this awareness is achieved, however, tends to be through a friend's or family member's disclosure of HIV infection or AIDS diagnosis. When HIV/AIDS comes home in this way, it is no longer possible to pretend that this public health crisis is someone else's problem. As the story of HIV/AIDS grows longer and more heterogeneous, unfortunately, fewer people must rely on print or television biographies to meet and know the HIV/AIDS epidemic face to face. As of December 1989, 14 percent of adults said that they know someone with HIV infection or AIDS. This percentage has increased steadily since the National Health Interview Survey began in August 1987. The proportion who knew someone with AIDS increased for several groups by December 1989: those 18–29 years of age (from 11% to 14%), females (from 12% to 15%), white adults (from 11% to 14%), black adults (from 13%

to 17%), and those with more than twelve years of education (from 17% to 20%). Not only is it increasingly likely that a person will know someone with HIV/AIDS; more and more people are experiencing the death of someone to AIDS.[2]

By the end of 1990, just months short of the official tenth anniversary of the epidemic in the United States, the death toll surpassed 100,000. Estimates of the number of people infected with the AIDS virus range between 750,000 and 1,500,000, thus guaranteeing that the disruption, debilitation, and death are far from over, given the current state of therapeutics and vaccine development. Against this background and in the light of a predictable future, preventing the spread of HIV disease and controlling the development of AIDS have become the highest public health priorities, both in the United States and in the 176 nations linked through the World Health Organization's Global Program on AIDS. Yet it is a mistake to consider the epidemic only from the perspective of public health.

Epidemics do not occur in a vacuum. They take place in a social context. The church is part of the social context of HIV/AIDS. The church has been and continues to be challenged by the specific characteristics of this epidemic to reflect on its identity and mission. The integrity and witness of the body of Christ are on the line in its collective and individual member responses to the HIV/AIDS crisis and particularly to people touched by HIV/AIDS. The initial failure to be a prophetic voice or a healing and comforting presence ought to be confessed and must not be perpetuated. There is no question about the church's responsibility in the midst of epidemic disease or the need for ministry it is called to offer. The church's willingness to acknowledge this responsibility beyond words and its readiness to give and receive ministry, however, may be less clear.

During the first five or six years of the epidemic, few denominations spoke officially about the rapidly worsening crisis. Popular preachers with access to the media, however, were quick to declare AIDS to be God's judgment on gay men and other sinners. The denominational silence that seemingly allowed these preachers to set a theological interpretation to the epidemic in the public mind began to break during 1986–1987. Declarations and resolutions calling for research, education, and compassion were issued by major denominations, providing, in effect, a countervoice to widely publicized judgments. However, the church was slow to speak in an enlightened manner or to forge a compassionate response to the HIV/AIDS epidemic. Although this is regrettable and inconsistent with the church's calling, it is not unprecedented.

Cultural Reactions to Infectious Disease

For the past 150 years in the United States, negative religious and moral attitudes have been a characteristic part of the social response to infectious diseases and the people who suffer them. Charles Rosenberg has chronicled the nation's response to the cholera epidemics in 1832, 1849, and 1866, for example. Cholera is a devastating disease characterized by diarrhea, acute spasmodic vomiting, painful cramps, consequent dehydration, cyanosis, and possibly death within hours or days following the onset of symptoms that appear without warning. Unlike HIV, the organism that causes cholera *(Vibrio cholerae)* is easily spread by any pathway to the digestive tract (food, water, hands). Also unlike AIDS, cholera claimed relatively few lives. But like AIDS, according to Rosenberg, "It was novel and terrifying, a crisis demanding a response in every area of American life and thought."[3]

During the epidemic of 1832, cholera was said by many Americans to be a scourge of the sinful. "Respectable" people had little to fear. Only intemperate, dirty people whose behavior predisposed them to cholera were at risk. This perception of the link between moral judgment and vulnerability to disease reflected and reinforced prevailing patterns of thought. Cholera was viewed as a consequence of sin, an inevitable and inescapable judgment of God upon people who violated the laws of God. Cholera was not seen as a public health problem; it was an indication of God's displeasure with the people who contracted the disease.[4]

In the epidemic of 1849, the connection between disease and vice still persisted. The belief endured that disease is an expression of God's judgment upon persons and nations corrupted by materialism and sin. But unlike the cholera epidemic of 1832, the needs of people orphaned or made destitute by the disease were not ignored by private charities and committees of "Christian gentlemen." Food, money, clothing, and other forms of assistance were collected and distributed. Some churches joined with these ad hoc committees of lay people, receiving collections for the sick and impoverished. These compassionate ministries were performed even though the victims of cholera were considered guilty of intemperance, gluttony, lechery, or alcoholism. The sickness or death of a so-called respectable person was considered anomalous and conveniently ignored.[5]

The nation's third epidemic of cholera, in 1866, was explained more in scientific than in moral terms. The theory that cholera was caused by a microorganism transmitted to the water supply in feces and vomit gained credibility but not full acceptance. Personal hygiene, sanitation, disinfection, and quarantine became important ways to control the emerging epidemic. Prayer and fasting, stalwarts of previous battles against cholera, were relied upon less in an era of developing scientific knowledge and increased power to combat infection. Thus, as physicians and public accepted an organic cause for cholera, the hand of God was no longer blamed, and the belief that moral failure predisposes people to disease lost influence.[6]

This interaction of religious values and social response to infectious disease has not been restricted to cholera. Allan M. Brandt has shown that this pattern of interpretation and reaction applies equally, if not more so, to venereal disease.[7] Within the past hundred years in the United States, it was commonly understood that sexually transmitted diseases, principally gonorrhea and syphilis, were divine punishment upon persons who willfully broke the moral code of sexual responsibility. When God is perceived as the dispenser of judgment, then efforts, and the people who undertake them, to control or eliminate the alleged punishment come to be regarded as anti-God. And when science defeats God with a cure or treatment, God finds a new way to express displeasure. Evangelist Billy Graham reflected this thinking as recently as in 1982: "We have the Pill. We have conquered venereal disease with penicillin. But then along comes Herpes Simplex II. Nature itself lashes back when we go against God."[8] It is implicit in this view that sexual restraint and behavior modification, due to fear if not conscience, are the preferred ways to control and combat sexually transmitted diseases. A consequence of this view is that people afflicted with a sexually transmitted disease suffer doubly: the physical effects of the disease itself and the psychological effects of being stigmatized.[9]

Scientific and therapeutic efforts are undermined when this attitude prevails. During the 1930s, people with syphilis were refused admission to hospitals, tacitly affirming the view that these people were morally tainted and less deserving of care. Afflicted persons, rather than (and in some instances in addition to) the etiologic biological organism, became the focus of attack.[10] By controlling the intemperate individuals seen to be carriers or transmitters of disease, the welfare of the rest of society could be protected. Respectable moral persons were felt to be safe until nonsexual means of transmission were discovered. Then calls for the social isolation of carriers were issued. Nevertheless, the attitude persisted that venereal disease was a disease that preeminently affected others—other races, other classes, other ethnic groups. Blame easily was placed on people different from the accuser. Women were favorite targets, because they were supposed to practice sexual restraint and to uphold prevailing sexual mores. When controlling prostitutes did not decrease the incidence of disease, the role of "good girls" was acknowledged—men totally escaped responsibility—and a profound change in American sexual morality had to be confronted during the 1930s and 1940s.[11]

Educating the public about the effectiveness of condoms as a means to prevent disease was inhibited because of the Roman Catholic Church's opposition to birth control. Fear of disease and pregnancy, not prophylaxis, was the standard weapon against disease. But fear was not very effective. Venereal disease spread. As more "innocents" (people infected by nonsexual routes) and respectable people (people not in some "other" category) were affected, the stigma of disease lessened. Nevertheless, the notion was not forgotten that the entire community was put at risk because of the moral failures of certain disvalued members.[12]

This general pattern of interpretation and response to gonorrhea and syphilis, both before and after 1932, when a cure was discovered, is echoed in the current discussion about HIV/AIDS. Medical, governmental, religious, and public concern tended to be anemic until the probable impact of HIV/AIDS on people everywhere was recognized. AIDS was initially described as a "gay disease." Some considered it appropriate punishment for men who violated natural law. Government funding for research and treatment was opposed by leaders of the religious right. Ronald S. Godwin, an executive of the now defunct Moral Majority, stated in June 1983, "What I see is a commitment to spend our tax dollars on research to allow these diseased homosexuals to go back to their perverted practices without any standards of accountability."[13] According to this punitive view, homosexuality, not a retrovirus, causes AIDS; AIDS will be eliminated when homosexual persons are eliminated; homosexual persons, not disease-causing organisms, are a threat to the health of society. AIDS, perhaps the ultimate venereal disease, is portrayed as a disease of sinners, an indication of moral decay.

It may not be surprising that people who condemn male homosexuality and other behaviors on religious or moral grounds would interpret HIV/AIDS as a divine corrective to an offending people. It is surprising, however, that secular institutions responsible for public health would or should be influenced by religious explanations or moral attitudes in the design and implementation of preventive and therapeutic programs in the midst of an epidemic. Although there may be reasonable disagreements about strategies to limit the impact of an epidemic, the criterion for judgment in a public health environment should be effective control. Negative feelings and judgments about the sexual and drug-use behaviors that place people at risk for HIV infection ought not impede effective disease-prevention practices or medical-scientific efforts to comfort and cure any person suffering disease, regardless of its cause.

As this brief overview of cultural reactions to infectious disease shows, moral condemnation and wishes that an organism will be confined to stigmatized people never have been and are not now effective means of controlling infection. Scapegoating certain groups and blaming the victims are equally ineffective. As medical historian Guenter B. Risse observes, "These social reactions reveal our ambiguities about the meaning of such diseases while furnishing convenient targets for projecting responsibilities and blame."[14] The link of disease to sin may provide a persuasive explanation to some people, and it may be powerful psychologically, but it is no magic bullet. It compounds suffering rather than alleviates it, as the history of society's response to sexually transmitted diseases shows.

The Response to AIDS

Between 1981 and 1983, few people other than those who could not or chose not to ignore AIDS expressed much interest in the syndrome or concern for people suffering with it. AIDS was a story, according to NBC science correspondent J. Robert Bazell, that could not be told when it first appeared because it was seen as a gay story.[15] James Kinsella, former editor for the Los Angeles *Herald Examiner* and Fellow at the Gannett Center for Media Studies, attributes the relative apathy of the media to the belief of key people within the industry that the deaths of gay men and intravenous drug users were not worth reporting.[16]

Public disregard for gay men took the form of indifference to a major emerging threat to public health, probably to the public's peril. Prejudice toward people who engaged in risky practices (gay men and intravenous drug users) joined with public fears of contagion to foster hysteria and panic. People with AIDS were fired from their jobs, evicted from their apartments, denied medical insurance payments, deserted by friends, and abandoned by family members. Funeral directors refused to handle their bodies. Nurses, medical technicians, and physicians refused to care for them. Scientific uncertainty and caution were manipulated by political and moral opportunists to further their respective agendas. People were told to avoid contact with stereotyped gay service providers: hairdressers, florists, designers, waiters. Children with AIDS were sent home from their schools.[17] Fear, ignorance, and hysteria replaced apathy as the public became increasingly aware that AIDS is caused by an infectious organism and that valued as well as disvalued persons were being stricken.[18]

Even as late as 1985, when the evidence was convincing to most people that the AIDS virus is not easily transmitted, AIDS and the group most identified with it, gay men, were being used as weapons of political warfare. The mayoral campaign in Houston, Texas, was a prime example of manipulation of prejudice. Incumbent Mayor Kathy Whitmire was challenged by Louie Welch, a former mayor and recently retired president of the Chamber of Commerce. Welch announced a four-point plan to control AIDS, one of which was to "shoot the queers."[19] When this remark was inadvertently broadcast live, his campaign managers boasted that record monetary contributions were received as a result, and pastors in his denomination gave him a standing ovation at their prayer breakfast. It is impossible to know whether this applause was merely polite or indicated agreement with his AIDS plan. Further, Welch has not stated publicly whether the famous quip expressed his true feelings or was only a poor attempt at humor. Nevertheless, he subsequently lost his electoral bid in an overwhelming defeat. Since then, however, he has been a member of the host committee for a special event raising funds for an adult day-care center, counseling center, and dental clinic serving people with HIV disease sponsored by a United Methodist congregation located in a neighborhood densely populated by gay men and burdened by a high incidence of HIV infection and AIDS. Welch's comments in 1985 were typical of a broader, national perverse delight with the HIV/AIDS epidemic.

Conservative columnist and then White House Director of Communications Patrick Buchanan fanned the flames of AIDS hysteria and homophobia when he wrote in 1985 that the "essence" of homosexual life is "runaway promiscuity," which leads to illness and death. "Call it nature's retribution, God's will, the wages of sin, paying the piper, ecological kickback, whatever phraseology you prefer," Buchanan continued.[20] Buchanan's comments misrepresent the lifestyle of the vast majority of homosexual people and reflect a poor understanding of science, philosophy, and theology. William F. Buckley, Jr., a conservative but less vituperative columnist, also had taken note of the AIDS crisis, proposing universal screening for AIDS. If the "AIDS test" is positive, that person "should be tattooed in the upper forearm, to protect common-needle users, and on the buttocks, to prevent the victimization of other homosexuals." These actions are warranted, according to Buckley, because "our society is generally threatened, and in order to fight AIDS, we need the civil equivalent of universal military training."[21] Like that of his colleague, Buckley's proposed solution is based on incorrect evidence. There is no such thing as an "AIDS test." The test to detect antibodies to the AIDS virus is not perfect and, when accurate, only indicates antibody level at the time of the test. The test only indicates that a person has been infected. Relying on a single antibody screen to safeguard the public from inadvertent infection, as counseled by Buckley, would provide a safety net that is full of holes.

Finally, followers of political extremist Lyndon LaRouche attempted to use fear of AIDS to gather support for and validate his political ambitions. The Prevent AIDS Now Initiative Committee (PANIC) successfully placed a proposition on the California ballot in 1986 that, if passed, could have barred infected people from certain jobs, mandated reporting infected persons to state health authorities, and possibly sanctioned quarantining persons with AIDS or people who are well but infected.[22] Like Buckley's proposal, PANIC's answer for AIDS would not provide effective protection and totally disregards the needs of people who are presently ill or infected. The proposition was not passed by the citizens of California.

The voices of religious leaders were part of the public discussion of AIDS during the middle years of the decade. Jerry Falwell speculated that AIDS could be God's judgment on homosexual persons and society. His disbanded political organization, Moral Majority, opposed government-funded research to find a cure for what it considered a gay problem.[23] In his *Liberty Report* for April 1987 he stated, "AIDS is a lethal judgment of God on America for endorsing this vulgar, perverted and reprobate lifestyle."[24] On the "Old Time Gospel Hour," after saddling the "national media, the national press, [and] the educational system in this country" with responsibility for AIDS, he asserted that the "sexual revolution" is being brought to an end by "God Almighty." He stated, "They [male homosexuals] are scared to walk near one of their kind right now. And what we [preachers] have been unable to do with our preaching, a God who hates sin has stopped dead in its tracks by saying do it and die. Do it and die."[25]

Less condemning and more compassionate religious views have been voiced. We were among the first to discuss the issues that AIDS presents to the church in a national ecumenical journal.[26] Eileen Flynn similarly called Catholics to stand with, console, and care for people with AIDS.[27] Bishop William E. Swing, Episcopal Diocese of California, has commented:

> When I read about Jesus Christ in Scriptures and try to understand something of the mind of God, I cannot identify even one occasion where he pictures his Father as occasionally becoming displeased and then hurling epidemics on nations. Especially in relation to sexual matters! Rather than hurling wrath when dealing with an adulteress, Jesus said, "Whoever is without sin, cast the first stone." . . . Thus I do not believe in the God who becomes displeased and decides to show his anger by murdering large numbers of people, or in this case homosexual people.[28]

Archbishop John R. Quinn, Roman Catholic Archdiocese of San Francisco, wrote:

> The Christian—the church—must not contribute to breaking the spirit of the sick and weakening their faith by harshness. . . . The presence of the church must be a presence of hope and grace, of healing and reconciliation, of love and perseverance to the end. . . . AIDS is a human disease. It affects everyone and it tests the quality of our faith and of our family and community relationships. Persons with AIDS and ARC [AIDS-related complex][29] are our brothers and sisters, members of our parishes. . . . "As disciples of Jesus who healed the sick and is Himself the compassion of God among us, we, too, must show our compassion to our brothers and sisters who are suffering."[30]

Similarly, Roman Catholic conservative Cardinal John J. O'Connor committed the Archdiocese of New York "to do its best to minister to every person who is ill, of whatever disorder, because of our commitment to the belief that *every* person is made in the Image and Likeness of God."[31]

Christian denominations have adopted resolutions and issued statements regarding the church's witness in the AIDS crisis. The first resolution by a church body was adopted in June 1983 by the Fourteenth General Synod of the United Church of Christ. The resolution took note of the slow and meager response of government to a rapidly spreading epidemic and foresaw that AIDS "constitutes a threat to the health of all Americans and to the entire human population worldwide." Through the resolution, the United Church of Christ declared, in part, "its compassionate concern and support for all who are victims of Acquired Immune Deficiency Syndrome and the opportunistic diseases it enables, their lovers, spouses, families, and friends." Congregations were called to support and provide ministries to people touched by AIDS. Finally, the resolution called upon various agencies of government to increase their efforts in combating AIDS' devastating effects.[32]

The 69th General Convention of the Episcopal Church in 1988 received a report on AIDS from its Commission on Human Affairs and Health. Following receipt of this report, the Convention adopted numerous resolutions calling for AIDS educational programs in every congregation, commending homosexual persons for their care of people with AIDS, and establishing an annual day of prayer and healing.[33]

The General Conference of the United Methodist Church adopted a comprehensive statement on HIV/AIDS in May 1988. Noting that "diseases spring from complex conditions, factors, and choices," the General Conference declared, "It is not helpful to speak of diseases in inflammatory terms like 'punishment for sin.' " The church confessed its tardy response to the epidemic and celebrated the existing ministries of care and education. It resolved that congregations should be open to and caring of people touched by HIV/AIDS, work for the acceptance of people with HIV/AIDS, develop specialized AIDS ministries, advocate the civil rights of adults and children with HIV infection, and encourage global cooperation in battling the epidemic. The statement concluded, observing: "The global AIDS pandemic provides a nearly unparalleled opportunity for witness to the Gospel and service to human need among persons many of whom would otherwise be alone and alienated from themselves, other people and from God. . . . We ask for God's guidance that we might respond in ways that bear witness always to Jesus' own compassionate ministry of healing and reconciliation; and that to this end we might love one another and care for one another with the same unmeasured and unconditional love that Jesus embodied."[34]

The Presbyterian Church (U.S.A.) passed a resolution on AIDS at its General Assembly in 1986. The resolution acknowledged that "certain leaders of Christian denominations and groups" and "certain persons seeking or holding political office or public position" were exploiting public fear and private suffering for individual advantage. In contrast, the 198th General Assembly declared that AIDS "is not punishment for behavior deemed immoral," called congregations to nonjudgmental ministry, urged increased funding for research, asked for legislation protecting civil rights of infected people, and called for "accurate, current AIDS information to diffuse the unfounded fears created by ignorance or false public information."[35]

The Southern Baptist Convention adopted a resolution in 1987 that differs in important ways from the statements by other large Protestant denominations. The Southern Baptist resolution mandates no action by any Convention agency and urges medical, legal, educational, and public officials to give greater attention to "biblical standards of decency and morality" when speaking about HIV/AIDS. The resolution states that "safe sex" education that promotes the use of condoms "seems to accept infidelity and adultery, as well as perversion, as an accepted fact of our American way of life." The Convention, in response to these observations, affirmed its belief "that obedience to God's laws of chastity before marriage and faithfulness in marriage would be a major step toward curtailing the threat of AIDS." Despite this moral stand regarding risk-reduction education, the Convention called for "Christlike compassion in dealing with the hurting victims of AIDS and their families."[36]

The Greek Orthodox Archdiocese of North and South America, in a pamphlet published in 1988 titled "AIDS and You," echoed the prevention approach favored by the Southern Baptist Convention (1987). The document states: "The Church has proclaimed her message, loud and clear: abstention and monogamous relationships should be the motto promoted by both the medical community and the government. Young people . . . should be taught that abstention from pre-marital sex is the only way to combat the disease." Education about condoms as a means to reduce the risk of HIV infection during sexual intercourse is opposed as a "band-aid approach. . . . Promoting condoms as a solution distorts the value of responsibility by suggesting that being responsible about one's sexuality simply means taking precautions against pregnancy and AIDS. The promotion of contraceptives distorts the values of mutual respect, of wanting what is best for someone else, by camouflaging as love what is often really exploitation."[37]

The response to HIV/AIDS by the U.S. Catholic Conference illustrates the difficulty that denominations may have in taking a position about HIV prevention education. An ad hoc committee of the Conference reminded Roman Catholics of their obligation to care for people suffering from HIV/AIDS. Abstention from sexual relations outside monogamous marriage was recommended as the primary means of prevention. However, the committee report issued in 1987, "The Many Faces of AIDS," permitted discussion about condoms with those people who would not or could not follow the church's primary moral teaching.[38] This position was justified by the doctrine that a lesser evil could be tolerated in order to prevent a greater evil. Several bishops objected to this apparent reversal or weakening of the church's historic opposition to contraception under any circumstance. As a consequence, the 1988 U.S. Catholic Conference issued a second statement on AIDS, "Called to Compassion and Responsibility: A Response to the HIV/AIDS Crisis." This statement agreed with the emphases of the first document except for the discussion of condoms as means of prevention. Abstinence was urged as the primary and only means of prevention. Condoms, "safe sex," and "safer sex" were not mentioned.[39] Because the second statement did not explicitly repudiate the first, it appears that both stand, speak with one voice about the duty to care for people with HIV/AIDS without discrimination, but present differing interpretations of allowable risk-avoidance and risk-reduction education.

The Church Council of the Evangelical Lutheran Church in America approved a statement in 1988 that, unlike the Southern Baptist Convention in 1987 and the Greek Orthodox Archdiocese, spoke about the crisis in general terms, steering away from a single focus on sexual routes of transmission. The statement notes that HIV/AIDS affects men, women, and children around the world. In response to disease, church members are called to remember their common humanity and are summoned to "compassion for, acceptance of and service with people affected by AIDS both within and outside our congregations." Further, Lutherans are urged to be educated and to participate in the complex public policy debates surrounding the disease.[40]

As the years have passed, more and more religious leaders and denominations are making statements embracing reason and compassion. These expressions of concern and calls to ministry are admirable, though generally issued belatedly, as some statements have acknowledged. Nevertheless, it is notable that when the denominations speak officially the notion that HIV/AIDS is punishment for specific sins is rejected. Moreover, the calls for compassionate engagement and support for the civil rights of people with HIV/AIDS may be remarkable given the general disapproval of nonmarital sexual intercourse and intravenous drug use. Christian denominations tend to be large institutions with many levels of organization and administration. As such, they can be slow to speak and act, whereas local congregations can respond to changing situations and needs more quickly. It is therefore often at the local congregational level that the church's most compassionate, intense, and effective response is manifested.

Individual Christians and congregations have provided spiritual and hands-on ministries beginning soon after the appearance of this new disease. These ministries have involved commitments of time and money. Some have been provided by individuals, acting alone or with friends. Some have been sponsored by single congregations; others have had diocesan or interfaith sponsorship. In sanctuaries, homes, hospitals, and hospices, some of the people of God have turned toward rather than away from persons caught in the crisis of AIDS. Neither the stigma of AIDS nor the stigma of homosexuality or drug use kept them from doing what their faith taught them to do.

The early history of AIDS ministries is difficult to reconstruct in detail because few reports were published in accessible places. The more recent history of individuals and congregational and denominational ministries is being written in secular and religious magazines, newspapers, and journals. Ministries are proliferating but, unfortunately, not at the same pace as the need. A quantitative gap continues to exist. Verbal confessions of love for a neighbor touched by AIDS have not tended to become acts of love for that same neighbor. The opportunities for ministry that AIDS presents vary among people and places. A question that must be answered by the faithful is whether and how these opportunities will be met. The call of God's people to loving witness is being heard and answered. As a result, perhaps the church soon will assume a leadership role in modeling a compassionate, reasoned, and reasonable response to the AIDS crisis that will be more broadly recognized. With this leadership, perhaps love will replace fear among the faithful and the public. Perhaps hope will replace despair among the sick and their loved ones. Perhaps AIDS will become an opportunity for reconciliation rather than estrangement.

AIDS is the latest of several diseases to evoke fear among people and to challenge the church to reflect on its identity and mission. Historians help us to appreciate that the individual, institutional, societal, and governmental responses to the HIV/AIDS epidemic have not been dramatically different from responses to previous epidemics throughout human history. Epidemics are part of the human condition that contemporary Americans conveniently dismissed prior to AIDS. We would be well served as we reflect on our experience with HIV/AIDS to prepare for the next epidemic that will challenge our collective character. As William H. McNeill concludes in his masterful study *Plagues and People*, "Infectious disease which antedated the emergence of humankind will last as long as humanity itself, and will surely remain, as it has been hitherto, one of the fundamental parameters and determinants of human history."[41] HIV/AIDS sets before the church a choice, either to respond in a manner that buttresses social divisions and prejudices or to be a prophetic, servant, and priestly community that comforts hurting humanity, reconciles estranged populations, and stands in solidarity with people oppressed and isolated by prejudice and fear.

Fear about HIV/AIDS is being reduced by a growing body of scientific and medical evidence. Failures in discipleship can be confessed and corrected. Calls to ministry can be answered with a witness that is obedient to and honors the Lord. It has not been easy to have a clear perception of what should be an appropriate response to

HIV/AIDS. The disease itself initially was shrouded in mystery. Scientists were not sure whether it might disappear as suddenly as it had appeared. Thus, in this respect the church's slow response may be understandable. But now it is clear that, although the virus is not easily communicated, HIV/AIDS is a growing, global health crisis that has an unprecedented potential to destroy lives. In the face of such an obvious crisis, God's people must mobilize, design, and implement a variety of sustaining ministries in the name of the Lord who commanded God's people to love one another.

The religious voices that condemn people touched by HIV/AIDS and counsel the church to abdicate its duty toward them are beginning to fade. People are listening less to those who use scripture as an instrument of repression. The arguments and conclusions that initially led to harsh, uncaring interpretations of AIDS are increasingly recognized as flawed, now that the epidemic increasingly affects other than gay people in this country, and its global demographics are becoming known. The true liberating, healing witness of scripture is being heard and followed as the faithful perceive the magnitude of human suffering wrought by HIV/AIDS and their obligations with respect to it. Education about HIV/AIDS and a broadening experience with it are destroying the myths, stereotypes, and prejudices that have inhibited an empathetic and supportive response. The barriers that partly hindered the church's response to HIV/AIDS during most of the first decade of the epidemic progressively are being broken. Moral attitudes about male homosexuality and intravenous drug use seem not to be preventing some denominations, congregations, and individuals from engaging in compassionate, nonjudgmental, sustaining ministries. Yet as the history of the epidemic lengthens and the demographic description of the affected population changes, it is likely that the church will be challenged once again to consider its obligations to people of color, women, the impoverished, their children, and those who cope with life's stresses by resort to drug use. The church also may have to confront charges of heterosexism, racism, classism, and elitism as it finds its way into and probably beyond the second decade of the HIV/AIDS epidemic in the United States.

This volume is a revised contribution to the church as it seeks to be God's agent in this crisis. It provides biblical, theological, and ecclesiastical analyses that articulate and justify a redemptive interpretation of HIV/AIDS and proposes for God's people a compassionate response to all touched by HIV disease.

Chapter 2 provides a scientific and epidemiological overview of HIV/AIDS. The survey continues in Chapter 3, focusing on the clinical and psychosocial effects of HIV/AIDS infection. Chapter 4 examines God's role in illness and the responsibilities of the faithful to sick people, concluding that AIDS is not God's retribution on any person or any group of persons and that God's people have a duty to care for the sick, regardless of the nature of the sickness or the means by which people become ill. Chapter 5 advances and defends the claim that people touched by HIV/AIDS are contemporary instances of the "poor" toward whom the people of God have a special mission. This mission is expressed in two ways: (1) by advocating the cause of the "HIV/AIDS population" where their voices are too weak to be heard and (2) by supporting them with direct, sustaining ministries. The analysis turns from interpretation to application in Chapter 6, where descriptive proposals for AIDS ministries are provided. In Chapter 7, we describe the worsening global impact of HIV/AIDS, suggesting that the mission of the church in the United States extends to the developing world.

The volume concludes in Chapter 8 with a summary defense of the claim that God's people have no option in the HIV/AIDS crisis but to design and implement a compassionate, healing, and prophetic ministry that sets an example for all of society to follow.

2

The HIV/AIDS Epidemic

When the clinical condition eventually named acquired immune deficiency syndrome, or AIDS, was first described in the United States during 1981, few people foresaw the magnitude of the sickness and death that was to come. Neither was the difficulty foreseen of discovering the cause of this new phenomenon, finding a cure, or developing a vaccine if the cause proved to be viral. The initial reports of unusual infections and malignancies among gay men generally were considered medical curiosities, not preliminary evidence of the destructive potential of a new virus being spread globally. Almost totally without public attention or concern, a new chapter in the history of medicine and public health had begun. No one knows yet when or how it will end. Until then, however, men, women, and children around the world face an epidemic with an unprecedented deadly potential.

AIDS is less mysterious today than it was in 1981. Much has been learned about the AIDS virus and its effects on the human body. Much more will have to be learned before the physical destruction it causes can be stopped. Moreover, the public needs to learn more about HIV/AIDS in order to transform ignorance into knowledge and indifference into compassion. The church can and should take a leadership role by becoming educated about HIV/AIDS and modeling a caring response toward people touched by it. Educating the church about AIDS is the focus of this chapter.

Early Observations and Theories and the Discovery of HIV

Beginning in June 1981, physicians in New York City and Los Angeles reported the appearance of *Pneumocystis carinii* pneumonia (PCP), other opportunistic infections (infections that result in clinical illness when the cellular immune system is weakened), and a disseminated form of malignancy called Kaposi's sarcoma in apparently previously healthy young gay men. Any one of these diseases would have been unusual in this group, but such a constellation of disorders was unprecedented. Medical scientists and epidemiologists soon realized that these reports were signaling the onset of an apparently new illness in this country. Speculation began immediately about its cause.[1]

Surveys of patients showed that they tended to be sexually active, engaging in practices involving fecal contact and having contact with large numbers of homosexual and bisexual men. This information suggested that perhaps an immunosuppressive substance was being used or an immunosuppressive pathogen was being transmitted from person to person through bodily fluids. Suspicion that the causative agent was immunosuppressive was based on laboratory data indicating an impaired cellular immune system, a system unable to counter infections with an effective defense. This is why infections indicative of AIDS are characterized as opportunistic—the illness is caused by a pathogen that would be controlled or destroyed by a competent cellular immune system. Thus opportunistic infections take advantage of the cellular immune system's impaired function, resulting in illness where otherwise none would occur.

Researchers tried to explain the observed impaired cellular immune response by studying the immunosuppressive effects of a commonly used inhalant (amyl and butyl nitrite, or "poppers") and of human semen absorbed into the bloodstream through small tears in the rectum during anal intercourse. These studies and other hypotheses related to lifestyle factors led nowhere. The appearance of AIDS among heterosexual intravenous drug users and heterosexual hemophilia patients using a blood clotting agent (Factor VIII concentrate) suggested that the etiologic agent of AIDS not only was transmitted sexually but also was transmissible by blood or blood products. If the causative agent could be carried by blood, it had to be small enough to escape being removed during the process of preparing Factor VIII. This finding ruled out bacteria and fungi, but not viruses. Consideration was given to Epstein-Barr virus and cytomegalovirus, members of the herpesvirus family, because evidence of these viruses was found in patients. However, neither virus was known to produce illnesses like AIDS, nor does either virus have an affinity for the CD4+ T cells of the cellular immune system. The CD4+ T, or T helper cell, is a white blood cell that has a key role in regulating the body's cellular immune system. Studies indicated that CD4+ T cells were decreased in quantity and quality in people with this new disease.

The search for the elusive virus continued. Because of what had been learned about the virus indirectly through patient interviews and laboratory studies, it was determined that the cause of AIDS was transmissible through whole blood, plasma, semen, vaginal secretions, and Factor VIII. Further, as infants born to women with AIDS developed similar illnesses, scientists concluded that the etiologic agent also had to be transmissible congenitally. The collected evidence suggested that the cause of AIDS was likely to be one of a large group of RNA viruses called retroviruses.

Luc Montagnier, head of the Viral Oncology Unit of the Pasteur Institute in Paris, and his colleagues were the first to isolate the retrovirus that was later shown to be the necessary cause of AIDS. In May 1983, the Paris group isolated a new virus from a patient with unexplained swollen lymph nodes, naming it lymphadenopathy-associated virus (LAV). Similar retroviruses were isolated from the blood of several AIDS patients, but the French were not very successful in growing the retrovirus, a necessary step in the process of identification.

At about the same time that the French were doing their research, Robert C. Gallo and his associates at the National Cancer Institute also were looking for a new retrovirus as the cause of AIDS. Gallo's group reported in May 1984 that they not only had isolated a retrovirus that attacked CD4+ T cells—designated human T-cell lymphotropic virus III (HTLV-III)—but they also were able to grow the retrovirus in sufficient quantities to warrant concluding that this retrovirus caused AIDS. Comparisons of LAV and HTLV-III were thought to show the two to be variants of the same virus. Thus, within three years of the description of AIDS in the United States, scientists had found the agent responsible for the destruction of CD4+ T cells and thus for the many secondary clinical illnesses resulting from this deficit in the cellular immune system.

As welcome as this discovery was in 1983–84, journalist Randy Shilts argues that isolating the retrovirus involved relatively basic laboratory work. The reason it took scientists at the National Cancer Institute three years to do so was a reluctance to look for it; that is, a lack of interest resulted in unnecessary delays.[2]

Controversy over the name of the virus resulted in a recommendation that these viruses be officially designated as human immunodeficiency viruses (HIV).[3] The word "virus" is plural because two variants of HIV appear capable of causing AIDS. HIV-2 is primarily present in Western Africa, whereas HIV-1 is more common and found throughout the world. This term, as well as the colloquial "AIDS virus," will be used here.

The controversy surrounding the identification of the cause of HIV/AIDS was not limited to its designation or name. The belief of Robert Gallo that HIV is another member of the HTLV family of viruses now has been discredited. The claim that Gallo discovered HIV independently of the work of Montagnier also has been questioned. Studies of the nucleotide sequence of Montagnier's LAV and Gallo's HTLV-III showed that the two were identical within 1.8 percent of nucleotides. The two were essentially identical twins. Some scientists have concluded, based on notes in Gallo's laboratory records, that "at the time of the supposed discovery of HTLV-III virus, his team had not yet succeeded in cultivating any permanent lines of the American isolate of this virus."[4] It appears that national pride, financial rewards, and professional ego may have entered the "objective" realm of science.

Additional internal investigations of this episode are being conducted at the National Institutes of Health as of this writing. Randy Shilts summarized the effect of Gallo's claims as follows: "Gallo had not only stolen credit from the French for discovering the AIDS virus, he had stolen the virus itself."[5] As intriguing as the politics of science in general and the politics of HIV/AIDS in particular are for this general inquiry, they are a distraction from the main task of this chapter.

The Cellular Immune System

Identifying the retroviral cause of HIV/AIDS was only one step in the process of finding a cure. Learning how HIV affects the body's cellular immune system was another step. Fortunately, HIV disease appeared at a time in the history of medicine when the technology to study viruses and the cellular immune system was becoming available. In order to appreciate the destructive potential of HIV, it is helpful to have a basic understanding of the cellular components of the human immune system.

The cellular immune system is a flexible but highly specialized defense mechanism that protects the body from invading microorganisms, destroys infected and malignant cells, and removes debris. The precise mechanism by which these tasks are performed is too intricate and complex to pursue here. (For a highly informative presentation of the cellular immune system, see *National Geographic,* vol. 169, June 1986, pp. 702–735.) The process by which infections are normally controlled, however, can be described in simple terms.

White blood cells (lymphocytes) are central to cellular immune response. There are two classes of lymphocytes: the B cells, which develop in the bone marrow, and the T cells, which also develop in the bone marrow but mature in the thymus gland. B cells produce potent chemical weapons called antibodies that identify antigens (substances that stimulate the production of antibodies) and aid in their removal or destruction. T cells perform three functions. The killer T cell destroys cancerous cells and body cells that have been invaded by foreign organisms. The CD4+ T cell, unlike B cells and killer T cells, does not directly confront the enemy, so to speak. It is the commander in chief of the cellular immune system. After being summoned to the site of a foreign organism by the macrophages (frontline troops of the body's defensive army), the CD4+ T cell stimulates the production of killer T cells and B cells to combat the intruder. After an intruder or infection has been defeated, a third type of T cell, the suppressor T cell, or CD8+ T cell, calls off the attack by killer T cells and B cells. Thus, CD4+ T cells turn on the immune response; macrophages, killer T cells, and B cells are combatants; and T suppressor (CD8+) cells turn off the cellular immune response. Following a successful defense, a population of T and B cells persists that "remembers" the invader. Should the invader appear again, the cellular immune response will be accelerated because the enemy is recognized more quickly.

Among the cells that constitute the cellular immune system, the CD4+ T cell has a key role in orchestrating a defense of the body against infections. Without an adequate quantity and quality of CD4+ T cells, the body's defensive forces are ineffectively mobilized, if at all, when challenged. The AIDS virus is able to defeat the body's cellular immune response by preemptively destroying its commander in chief. When the CD4+ T cell is infected by HIV, it becomes a factory within which additional HIV is produced. As an HIV-laden cell dies, viruses escape to conquer other cells with appropriate chemical receptors that allow entry, including macrophages. It should be noted that HIV can infect any cell having the CD4+ molecule on its membrane, including monocytes of the lung and brain. Even though HIV has a pathogenic effect on these organs, most attention is given to its deleterious effect on the cellular immune system.[6] The number of CD4+ T cells, which normally constitute between 60 and 80 percent of the circulating T cells, can be reduced in AIDS to a level where they are too few to be detected. Thus, as more CD4+ T cells are infected, harbor the replicating virus, die, and release more of the virus to attack the remaining competent CD4+ T cells, the cellular immune system becomes progressively impaired, rendering the body vulnerable to microorganisms and physiological processes that otherwise would not result in clinical illness.

Origin and Transmission of HIV

Identifying the retroviral cause of HIV/AIDS and learning about the effect of HIV on the body's cellular immune response are important discoveries. The official clinical story of HIV/AIDS began in the United States in 1981, but investigators have learned that these were not the first cases of HIV/AIDS. The first case or cases probably never will be known with certainty. Like other first phenomena in medicine, the first people with HIV/AIDS were assigned other diagnoses, treated reasonably, and given a mistaken diagnosis; their deaths were attributed to an opportunistic disease or wasting disorder of unknown etiology.[7]

As soon as reports of AIDS from the United States reached Europe in 1981, physicians in Denmark, Belgium, and France recalled patients who, as early as 1976, were treated for mysterious infections following time spent in equatorial Africa. Other probable cases have been identified in Germany, also as early as 1976. An earlier cluster of cases appeared in Norway in 1966. A Norwegian sailor who had traveled extensively in Europe and Africa developed persistent lymphadenopathy, musculo-skeletal pain, and dark spots on his skin. At the time of his death in 1976, his wife had experienced HIV-related symptoms since 1967, and she died eight months after her husband. His daughter died four months before him, following a series of major infections beginning at age two. Blood studies performed in 1988 confirmed the presence of HIV antibodies in tissue samples retained from all three people. The child in this family is the earliest proven diagnosis of pediatric AIDS. Two older children are well, seronegative, and have no signs of immunodeficiency.

Even earlier instances of HIV/AIDS now have been documented. An English sailor died in Manchester in 1959, a girl died in England in 1961, and another girl died in Sweden in 1967. The history of HIV/AIDS in the United States also began before 1981. Medical journals contain at least sixteen case reports that fit the present clinical definition of HIV/AIDS. Perhaps the earliest case report was in 1952, involving a 28-year-old male with a diagnosis of viral pneumonia at Baptist Memorial Hospital in Memphis, Tennessee. Tissue samples were preserved at autopsy and stored. Further examination of these tissues in 1982 confirmed an earlier review that rendered a diagnosis of *Pneumocystis carinii* pneumonia superimposed on a cytomegalovirus infection. Another case involved a 15-year-old black male in St. Louis. Treatment began in 1968 for a variety of complications of immunodeficiency. He died in May 1969. Autopsy revealed Kaposi's sarcoma and anal trauma. He never had been out of the United States, and no contact with foreigners has been established. In 1987, this young man's blood and lymph samples were tested and found positive for HIV-1. Moreover, the identified antigens are related to a present strain of HIV-1.

There is evidence, as well, of HIV in humans in South America as early as 1968. Blood was taken from 224 aboriginal Amazonian Indians living in the Orinoco River Valley of Venezuela. Four percent of the blood samples, five females and four males, contained antibodies to HIV-1 by Western blot assay. Clinical and serological evidence from Africa further suggests that HIV-1 was present in humans on several continents prior to the epidemic's official birth in 1981. HIV/AIDS probably assumed epidemic levels in Africa between 1961 and 1980. By 1977, the earliest AIDS cases were seen in Zaire—a woman from Kinshasa and her daughter—as well as a family (mother and children) from Rwanda. In addition, a Canadian received a blood transfusion in Zaire in 1976, and he died two years later with a retrospective diagnosis of AIDS.

The conditions of medical care and research in much of Africa make it difficult to know with any certainty when AIDS was first seen by physicians. The incidence of opportunistic infections in tropical Africa and technologically less advanced diagnostic facilities made conclusions difficult to reach. Retrospective studies of stored blood from the Belgian Congo, southern Sudan, Rwanda, Burundi, Mozambique, and Zaire yield several conclusions: (1) HIV-1 or a virus with similar antigenic properties was present in Zaire as early as 1959; (2) nevertheless, the HIV/AIDS epidemic is relatively new in Africa, with seroprevalence relatively low until 1982; and (3) the standard antibody test (ELISA) is unreliable on frozen plasma stored for ten or more years.[8]

The identity of the first person infected by HIV remains unknown. Despite Randy Shilts's fascinating story of Gaetan Dugas, a Canadian flight attendant, as "patient zero,"[9] the history of the first people with AIDS is fragmentary and, in some instances, presumptive. However, such evidence as is available (for example, HIV-1 and HIV-2 antibodies found in blood from eleven African countries as early as 1966) suggests that HIV-1 and HIV-2 infection in humans was resulting in clinical disease and death on several continents simultaneously, beginning in the 1960s, increasing in the 1970s, and reaching a critical level for classification or description as a "new" disease in the first years of the 1980s.

Determining the origin of HIV/AIDS in nature may be as inconclusive as identifying the first person to develop HIV disease. Soon after AIDS was described in humans, there were reports of captive Asian macaques in the United States developing severe infections, wasting disease, and dying. Subsequently designated simian AIDS or SAIDS, the infectious origin was named simian immunodeficiency virus, or SIV, in 1984.[10] Studies of wild monkeys in Asia (the original location of macaques) showed no trace of SIV. African chimpanzees and baboons in the wild were also negative for SIV. However, over 50 percent of examined captive African green monkeys had SIV antibodies in their blood. Several strains of SIV have been isolated, though this species of monkey in the wild remained without disease. Moreover, a strain of SIV taken from a healthy mangabey monkey produced chronic illness in an infected macaque similar to minor forms of AIDS in humans. The agent became more virulent as it was passed from one macaque to another. When the strengthened virus was inoculated into a healthy mangabey, the animal became ill despite its previous natural resistance.[11] This experience is significant as an animal model, indicating the possibility that the virulence of HIV-1 was potentiated by an analogous process in humans.

Pathogenic viruses evolve from ancestors and replicate either in animal or human hosts. Scientists are able to establish viral pedigrees. The origins of retroviruses will never be known; they are "lost in the depths of time."[12] The lineage of HIV appears to be more subject to investigation, however. Genetic analyses show that HIV is related to the lentiviruses that infect a wide variety of mammals. HIV and SIV form a branch of the lentiviruses distinct from the branches that infect horses, sheep, and cattle. Researchers think that the common ancestor out of which SIV and HIV evolved is between 140 and 280 years old. HIV was not necessarily pathogenic in its ancestral form. Genetic studies of SIV, HIV-1, and HIV-2 suggest that SIV is a distant cousin of HIV-1, that HIV-1 and HIV-2 did not descend from each other, and that HIV-1 (the more prevalent HIV infection in humans) did not descend from most known strains of SIV. Finally, comparative studies of HIV-1 strains isolated in the United States, Africa, and Europe show that the European strain is more similar to the American strain than to the African strain. Calculations based on the rate of 10^3 nucleotide substitutions per year suggest that HIV-1 has been a parasite in humans for 20–100 years. The history of HIV-2 in humans may be longer.[13]

Despite what is known or reasonably believed about the evolutionary history of HIV and the first disease or death resulting from HIV infection in humans, certain or definitive answers to questions of where, when, and how HIV entered humans elude scientists. From an epidemiological perspective, however, HIV/AIDS escaped the attention of medicine prior to 1980–1981. Whether the epidemic began in Africa or America is less important epidemiologically, given the evidence of HIV on several continents, than the fact that AIDS as an epidemic was new on both the African and North American continents by 1981.

This review of the origins of HIV and the retrospective diagnosis of AIDS on several continents prior to 1981 constitute a corrective to a major myth about AIDS. AIDS was not in 1981 a "gay" disease, even though the first diagnoses in the United States were made among gay men and male-to-male sexual contact is a mode of possible infection. Neither is AIDS a "drug addict's" disease, even though sharing drug-injecting equipment may result in infection. Rather, HIV/AIDS is a probable consequence, given the current state of therapeutics, of infection by HIV-1 or HIV-2 in any person, without regard for any identifying characteristic or location. Homosexual and heterosexual people, male and female, white and black, young and old are all equally subject to infection if virus particles or infected cells gain direct access to the bloodstream. Certain practices permit this to happen: anal intercourse (the passive partner is at greater risk), vaginal intercourse (male-to-female and female-to-male transmission have been documented), use of nonsterile needles, receipt of contaminated blood or blood products, and transmission from a mother to her fetus. These are most prevalent ways by which the AIDS virus is spread.

Infected blood, semen, and cervico-vaginal secretions appear to be the only bodily fluids by which HIV can be transmitted, provided the virus has entry into the bloodstream. HIV has been isolated in tears, cerebro-spinal fluid, breast milk, and saliva. The quantity of virus possibly present in tears and saliva of infected individuals probably is too low to be damaging. Whether breast milk is a means of HIV transmission from a mother to her nursing infant is debated. Postnatal infection has been reported. It is unclear whether infection occurred through breast feeding or was already present but undetectable by standard techniques. The polymerase chain reaction (PCR) test,[14] which is more sensitive than the standard antibody test, may resolve this question. It should be noted, as well, that there is no evidence that the virus penetrates the intact skin, epithelial cells lining the respiratory tract, or mucosa of the digestive tract. Thus, casual contact, coughs, sneezes, and consumption of food prepared by infected persons present no known risk of infection. Transmission by insects is unlikely and has not been demonstrated. Although people are becoming better educated about HIV/AIDS with the passage of time and more extensive information campaigns, certain mistaken beliefs persist. For example, adults were asked in December 1989 whether HIV infection was likely by a variety of behaviors involving another person with HIV infection or AIDS. Fifty-four percent thought infection was likely by kissing involving exchange of saliva, 27 percent by being coughed or sneezed on, 24 percent by eating in a restaurant, 18 percent by sharing eating utensils or using public toilets, and 8 percent by shaking hands, touching, or kissing on the cheek. Finally, 27 percent thought mosquitoes or other insects are likely vectors for HIV transmission. It should be emphasized that none of these activities is known to transmit HIV. The survey showed that adults were setting aside certain earlier mistaken beliefs. Only 4 percent thought infection likely by living near someone, 11 percent by working near someone, and 7 percent by attending school where a child has HIV disease. Further, 62 percent had discussed AIDS with their children between 10 and 17 years of age.[15] There is no risk of infection by donating blood at centers where sterile procedures are used. Though HIV has a potent destructive effect over time once it enters the body, it is fragile outside the body. Most household detergents, common disinfectants, and moderate heat (158 + °F for ten minutes) can kill the virus. Studies of health care personnel and families of patients indicate that none has been infected as a result of casual, even daily, contact with infected individuals.

Health care personnel have been infected as a result of other types of exposure to infected bodily fluids. As of November 1989, nineteen occupational infections were documented in the world medical literature. Needle-stick exposure or lacerations contaminated by infected blood resulted in twelve infections. Four infections followed parenteral exposure to infected blood through breaks in the skin or mucous membrane inoculation with blood. Exposure to virus concentrate in research laboratories produced infection in two workers (parenteral and nonintact skin contamination). The mode of infection in one instance is unknown, but followed extensive unprotected contact with infected blood and other body fluids. There may be more occupational infections than these, because HIV infection, as opposed to an HIV/AIDS diagnosis, is not a reportable condition.

The risk of infection following occupational exposure appears minimal. Over four thousand health care workers have been enrolled in surveillance studies following exposure to HIV. A variety of poorly defined factors may influence the risk for infection (e.g., volume of the inoculant, duration of contact, portal of entry, or stage of infection in the source patient). Even though the risk to health care workers is real, the risk can be reduced and nearly eliminated by consistently following recommended universal precautions (i.e., wearing latex gloves for procedures involving contact with blood, bloody body fluids, and certain other fluids; wearing protective eyewear when splatter of these body fluids is possible; and wearing protective garments when clothing is likely to be soiled).[16]

Infection in health care settings can be from clinician to patient as well as from patient to clinician. No HIV infection from a health care provider to a patient was documented in the United States until July 1990. A woman in Florida, Kimberly Bergalis, was diagnosed with AIDS. Epidemiologic investigation of her case found no source for her HIV infection. However, it was revealed that twenty-four months prior to her diagnosis she had two teeth extracted by a dentist, David Acer, who was diagnosed with AIDS three months before the procedure. Blood specimens from the young woman and the dentist were studied. These analyses, according to the Centers for Disease Control (CDC), "showed a similarity between the [viral protein] sequences from the patient and the dentist that was comparable to what has been observed for cases that have been epidemiologically linked. . . . Although the viral sequences from the dentist and the patient could be distinguished from each other, they were closer than what has been observed for pairwise comparisons of sequences taken from the other North American isolates studied."[17] Tests of other patients of Dr. Acer indicated that three others were infected through procedures.[18]

By February 1991, the CDC estimated that, based on

a number of assumptions, as few as 13 or as many as 128 Americans have been infected with HIV by their dentists or surgeons. The estimated risk that an infected surgeon would transmit HIV to a single patient was calculated to range from 1:41,667 to 1:416,667. The estimated risk that an infected dentist would transmit HIV to a single patient during a procedure where bleeding occurs ranged from 1:263,158 to 1:2,631,579. In order for these *estimated* risks to be put into perspective, it should be remembered that 1 in 10,000 patients die in reaction to anesthesia, allergy to penicillin kills about 1 in 100,000 patients, and 3 in 1,000 health care workers have been infected following a needle-stick injury involving an HIV-infected patient.[19]

Publicity about the risks for HIV infection among patients and clinicians has reminded people that health care settings can be dangerous! A risk for HIV infection is only one of the potential adverse effects of health care. People tend to minimize familiar risks and exaggerate new risks. Health professionals have examined their professional responsibilities to care for people with infectious disease.[20] The American Medical Association and the American Dental Association have asked their HIV-infected members to warn patients about their conditions or cease performing surgery. Some public health officials, like New York State Health Commissioner Dr. David Axelrod and others, have responded that the recommended disclosures or changes in practice are unnecessary. Consumers of health care are being forced to acknowledge that medical personnel can be agents of harm as well as agents of healing and comfort. So what is new?

Epidemiology

HIV/AIDS is an epidemic both in the sense of the estimated number of people worldwide infected with HIV and in the sense of the number of people with a confirmed diagnosis of AIDS. For example, at the beginning of the decade of the 1980s, about 100,000 people worldwide were infected with HIV. By the beginning of the second decade of the world's recognition of HIV in humans, the number of people worldwide estimated to be infected increased to 10 million. One-half of those infected (5 million) are in Africa, 40 percent (4 million) in the Americas, 1 million in Europe, and about 200,000 in Asia and Oceania. As sobering as these data are, there is little reason to believe that new infections will cease or that regions of the world previously unaffected or only slightly affected by HIV/AIDS will remain untouched. In June 1989, Jonathan Mann, then director of the World Health Organization's (WHO) Global Program on AIDS, predicted that the cumulative global total of AIDS cases would double by the end of 1991.[21] (More will be said about the global dimensions of the HIV/AIDS pandemic in Chapter 7.) These estimates and projections should remind us that the epidemic in the United States is but one part of an expanding global crisis.

The United States Public Health Service (PHS) at the end of 1989 estimated the prevalence of HIV infection in the United States at approximately 1 million people. This estimate was a revision of a 1986 estimate of 1–1.5 million people infected. By 1991, it was thought that approximately 750,000 people were actually infected in 1986. If the revised estimates for 1986 and 1989 are accurate, 250,000 new infections occurred in three years, despite risk-avoidance and risk-reduction educational campaigns. Not only has the number of new infections continued to increase, the number of diagnosed AIDS cases continues to grow. The PHS estimated in 1989 that 52,000–57,000 new AIDS diagnoses would be made during 1990 and that this number would rise to 61,000–98,000 new diagnoses during 1993. The cumulative total of AIDS diagnoses will be between 390,000 and 480,000 by the end of 1993. At the beginning of 1991, the cumulative count was less than half that projected for 36 months later. That is, more people will be diagnosed with AIDS between 1991 and 1993 than were diagnosed during the previous ten years! The total number of people diagnosed with AIDS in each of the current principal transmission categories (male-to-male, intravenous drug use, heterosexual intercourse, and perinatal) will continue to increase through 1993.[22]

The Committee on AIDS Research and the Social, Behavioral, and Statistical Sciences of the National Academy of Sciences has monitored the progression of the HIV/AIDS epidemic in the United States. The Committee notes that the primary bearers of HIV disease are the nation's most productive population, namely, 20–40-year-old adults. The percentage of adult AIDS diagnoses linked to male-to-male sexual transmission has fallen since 1984. However, decreasing proportions do not mean decreasing numbers of cases. A smaller proportion of an increasing whole still results in increasing morbidity. The proportion of cases linked to intravenous drug use (IVDU) and heterosexual contact has increased, approximately doubling between 1981 and 1989. Among IVDUs, the burden of AIDS has fallen most heavily on minorities. "Crack" cocaine is now joining injectable drugs as a risk factor for HIV infection owing to the tendency of "crack" users to engage in unsafe sexual activity. Many male "crack" smokers report intensified sexual arousal and pleasure. Some women who are dependent on the drug seem more willing to exchange sex for more of the drug or for money to buy the drug. The use of other drugs also has been linked to the transmission of HIV. The disinhibiting effects of alcohol, marijuana, and other noninjected drugs appear to increase the likelihood that people will engage in unprotected sexual intercourse.[23]

The majority of males with AIDS have been linked to same-gender sexual contact. The major transmission category for women, however, is IV drug use. Further, women are at greater risk than men for infection through heterosexual contact. Most heterosexual females with AIDS were infected during intercourse with infected male IVDUs. The distribution of AIDS cases through 1989 among women thirteen years and older by exposure category and ethnic group demonstrates the differential risk of AIDS among minority women.[24] About 30 percent of infants born to HIV-infected women also are infected with HIV. During 1989, between 1,500 and 2,000 infants were born with HIV disease, representing approximately 0.05 percent of all births in the United States.[25] HIV infection following transfusion of blood or blood products has declined since March 1985, when screening of donated blood for HIV infection began. Nevertheless, not all infected blood is detected by standard screening techniques.[26] Blood donated after the donor became infected and before the development of a detectable antibody response might not be identified. This period of danger generally is no more than a few months, but one study found that twenty-seven infected men did not produce detectable antibodies for as long as thirty-six months after the initial positive virus culture. Nevertheless, the blood supply is much safer now than before March 1985. New methods for screening donated blood are being investigated, and improved donor screening and recruitment methods should further reduce the risk for HIV infection through blood transfusion.[27]

There was concern during most of the first decade of the epidemic that female prostitutes would become infected and spread HIV to their male customers, thereby constituting a bridge for infection from promiscuous or drug-injecting populations to "mainstream" married men, their unsuspecting wives, and newborn infants. This fear appears so far to be unfounded in the United States. Studies of female prostitutes have not been easy because of the illegal and stigmatized character of their activity. The women most easily studied are poor, inexperienced, minority, use drugs, or work the streets and, as a consequence, are in contact with the criminal justice system. Little reliable evidence exists on the HIV infection status of male prostitutes and female prostitutes who have escaped legal prosecution. Of female sex workers studied, it appears that their risk for infection is "more closely associated with drug use than with multiple sexual clients. The evidence also indicates that the risk of transmission through sexual contact is greater in . . . personal relationships . . . than in their paying ones,"[28] principally because condom use is less frequent and the repertoire of sexual activity may be more extensive and carry a greater risk for HIV transmission. These data do not mean that unprotected sex with female prostitutes necessarily carries little or no risk for HIV infection. The risk exists and is comparable to that associated with unprotected intercourse with sexually active or drug-injecting partners.

Who is HIV+ (HIV positive) or is at risk for HIV infection is becoming clearer as survey techniques are improved and refined. The demographics of the HIV/AIDS epidemic have changed between 1981 and 1991. Unless a "second wave" of new infections occurs among younger men who have sex with men, the sexual transmission of HIV in the United States will begin to parallel more closely the epidemic in developing countries, that is, by heterosexual intercourse. Not only do the epidemiological data over time show that the demographics of the HIV epidemic are changing; they indicate that the geography of HIV/AIDS is changing. The epidemic has been centered in large urban areas such as New York, San Francisco, Miami, Houston, Washington, D.C., and Los Angeles, a few of the so-called hyperendemic cities. There is emerging evidence, however, that the prevalence of HIV infection in smaller cities and rural areas is rising. Reports on the HIV serostatus of applicants for military service point to this conclusion. The HIV test results of applicants from the seven most populous states (New York, California, Texas, Pennsylvania, Illinois, Ohio, Florida) between October 1985 and September 1987 have been analyzed. Of 435,146 applicants (86% male, 73% white), 1.89/1,000 were HIV+. The prevalence rate for whites born between 1962 and 1969 was 0.67/1,000; for blacks born between 1962 and 1969, the rate was 3.43/1,000, and for all races born between 1937 and 1961, the rate was 4.98/1,000. These rates may underestimate the seroprevalence rates of the general population because gay and bisexual men and intravenous drug users are likely not to apply for military service. Further analysis of HIV+ applicants indicates that the total rate of HIV seroprevalence increased from 1.21/1,000 from 1985–1986 to 1.49/1,000 during 1986–1987 in nonepidemic areas outside urban areas where the epidemic has been centered. The authors of this study conclude: "These military applicant HIV antibody data document that HIV infection transmission was occurring in cities (and nonurban locations) outside the original AIDS epidemic centers as early as 2 years ago [1987]. Furthermore, the data indicate that transmission was occurring among adolescents and young adults both black and white, and across all regions of the U.S. If these findings can be replicated with more recent HIV seroprevalence data, it can be concluded that observations on the increasing proportion of AIDS cases in small cities are a significant development with serious health care ramifications for the future."[29]

Estimates of the number of people infected, projections of the number of people who will be diagnosed with HIV/AIDS in the next several years, and discussion of the diversification and dispersal of the population with HIV disease separately and collectively present a daunting picture of past, current, and future morbidity.

It should not be forgotten that people die with AIDS. By the end of 1990, the official death toll was 100,777. About one-third (31,196) of these deaths were reported during 1990! By 1988, HIV/AIDS became the third leading cause of death among men aged 25–44 years. It surpassed heart disease, cancer, suicide, and homicide to become the second leading cause of death among this age-group by 1989. In fact, the steady decline in death rates among men 25–44 years of age began to reverse by 1987. This reversal is attributed to the increased mortality among men this age due to HIV/AIDS.[30] HIV/AIDS was the eighth leading cause of death among women

25–44 years of age in 1988. By the end of 1991, HIV/AIDS will be among the five leading causes of death for women of this age-group.

Gay and bisexual men account for 59 percent of cumulative deaths. Women and heterosexual male IVDUs constitute an additional 21 percent. Although whites represent approximately 55 percent of all deaths due to HIV/AIDS (8.7/100,000 population), by 1990 reported deaths were highest for blacks (29.3/100,000) and Hispanics (22.2/100,000). Children also die from AIDS. By the end of 1990, 1,141 children under age five and 308 between the ages of five and fourteen had died.

Mortality due to HIV/AIDS varies across the country. HIV/AIDS is the leading cause of death among young adult men in San Francisco, Los Angeles, and New York City. It is the leading cause of death among black women 15–44 years of age in New York State and New Jersey. In 1988 in New York State, it was the leading cause of death among Hispanic children and the second leading cause of death among black children 1–4 years of age. Of the estimated one million people now infected with HIV in the United States, the CDC projects that 165,000–215,000 will die during 1991–1993.[31]

The capacity to confirm infection was greatly enhanced during 1985 with the approval of a blood-testing process called enzyme-linked immunosorbent assay (ELISA).[32] This relatively simple and inexpensive test was developed to screen donated blood for antibodies to the AIDS virus, thus reducing the risk of infection by transfusion or use of blood products. The ELISA is also used to determine the infection status of people in clinical settings. A positive ELISA generally is followed by another blood test, Western blot, to increase the confidence level that the ELISA result was a true positive.[33] The ELISA test, if positive, indicates the presence of antibodies to the AIDS virus at a sufficient level to activate the test at the time the tested blood was drawn. If the test is negative, it means that the tested blood does not have a sufficient level of

HIV antibodies to activate the test. A person may, nevertheless, be infected. Thus, it is recommended that people at risk for infection be tested every six months if they wish to monitor their infection status. When a person is antibody-positive for the AIDS virus, he or she should be considered infectious and take precautions not to infect others. With the ELISA, it could be possible to determine the actual incidence of infection in the population, but public health authorities have decided against universal testing.

During the decade of the 1980s, the spread of HIV on several continents during prior decades became manifest. The first few case reports in New York City and Los Angeles signaled a new era in the history of infectious diseases and public health. The speed and severity of the impact of this new epidemic initially experienced by gay men in the United States increasingly are being felt by other identifiable populations in this country and abroad. More is known about the epidemic in developed countries than in those of the developing world because of the medical, scientific, and social science resources of the former. Nevertheless, the emerging global picture of the epidemic ought to command the attention of people everywhere. The morbidity and mortality owing to HIV/AIDS during the first official decade of the epidemic are only a harbinger of even greater destruction of human life to come, given current therapeutics and probable advances during the decade of the 1990s. The fate of people now infected or who will become infected in the future can be seen by looking at those people already suffering because of HIV/AIDS. Effective risk-avoidance and risk-reduction educational campaigns throughout the world might decrease the human toll in the future. Information without the resources to act upon it, however, is a scandal. Thus, we remain pessimistic about the prospect of new infections decreasing in the developing world and only slightly more optimistic about the epidemic of infection abating in the developed world during the next several years. It appears that HIV and AIDS will be part of the world's vocabulary and a crisis of varying magnitude into the twenty-first century.

3

Clinical and Psychosocial Effects of HIV/AIDS

AIDS is the most widely known clinical diagnosis that may follow infection by HIV. It is not generally understood among the public, however, that AIDS is not the most common HIV-related diagnosis. Two additional clinical diagnoses of HIV disease are more common but less publicized: asymptomatic HIV disease and symptomatic HIV disease. The most common clinical category, as can be inferred from the epidemiological data in the preceding chapter, is either asymptomatic HIV disease, that is, HIV antibody-positive, or HIV seropositive (each term refers to presence of antibodies to HIV in the blood).

According to the Centers for Disease Control (CDC) revised surveillance definition, the diagnosis of AIDS is reserved for cases with one or more well-defined life-threatening conditions that are related to an underlying HIV-induced cellular immune suppression or a CD4+ T cell count of two hundred or less per cubic millimeter. The surveillance definition allows for an AIDS diagnosis in situations where laboratory evidence of HIV infection is available and where it is lacking but no other cause of immunodeficiency is found. A number of specific diagnoses in addition to laboratory or presumptive evidence of HIV infection will trigger an AIDS diagnosis. In general, indicator diseases of AIDS include candidiasis, cryptococcosis, cryptosporidiosis, cytomegalovirus disease, herpes simplex virus infection, Kaposi's sarcoma, lymphoma of the brain, lymphoid interstitial pneumonia and pulmonary lymphoid hyperplasia in a child under thirteen years of age, *Mycobacterium avium* complex or *Mycobacterium kansasii* disease, *Pneumocystis carinii* pneumonia, progressive multifocal leukoencephalopathy, toxoplasmosis of the brain, certain multiple or recurrent bacterial infections in a child under thirteen years of age, coccidioidomycosis, HIV encephalopathy, histoplasmosis, isosporiasis, non-Hodgkin's lymphoma of B cells, small noncleaved lymphoma, immunoblastic sarcoma, extrapulmonary disease caused by *Mycobacterium tuberculosis*, *Salmonella* septicemia, and HIV wasting syndrome.

The current CDC surveillance definition includes severe noninfectious and noncancerous HIV-associated conditions that were omitted from earlier definitions.[1] Another change is the inclusion of conditions indicative of pediatric AIDS in the surveillance definition. Prior to the most recent revision, pediatric AIDS was a separately defined condition. With the passage of time and an improved understanding of HIV disease, epidemiologists and physicians are able more accurately to characterize the spectrum of disease.

A detailed explanation of each of the indicator diseases would not be helpful here. What is important is that each disease, in its own way, exacts a heavy toll on a person whose cellular immune system is compromised by HIV infection. Also, it is common for people with AIDS to have two or more of these conditions active at the same time. AIDS-related infections typically affect the lungs, gastrointestinal system, bone marrow, and central nervous system. Kaposi's sarcoma typically appears first on the skin but can spread to the lymph nodes, lungs, or gastrointestinal tract. The lymphomas in AIDS tend to appear most commonly in the central nervous system, bone marrow, and bowel, but also in other sites.[2]

Some of these diseases are responsive to conventional or experimental prophylactic or curative interventions.[3] It should be emphasized, however, that recovery does not mean that a particular disease will not reappear later. Many patients have recurring acute episodes of the same disease, or the disease becomes chronic. This phenomenon of multiple, sequential, major acute illnesses, alone or in combination with chronic illnesses typical of HIV/AIDS, results in a course that often is unpredictable. Patients may deteriorate gradually or rapidly. Their loss of control over their bodies and lives mirrors, in most instances, the features and rate of their deterioration.

Unfortunately, there is still no cure for HIV/AIDS, and death remains the ultimate prognosis. This is not to say, however, that AIDS is equivalent to a sentence of imminent death. Therapeutic advances since 1985 appear to be contributing to longer and improved survival for people who can access and tolerate them. Prophylactic treatment for *Pneumocystis carinii* pneumonia (PCP) with aerosolized pentamidine or sulfamethoxazole-trimethoprim and antiretroviral treatment with AZT or Retrovir, earlier diagnosis by physicians experienced in managing HIV/AIDS, and more aggressive therapeutic and prophylactic interventions all may have a role in the improving survival statistics.

Numerous reports of median survival with HIV/AIDS have appeared in the world medical literature. Despite recent advances in treatment, median survival following diagnosis with AIDS is still measured in months rather than years. Median survival times are influenced by factors such as sex, age, race or ethnicity, risk factor, and manifestation of disease at diagnosis. A study of people with AIDS in San Francisco, where state-of-the-art services generally are accessible to all, showed median survival for all patients to be 12.5 months, as of December 1988. The five-year survival rate was 3.4 percent.[4] A similar study of patients at Montefiore Medical Center in Bronx, New York, showed a median survival of 12.8 months for people presenting with Kaposi's sarcoma,

10.9 months for people presenting with PCP, and 4.8 months for people presenting with other infections or neoplasms.[5]

The relevance of this latter study for people living with HIV/AIDS may be limited because it was completed in 1987. Dr. Richard Chaisson of the Johns Hopkins University School of Medicine, in a 1990 review of median survival reports, agreed that improvements in survival are occurring in all demographic categories. However, he cautions against becoming euphoric about these small improvements. Characterizations of HIV infection as a "chronic manageable disease" may be misleading in light of available data. HIV infection is chronic and treatable in the sense that treatment "significantly slows, but does not reverse, the progress of the disease. . . . While 2-year survival after AIDS has increased dramatically, 5-year survival remains low. In the absence of therapy that restores cellular immunocompetence, mortality, while slowed, will remain high."[6] Although more current studies of median survival are unavailable as of this writing, the trend appears to be toward longer and improved survival, particularly for white men with access to therapy and services. The improvements do not appear as dramatic among minorities, women, and children whose health care needs in urban areas tend to be met inadequately.

A diagnosis of HIV/AIDS denotes the point within the progression of HIV infection that life is threatened. The median survival data reviewed above seem to validate this characterization, though recent reports indicate that some people live with HIV infection for years prior to advancing to AIDS. A cohort of homosexual and bisexual men in San Francisco were estimated to have a median incubation period (time from HIV infection to AIDS) of 11.0 years and a mean (average) incubation period of 11.8 years.[7] It appears that the rate of disease progression is affected by any number of poorly understood biological, physical, socioeconomic, and lifestyle variables.[8] Some people with HIV infection progress to

AIDS relatively quickly, whereas others do not. Laboratory and clinical predictors are being discovered and used to trigger initiation of antiretroviral chemotherapy and chemoprophylaxis for infections.[9]

HIV infection in children, particularly newborn infants, tends to differ from the course of adults with HIV disease. Antibody tests of infants newly born to HIV+ mothers may detect passively transferred maternal antibodies to HIV. These passively transferred antibodies may persist for 12–15 months. Thus, in the absence of symptoms, a positive ELISA may be misleading, indicating the need for other tests to determine if an infant is truly infected with HIV. Among HIV-infected infants, symptoms usually appear between 4 and 8 months, with progression to AIDS during the first year of life for approximately 50 percent of infants and by age three for approximately 80 percent. The onset of AIDS may be delayed until school age in some children with congenitally acquired infection.[10] Median survival for 172 children studied in Miami, Florida, was thirty-eight months after symptoms appeared. Mortality was highest during the first year of life (17%).[11] About 75 percent of children with HIV disease die within two years. The clinical course of young children with HIV infection tends to deteriorate much more rapidly than among adults.

AIDS-related complex (ARC) and lymphadenopathy syndrome (LAS) were commonly used clinical designations for disorders associated with HIV infection that were not life threatening. These clinical terms are now rarely used because the criteria for each were not uniform, rendering comparison of data nearly impossible. The practice now is to refer to non-AIDS HIV disease as symptomatic or asymptomatic. Symptomatic HIV disease includes such physical findings as diarrhea, unintended weight loss, malaise, fatigue, night sweats, unexplained fever, skin rashes, and swollen lymph nodes. Laboratory findings of cellular immunosuppression, like physical symptoms, indicate that regular monitoring by an HIV-informed physician is wise. Asymptomatic HIV disease excludes signs or symptoms of HIV infection, but includes abnormal laboratory studies of cellular immunocompetence. People who are asymptomatic simply are said to be HIV seropositive, capable of living as normally as if not infected with HIV. An important exception to this generalization, however, is that *all* HIV-infected people, including asymptomatic individuals, are considered infectious. Risk-reduction measures are advised when in contact with potentially infectious bodily fluids.

As noted above, based on available evidence, HIV infection constitutes a chronic, progressive condition. Any prediction of rates or time for progression from infection to symptoms, AIDS, or death is speculative. Retrospective and longitudinal studies of HIV+ people are instructive, providing over time a picture of the natural history of HIV infection in humans. There is consensus among experts that, in light of known data and in the absence of more effective or immuno-stimulating treatments, progression to AIDS is likely within an indefinite period.

Before we discuss other features of the HIV/AIDS epidemic, it is important to look briefly at the psychiatric and neurologic complications of HIV infection. We saw that HIV has a devastating effect on the cellular immune system by destroying the quantity and effectiveness of a key cell, the CD4+ T cell. HIV infects this cell because it has a chemical receptor on its surface that permits the virus to penetrate it. It should not be overlooked, however, that HIV can invade other cells in the body with CD4+ receptors to allow it entry. This means that HIV not only causes certain illnesses; it also creates the conditions in which other organisms may produce illness. This process of HIV-induced illness is seen dramatically in the central nervous system.

HIV was first detected in brain (glial) cells and in spinal cord tissues in 1984. This discovery is significant for several reasons. First, it confirms the suspicion that HIV, like other retroviruses, can cause neurological disease. This means that HIV may be capable of incubating in the body as long as fifteen years before symptoms of neurological disease appear. Second, antiretroviral agents must be able to penetrate the blood–brain barrier in order to be successful. Therapies that only inhibit viral replication in blood and blood cells will not be adequate. A cure must also entail removing HIV from brain cells in a way that is nontoxic to brain tissues. Third, neurological impairments related to or caused by HIV will place additional strains on the health care system. This potentially large population eventually could exhibit major physical impairments and severe neurological disabilities that require intensive medical and custodial care.

The psychiatric and neurological complications of HIV infection may range from minor to severe, even lethal.[12] In addition to opportunistic infections and neoplasms of the central nervous system, patients often develop some level of dementia, psychosis-like illnesses, and other neurological syndromes, such as multiple sclerosis. Common neurological complaints of patients are memory loss, confusion, mental slowing, leg weakness, unsteady gait, tremor, agitation, apathy, peripheral neuropathies, seizures, and decreased coordination. The most common central nervous system complication of HIV infection is the AIDS dementia complex. The majority of AIDS patients are likely to develop this complication in the later stages of disease progression. Few complications of HIV infection are dreaded more than the deterioration or loss of one's mental capacities. The possible severity and incidence of neuropsychiatric disorders underscore the extensive, devastating potential of HIV to infected individuals and those involved in their care.

Psychosocial Aspects and the Economic Impact of AIDS

The physical and mental manifestations of HIV infection tend to be most severe and debilitating with full-blown AIDS. The debility and dependency that accompany the progression of disease in the body can have a correspondingly severe effect on the family and friends of a person with AIDS and on the public at large. In some instances, the psychosocial consequences of an AIDS or HIV-related diagnosis can be as devastating as the disease itself.[13] The discussion of these matters will be divided into five parts, with each part focusing on different broad groups touched by the HIV/AIDS epidemic.

People with HIV Disease, Their Relatives and Friends

When a person is told by a physician that she or he has AIDS or HIV infection, a series of adjustments are set in motion, adjustments that affect every aspect of the person's life. Family and other intimate relationships, romantic involvements, friendships, and occupational ties suddenly are cast in a new light. Perspectives and priorities may change. Decisions about oneself and plans for the future require reexamination. Obviously, these matters generally appear more urgent to people with AIDS and symptomatic HIV disease than to people who are asymptomatic. Because HIV/AIDS in the United States is most prevalent among young adults, who normally are not anticipating debility and death, their diagnosis tends to set in motion a transition from being vigorous to being debilitated, symptom-ridden, and probably dying within an uncertain span of time. This abrupt change in status and self-perception requires a massive adjustment. It tends to be easier for people who were psychologically stable before the diagnosis and who have loyal and cohesive support systems.

People frequently use the defense mechanism of denial to exercise control over how and when they will face the matter of their own mortality. Denial tends to be less effective among people with AIDS because the lethal character of their diagnosis is reinforced by frequent media reports, discouraging medical developments, and the deaths of friends. It may be difficult to be hopeful about the future. The sense of insecurity (because prophylactic and curative treatments and other therapeutic interventions appear to have limited efficacies) is heightened by financial, career, and relational limitations common to young adults. Fears about infecting others and guilt about transmitting HIV to past sexual partners also may have a role in the adjustment process. IV drug users and men who have sex with men and have kept this conduct secret may have to disclose to family and friends this feature of their lives, not knowing for certain how others will respond. The threat of condemnation and abandonment intensifies the distress of people in these situations.

Diminished self-esteem and depression are common. The stigma attached to AIDS; concern about a loss of autonomy due to physical weakness and mental deficits; social rebuke and rejection; and discrimination in work, housing, insurance, and social services contribute to the psychological trauma of the diagnosis.[14] Having watched a lover or friend struggle against the dignity-robbing effects of AIDS, some people approach their illness with dread, fearful of the disfigurement, debilitation, wasting, and death that may already be all too familiar. The appearance of Kaposi's sarcoma lesions on visible parts of the body may provoke anger, anxiety, and, for some, resignation to a self-imposed, if not externally imposed, isolation. Abandonment or fears of abandonment may compound the anxiety that people experience about their present and future state. Living alone, perhaps with little or no support from friends or family, HIV+ people may worry about what will happen when they are unable to care for themselves. Nursing homes and hospices may not be available because of a lack of funds or because the doors are not open to them. Finally, knowing that they are infectious but still desiring intimate contact to meet a variety of psychological and emotional needs can create distress and anxiety. Some feel unattractive and untouchable, even though they have a significant need and desire for affirmation and affection, which often can be shown by a simple pat on the shoulder, a kind word, or a hug.

In contrast to the trend during most of the first decade of HIV/AIDS, activists within heavily affected populations, principally gay men, and the health care establishment now encourage all people with histories of HIV risk behavior to be tested. As of December 1989, 21 percent of adults have been tested at least once for antibody to HIV. Most tests were performed in the process of donating blood (67%), but 19 percent voluntarily sought the test.[15] The rationale for this change depends upon the availability of chemotherapies that, particularly in combination with the adoption of healthier lifestyles, appear to inhibit disease progression. HIV testing usually is linked to pre- and post-test counseling to educate the person about the test and to provide support and guidance upon learning the test results. Reactions when the test is positive for antibodies to HIV infection may include shock, grief, denial, anxiety, and depression. The prospect of delayed progression to symptoms or AIDS, however, may ameliorate the emotional response. Counselors at the testing site or at other centers usually are available to help newly diagnosed HIV+ people adjust and plan to *live* with HIV disease. An important aspect of this adjustment process is the development of negotiating skills regarding sexual interests, because most people in this situation are young adults who desire sexual intimacy. "Safer sex" education, accordingly, becomes part of an HIV+ person's continuing education.[16]

The psychosocial aspects of an AIDS or related diagnosis for relatives are in some ways unique. Many families must deal with the same fears and anxieties about AIDS that the general public confronts.[17] In addition, they may have to respond to disclosures regarding the family member's lifestyle and the resulting strain on relationships. Relatives, too, may feel stigmatized and isolated because of their relationship to a loved one with HIV/AIDS, who also may be homosexual, bisexual, or an IV drug user. Fears of criticism, ostracism, and embarrassment may prevent families from sharing their burden with others and, as a consequence, deny them the support that otherwise would be provided if the family member's illness were other than HIV/AIDS-related.

Relatives may be angry, feeling that the loved one has been irresponsible or sinful and has unnecessarily burdened them. Prejudice against gay and bisexual men suddenly may be directed toward a loved one, thereby threatening the relationship and generating internal conflicts in family members who are not understanding or sympathetic. Ambivalence toward a loved one's friends or gay lover may be an additional source of stress. In particular, family disapproval or rejection of a lover may lead a gay man to feel that he has to choose between his lover and his family at a time when he needs the loving support and affirmation of all people important to him.

Similar stresses may follow a family's discovery that a loved one had sexual contact with IV drug users or has engaged in nonmarital or extramarital sexual activity. Disappointment, anger, and feelings of betrayal may accompany or distort feelings of concern for the one newly diagnosed as HIV+. A spouse may experience a wide variety of feelings about a marital partner and self in light of a discovery of his or her risk behavior and the HIV infection that followed. Children of an infected parent require sensitive counseling as the household adjusts to the news and develops contingency plans. As HIV spreads among heterosexual women of child-bearing age, a woman's discovery of her infection may come at the birth of a child. The immediate and extended family then may be called upon to accommodate the HIV infection of mother, child, and, perhaps, father. They also may be forced to confront the anticipated death of the whole immediate family from HIV/AIDS.[18]

The threat of death carried by HIV/AIDS means disruption of the life plans of both HIV+ people and their relatives. Parental concerns for the welfare of an adult child whose death is foreseen as imminent involve concerns for themselves as well. They mourn the anticipated and actual death. They also grieve the loss of the potential security which that child represented to their old age.

Parents frequently say, "This isn't natural," or, "This isn't the way it's supposed to be." Children are to bury parents, rather than parents burying children. Death vigils may be complicated by family members who are afraid to hold or kiss their dying loved one. Although a spoken good-bye may be sufficient for some family members, a good-bye that forgoes physical contact may be an occasion for remorse and guilt later. Another complication in family relationships before and after death may develop if the person with AIDS has attempted to protect relatives by not disclosing the true diagnosis or has allowed the truth to be told too late for meaningful conversations to take place. Family members may feel they have not been trusted and may search to identify where they "failed" the loved one. Feelings of rejection, neglect, and abandonment are not uncommon in these situations. Feelings of guilt may develop if a family fears to take the patient home to die because friends, neighbors, and church members would learn the truth. And finally, the healing process of bereavement may be frustrated because the usual support from friends and family may be forgone or not available.

Lovers of gay men with AIDS may be a source of conflict with families if the relationship between the two men is difficult to accept. Families may not accept the lover as a person whose significance to the patient is comparable to a spouse in a heterosexual marriage. The stresses typically associated with situations of serious illness may be increased by tensions related to a gay relationship. In addition, a gay patient may legally empower his lover to make decisions about treatment during periods of the patient's incompetence, and families may resent being displaced in this fashion. Issues of control and dissatisfaction with one's sense of emotional importance to the person can become points of contention between lover, the person with AIDS, and the family.

Lovers tend to have emotional and psychological reactions to their loved one's illness comparable to that experienced by heterosexual spouses. These include anger, grief, and fear. Chronic illness, debility, and premature death are not within the normal expectations of young adults. The stresses imposed on the relationship create needs for support and understanding. The burden of care can be exhausting, physically and emotionally. Plans, dreams, and hopes that will not be fulfilled become sources of grief. The situation at home may be unknown to family and co-workers. For example, lies and excuses explaining exhaustion, irritability, and poor performance may not be satisfactory to an employer. Similarly, absence from work may be difficult to explain without disclosing personal information that could place one's employment in jeopardy. Finally, when death occurs, co-workers may be denied the opportunity to be supportive, and the grieving lover may not be excused from daily activities to mourn.

Friends of people with AIDS have many of the same feelings and reactions as families and lovers. At times, friends respond by avoiding the person with an HIV infection, especially if AIDS is diagnosed. In other situations, friends remain loyal, understanding, supportive, and compassionate. People who share risk histories, such as gay men, may have experienced the death of many friends. Chronic grief is not an uncommon phenomenon. The cumulative loss and pain can become so intense that they seek to avoid any future hurt by disengaging from sick friends. This response may not be callous but rather self-protective. Gay men have said they feel like soldiers watching the rest of their platoon fall in battle one after another.

People who have sojourned with and survived the deaths of many friends may discover that they are incapable of sustaining additional losses. Gay men, for example, who have seen twenty, thirty, forty, or more friends die may be incapable of supporting one more during a period of decline and death. Their loyalty or commitment seems steadfast, but their capacity to bear the burden one more time may be lacking. Withdrawal or decreased attentiveness in these circumstances may be self-protective, understandable, and appropriate. Nevertheless, anger and feelings of betrayal among those who need, value, and expect the absent person's care equally are understandable and appropriate. This situation is just one more reason for grief in lives already overburdened with grief. Moreover, it should be expected that people who draw back in emotional, physical, and spiritual exhaustion may feel shame and guilt about their decision. This dynamic tends to be more complex when the person who withdraws from the care of others is HIV+, symptomatic, or diagnosed with AIDS. The perception that a person is seeing one's future in others with more advanced disease is not the sort of encouragement one may need to live as normally as possible and with hope.

Health Care Personnel

Because people with HIV infection, especially AIDS and HIV symptomatic disease, frequently require medical attention and hospitalization, bonding often occurs with health care personnel. This takes place in both directions, patient to personnel and personnel to patient. Watching patients deteriorate and die in their prime is emotionally draining. There are no major victories in AIDS treatment at present, only minor ones. This situation is discomforting to professionals accustomed to cures, palliation, or remission. Chronic grief is common, and so is physical exhaustion. AIDS patients during acute illnesses tend to require frequent therapeutic interventions and diagnostic procedures. The needs of AIDS patients can seem all-consuming, especially when resources are limited and the needs for care are extensive. Finally, communicating with a patient can be complicated by a patient's neurological condition. Informing a patient about his or her status, explaining options, and responding to questions can be time-consuming, especially if a physician treats many AIDS patients. The time required to provide emotional support to patients, families, and friends places even greater demands on the time and energy of health care personnel. Prejudice toward at-risk groups and fear for personal safety may lessen the quality and character of care provided by personnel who may serve AIDS patients involuntarily—nurses, resident physicians, and technicians. Some personnel feel ambivalent about their work with these patients and are torn between a sense of professional duty toward the sick and negative feelings about conduct related to HIV infection. Finally, health care personnel may be isolated by peers and friends. Colleagues and friends may not value the investment in people with HIV-related diagnoses. Subtle and overt expressions of disapproval of one's professional and moral sense of duty may generate doubts about the worthiness of one's work and ambivalence toward the population served.[19]

Families with HIV Disease

The epidemiological data reviewed in Chapter 2 signals an important, gradually accelerating shift in the population with HIV disease. Single adults will continue to be the largest population with AIDS for several years because of their early infection and the long incubation period (perhaps ten years or longer) in some adults. However, as people infected with HIV, either as a result of heterosexual intercourse, IV drug use, or receipt of blood or blood products, marry or cohabit, an uninfected partner may become infected. In addition, children born to an infected woman have about a 30 percent probability of being born with HIV infection. The scenario of a whole family unit having HIV disease is becoming more common, particularly in urban areas where HIV is endemic due to lifestyle factors, that is, IV drug use and sexual intercourse with people who inject drugs with shared equipment.

The general, but by no means exclusive, picture of families with HIV/AIDS mirrors the demographic description of densely populated inner cities. These families tend to be people of color, people who are poor, have limited education, live in varied family structures, move frequently, and are affected by drugs directly or indirectly. Their histories have resulted in their having poor communication skills, embracing diverse value systems, suspecting authority figures, and being adept at manipulation in order to survive. This picture tends to contrast sharply with the psychosocial situation of families affected by hemophilia or blood transfusion and HIV/AIDS. In particular, hemophilia families generally have much confidence in medical authorities, and are self-determining, educated, and adept at accessing needed social and health care services. The two populations tend to share a concern for secrecy about their situations and feelings of being victimized by one or another oppressive force.

The parent or parents in these situations experience numerous impediments to the ability to live normally within their socioeconomic constraints. The health care of the family may be fragmented, adults being treated at one site and the children receiving care at another site. Agencies providing social services may be geographically dispersed, making access to services difficult when transportation is unavailable or unaffordable. The parent's physical condition may make employment impossible. It also may impair his or her ability to care continuously for a child. A shortage of physical and material resources among the adults in these settings may intensify feelings of loss, anger, frustration, hopelessness, and grief typically associated with illness and the prospect of death. Parents tend to worry about who will care for them when they are ill and who will tend a child during these times. Moreover, who will assume parental responsibility for a child, either HIV+ or not, if one or both parents succumb to AIDS? There will be grief occasioned by the prospect of not being able to watch a child grow up or the prospect of watching one's young child die. There may be questions of how and what to tell children about the physical status of the parent or parents. Similar questions often are raised regarding disclosures to an HIV-infected child or to the infected child's uninfected siblings. Finally, if an HIV+ mother becomes pregnant, whether to bring the pregnancy to term with the 30 percent chance that the newborn will be infected or to terminate the pregnancy is a difficult question for the woman to answer. The situation of families with HIV/AIDS tends to be more complex than that of single adults because of the larger number of people involved and the presence of dependent children. The plight of families is no more or less tragic than that of single adults; it simply is different.[20]

The Public at Large

The public justifiably is concerned about the present and potential impact of HIV/AIDS. Apart from reports of fearful reactions to people with HIV/AIDS, the disease generally was a matter of marginal concern until it was perceived as a threat to heterosexual people who are not IV drug users. The voices of scientists calling attention to the growing magnitude of the epidemic finally are being heard. Yet the unavailability of absolute answers to some questions regarding transmission of HIV and conflicting interpretations of available data generate confusion. This confusion seems to impede a comprehensive, informed, and coordinated response to HIV/AIDS, in terms of research, treatment, and prevention.

Public education activities have been constrained by a variety of concerns. For example, informing people about the means of HIV infection requires discussing sexuality and IV drug use, and both subjects are potentially explosive. Also, condoms, which decrease the risk of infection, are also contraceptive when used during heterosexual intercourse—another morally controversial topic among some people. The dilemma the public faces ought not be underestimated. Massive educational programs aimed at prevention are imperative. Yet the goal of prevention may be at odds with the moral values of certain segments of the population.

The Centers for Disease Control (CDC) is the federal agency most involved in the campaign to educate the public about the risk of HIV infection and how this risk can be avoided or decreased. The CDC has recognized the strategic role that religious organizations could have in a comprehensive disease prevention program through its National Partnerships Development Activity. Among characteristics of religious communities that signal their potential importance to HIV/AIDS education efforts are broad access to significant populations (including leaders in all sectors of life—workplace, education, civic life), influence and control of significant resources, respect by and credibility to very large segments of the population, and effective communication networks.[21]

Another area of public concern involves the response to people presently suffering with AIDS and HIV-related diagnoses. When the extent of suffering is made known, even if the ones suffering are not highly regarded, people tend to be moved to compassion. Informing the public of this situation without unnecessarily exposing the wasting bodies and minds of people with AIDS may be difficult. Verbal descriptions are not as compelling as personal testimonies and visual images. But once moved to compassion, the public must consider the claims of the AIDS population for care in relation to the claims of people struggling with other illnesses. Profound issues of distributive justice, as well as mercy, warrant consideration. Here the economic impact of AIDS becomes pointedly relevant.

Economic Impact of AIDS

Early estimates of the dollar and economic costs of AIDS in the United States were ominous. Analyses of the first 10,000 cases of AIDS indicated that hospitalization costs would be about $1.4 billion, and the economic loss from future earnings due to premature death would be $4.6 billion.[22] More recent studies indicate that the total lifetime hospitalization costs per AIDS patient will be about $75,000 in 1988 dollars.[23] This estimate is higher than earlier estimates of $42,000 to $50,000. Fred Hellinger, senior economist at the National Center for Health Services Research and Health Care Technology Assessment, has predicted that "the cumulative lifetime medical care costs of treating all people diagnosed with AIDS during a given year will be about $3.3 billion in 1989, $4.3 billion in 1990, $5.3 billion in 1991, $6.5 billion in 1992, and $7.8 billion in 1993."[24]

It should be noted that these estimates of current and projected expenditures do not account for lost earnings. Nor do they reflect expenditures for testing, screening, monitoring, and treating people with HIV symptomatic disease. Finally, neither the early nor the more recent analyses measure the intangible costs of pain, suffering, adverse effects on relationships, and social stigmatization. Clearly, the impact of HIV/AIDS on the demand for hospital beds, professional services, drugs, supportive services, and hospice care is already significant and will grow. Public education programs and social programs aimed at risk reduction will add to the economic burden.

This selected overview of the psychosocial aspects and economic impact of HIV/AIDS touches only the surface of the ever-widening effect of HIV. The picture of pain, suffering, and death truly is overwhelming when the experience in the United States is extended to include the rest of the world. There may be no other microorganism in history to equal the sweeping destructive effect of HIV/AIDS.

Prevention and Prospect for Treatment

It should be obvious that education to help reduce risks is at present the best defense against HIV. But several questions must be answered before these efforts can be expected to succeed. What should be the content of public education? What are the aims of public education? Who needs education? Who should do the educating? How should educational programs be funded and evaluated? These are vexing questions that raise complex and profound issues of public policy and ethics.[25] The difficulties foreseen in responding to these concerns ought not, however, be used as an excuse to ignore the public health crisis that prompts them.

Preventing or slowing the HIV/AIDS epidemic through education must be a high priority. However, this objective ought to be a companion to two other objectives: effective therapies for complications of HIV infection and a cure for HIV infection. Many of the acute illnesses associated with HIV/AIDS are treatable by conventional therapies. These treatments frequently restore people to a relative state of health that provides an acceptable quality of life. Unfortunately, either some complications of HIV infection are not treatable or the treatments are less effective. These therapeutic responses to acute and chronic illnesses may cure or lessen the effects of a particular secondary disease, but they do not address the underlying immune deficit that permits these illnesses to develop. Clearly, the primary objective of research is eradication of HIV and its destructive effect on the cellular immune system and the central nervous system, without becoming inattentive to treating complications.

The experience of scientists and physicians since 1981 suggests that finding a cure is a formidable task. There is no doubt that the basic science and therapeutics of viral diseases are improving. Treatments for herpes, papilloma virus (wart virus), and cytomegalovirus are reducing or preventing the acute signs of infection, if not providing a cure. This experience with less lethal viruses is proving valuable in the fight against HIV. But HIV is a virus hard to combat because it infects not only blood cells but also brain and probably other types of cells. Thus, ridding the body of HIV may be an unattainable objective, because to destroy the virus in cells may require destroying brain cells that cannot be replaced. Suppressing viral replication and preventing the infection of new cells may be the most practical approach, given the action of the retrovirus in the body. Antiretroviral drugs must, as a consequence, cross the blood–brain barrier, be safe for long-term use, and be administered orally, so patients are not tied to intravenous modes of treatment, adversely affecting quality of life and straining the health care system. Finally, effective therapy should be low-cost, because there is an urgent need for therapy in poor countries.

Efforts to identify, develop, and test drugs that safely inhibit virus replication thus far have produced limited positive results. We already have drawn attention to the relative efficacy and toxic side effects of AZT or Retrovir, the first antiretroviral drug approved in the United States for general use in the treatment of HIV infection. This drug appears partly responsible for the improved and extended life of some people with HIV disease. Nevertheless, it is an expensive drug that has been the subject of much scientific, regulatory, consumer, and commercial controversy.[26] The slow pace of antiretroviral drug development and dissatisfaction with the design and conduct of clinical trials of experimental drugs have resulted in affected populations organizing to take more control over treatment. Buyers' clubs import drugs for people, and networks through which treatment information is exchanged have become highly visible parts of the HIV/AIDS therapeutic arena. Alternative treatments and underground drugs are often part of the self-prescribed therapeutic regimen of people who are not willing to wait for a medically orthodox cure to be found. In situations where conventional authorities and gatekeepers are unable to provide the desired relief, people who feel desperate tend to seek help elsewhere. The urgency felt by HIV+ people in general and those whose infection has advanced to AIDS in particular should extend to those in positions to move research and therapy forward with all deliberate speed.

Many scientists and physicians believe that a two-pronged attack will be required: one or more antiretroviral drugs, and one or more immune-stimulating drugs. The first offensive, antiretroviral drugs, would inhibit the destructive effect of HIV. The second offensive, immune stimulators, would help rebuild or stimulate the cellular immune system. Until a cure of whatever description is found, physicians caring for symptomatic people and people with AIDS will be able to respond to acute and chronic complications of HIV infection only with the most effective therapies presently available.

For the population not infected by HIV, a protective vaccine is urgently needed in order to abort a rapidly exploding epidemic. There are several feasible approaches to the development of a retroviral vaccine. Limited clinical trials in humans are being conducted at several sites in the United States and in other countries.[27] Which of these approaches, if any, will be perfected is impossible to predict now. It is clear, however, that demonstrating the efficacy of any candidate vaccine may require years of observation. The development of a safe and effective vaccine will be an important step in the process of ending the HIV epidemic. However, a vaccine is not a solution to the present global crisis of AIDS and HIV-related diseases.

HIV and its clinical manifestations present an awesome and complex challenge to scientists and physicians. Intensive efforts are under way within the scientific community to develop a protective vaccine and to overcome the barriers to a cure for HIV infection. While these goals are being pursued, the pain, suffering, and death produced by HIV cannot be ignored. A compassionate response to everyone directly or indirectly experiencing the destructive effects of HIV is indicated. Such a response to people tragically touched by this insidious virus is an obligation, not an option, for the people of God.

4

Illness in Christian Perspective

The question of how to account for the existence of illness, suffering, and tragedy as integral parts of daily life has preoccupied the human psyche throughout history. In particular, the Christian church has struggled with the relationship of illness to faith. The Gospels provide little insight regarding the role of illness and suffering in creation. Issues of how to justify the ways of God seem to have been unimportant to Jesus, who clearly gave priority to the urgency of proclaiming the gospel. We seemingly cannot forgo our human preoccupation with attempts to explain illness and suffering, but apparently Jesus did not join these discussions. He was too busy going about healing the sick, casting out demons, and, in so doing, manifesting God's compassion and love toward the afflicted. The church attempts to keep a balance between these two functions, engaging in acts of compassion and support to people in need and reflecting theologically on the relationship of this ministry to the church's confession and mission. If the New Testament is a guide, ministry must remain in the forefront of the church's activity. But theology as critical reflection on the work of ministry is not a secondary function. Rather, each function informs and corrects the other; each fulfills a servant role, so that the church's work may be done.[1]

It is important to pursue this interrelationship with respect to the AIDS epidemic. The dimensions of this crisis, the needs of people with AIDS, and societal reactions to people with AIDS demand a response from the church. We must discover the appropriate form such a response must take, as to both the nature of compassionate ministry and the theological imperatives by which care and concern are shaped and corrected. In the course of exploring these issues, we will discover that the scriptures do not offer simple answers to questions related to the existence of illness and suffering. Rather, they call the people of God to serve their neighbors. At this moment, that includes people with AIDS.

New Testament Perceptions of Suffering

The New Testament recognizes suffering as a part of daily living that must be accepted and endured with fortitude. The troubles to be borne in this earthly existence are of little consequence compared to the life that is "hidden with Christ in God" (Col. 3:3). The New Testament, however, addresses sufferings at three levels. First, some afflictions clearly were the consequences of imprisonment and persecution because of the believer's witness to faith in Jesus Christ as Lord. Thus was Stephen stoned to death. Second, suffering may be the result of oppression by one person or group of another person or group. The most frequently cited biblical example is the oppression of the weak and helpless by the wealthy and powerful. Third, pain and suffering may be due to disease or physical or mental disability.

Suffering "for Christ's Sake"

Peter refers to suffering "for Christ's sake," for example, when he warns his readers that they may suffer "trials of many kinds." These trials come so that their faith "may prove itself worthy of all praise, glory, and honour when Jesus Christ is revealed" (1 Peter 1:6–7). Paul expresses the same thought frequently. Writing to the Corinthians, he offers the example of his faithful witness:

> As God's servants, we try to recommend ourselves in all circumstances by our steadfast endurance: in distress, hardships, and dire straits; flogged, imprisoned, mobbed; overworked, sleepless, starving. . . . Dying we still live on; disciplined by suffering, we are not done to death; in our sorrows we have always cause for joy; poor ourselves, we bring wealth to many; penniless, we own the world."
>
> (2 Cor. 6:4–5, 9–10)

One of the richest sources of this image is in the eleventh chapter of the same letter:

> Five times the Jews have given me the thirty-nine strokes; three times I have been beaten with rods; once I was stoned; three times I have been shipwrecked, and for twenty-four hours I was adrift on the open sea. I have been constantly on the road; I have met dangers from rivers, dangers from robbers, dangers from my fellow-countrymen, dangers from foreigners, dangers in towns, dangers in the country, dangers at sea, dangers from false friends.
>
> (2 Cor. 11:24–26; see also, for example, Rom. 8:19; 13–19; 1 Cor. 4:9–13; 2 Cor. 1:8–11; 4:8–12, 16–18)

These "trials of many kinds" were anticipated in phrases attributed to Jesus in the Beatitudes: "How blest you are, when you suffer insults and persecution and every kind of calumny for my sake. Accept it with gladness and exultation, for you have a rich reward in heaven; in the same way they persecuted the prophets before you" (Matt. 5:11–12). Suffering "for Christ's sake" on the part of his followers is thus incorporated into the suffering for the sake of righteousness that characterizes both Old and New Testaments. In the Jewish scriptures, it is linked to the concept of the Suffering Servant. In the New Testament, Peter recognizes that such human suffering participates in the suffering of Christ:

> My dear friends, do not be bewildered by the fiery ordeal that is upon you, as though it were something extraordinary. It gives you a share in Christ's sufferings, and that is cause for joy; and when his glory is revealed, your joy will be triumphant. . . . If anyone suffers as a Christian, he should feel it no disgrace, but confess that name to the honour of God.
>
> (1 Peter 4:12–13, 16)

Such passages often seem to be advanced in support of the claim that when suffering in the form of physical illness is experienced, it ought to be accepted and endured as an ordeal in the sense intended by Peter; that is, a trial sent to test the believer's faith. A clear distinction, however, should be made as to the reason for suffering before physical hardship and illness are so linked, as will be noted.

Suffering as the Result of Oppression

The Gospels note a second source of suffering against which Jesus cried out in protest, and which is to be opposed at every point: suffering that results from human injustice and oppression of the poor. Luke begins his record of Jesus' ministry with the account of the visit to Nazareth. The words from Isaiah 61 are applied to the ministry of Jesus: "[The Lord] has sent me to announce good news to the poor" (Luke 4:18). The announcement is clearly intended to address the concerns that so roused the prophets: the need to proclaim liberation to broken victims and release to the captives. It is usual to link with these phrases the complementary passages from Isaiah. Thus, the Gospel calls for the loosing of the fetters of injustice, untying the knots of the yoke, snapping every yoke, and setting free those who have been crushed. To the cry for compassion toward the crushed is added the call to proclaim recovery of sight to the blind and to clothe the naked, provide hospitality to the homeless poor, feed the hungry, and satisfy the needs of the wretched (Isa. 58:6–10). In denouncing the authorities, Jesus pointed to their greed: "Beware of the doctors of the law. . . . These are the men who eat up the property of widows, while they say long prayers for appearance' sake; and they will receive the severest sentence" (Luke 20:45–47. Cf. Isa. 1:1ff.; Jer. 7:1–15).

Luke is not alone among the Evangelists in identifying Jesus as championing the cause of the poor and oppressed, but his Gospel is noteworthy for this emphasis. With Matthew, Luke cites Jesus' reply to John's disciples, who sought confirmation that Jesus was really "the coming one." Jesus' ministries of healing and liberation were explicit signs of the reign of God—for those who had eyes of faith to see. The fact that, in the liberating actions of Jesus, John possessed all the evidence he needed to satisfy his uncertainty leads to only one conclusion: the power of God is present in Jesus. In its presence, evil—in the form of oppression of the innocent, injustice levied against those too weak to speak for themselves, or exclusion of the humble from the community's concern and care—is being overturned. The message is clear. Evil cannot continue to exist in the presence of God's love.

The hospitality of the kingdom is extended without hesitation to those whom society has oppressed or ignored: the poor, the crippled, the lame, and the blind (Luke 14:21), those whose homes are the city's streets and alleys (v. 21) or the roads and hedges of the countryside (vs. 23–24). Such gracious acts are extended to people who, because of their very weakness, even their failure to thrive, are unable to return the gift of hospitality. That they cannot is the best reason for inviting them. The inability of the poor to return the kindness is the measure of their need of it. The words and actions of Jesus are those of confrontation: the causes and consequences of poverty, injustice, and exclusion from the community are to be opposed. Not only will those who oppress the poor not inherit the kingdom; even those who fail to minister to the least of the Lord's brothers and sisters will go away to eternal punishment, "to the eternal fire that is ready for the devil and his angels" (Matt. 25:41). Jesus accused the authorities of having no care for justice and the love of God, and the lawyers of loading people with intolerable burdens (Luke 11:42, 46). The scene in the temple in which the money-changers' tables were overthrown and the pigeons freed from their cages expresses the same sense of outrage at the afflictions imposed on the poor. For the robbery being practiced involved not only the fraudulent activities of the money-changers against worshipers, but the stealing of this house from God. "Moreover, the thefts from men were not limited to the Temple precincts, as Jeremiah knew, but included the dog-eat-dog practices outside the Temple by men who then took part in the worship" (Jer. 7:8–15).[2]

Jesus' work in the Temple was a prophetic sign of God's wrath, in accordance with God's desire to make God's house a place of worship for all nations. God had promised to bring foreigners and gather the outcasts to rejoice in the benefits of the Temple (Isa. 56:6–8). "It was this promise which Jesus fulfilled and which the priests repudiated, so that this episode becomes an epitome of the Messiah's whole career."[3] Jesus was addressing religious leaders in his society—but the same warnings apply to God's people in every age, as Matthew 25:31ff. reminds us. Woe to us, also, if having ears, we do not hear. As a result, God's people are not to accept or tolerate such affliction with passive resignation; we are bidden to lift the yoke of oppression and to fill the role of champions of the downtrodden. We walk in his footsteps only if we are filled with a like concern for the poor, a theme that is discussed more comprehensively in Chapter 5.

Suffering Due to Disease or Disability

Just as injustice cannot exist in the presence of the Lord's anointed, neither can sickness endure against God's power. The citing of the Isaianic passages (Luke

4:18–19) signals Luke's emphasis on Jesus' ministry to the poor and oppressed, among whom the Jewish scriptures identify the sick and disabled in body and mind. This aspect of the discussion should be set in the context of the attribution of causality for sickness and affliction, and the perceived relationship between illness or disability and ritual defilement, that has characterized Judeo-Christian thought. Judaism struggled with the notion that sickness was a consequence of sin and therefore a punishment. Acts of healing were acknowledged by proving to a priest that the symptoms of disease or disability had vanished, whereupon the priest declared that the defilement was lifted and the formerly disabled person was restored to the community and to the full benefits of the law. Ritual defilement resulted from any affliction, because it was axiomatic that the disease would not have occurred if the victim's relationship with God was not disordered.[4]

It is in this context that the ministry of Jesus to the sick should be set. Jesus was at pains to discard the ancient attribution of illness or disability as punishment for some act of disobedience of God's law, that is, as God's retribution for human sin. The tradition was long and deep. Sirach, or ben Sira, the author of Ecclesiasticus, declared in the second century B.C. that

> From the beginning good things were created for the good,
> and evils for sinners.
> The chief necessities of human life
> are water, fire, iron, and salt,
> flour, honey, and milk,
> the juice of the grape, oil, and clothing.
> All these are good for the godfearing,
> but turn to evil for sinners.
>
> There are winds created to be agents of retribution,
> with great whips to give play to their fury;
> on the day of reckoning, they exert their force
> and give full vent to the anger of their Maker.
> Fire and hail, famine and *deadly disease,*
> all these were created for retribution;

beasts of prey, scorpions and vipers,
and the avenging sword that destroys the wicked.
They delight in carrying out his orders,
always standing ready for his service on the earth;
and when their time comes, they never disobey.

(Ecclus. 39:25–31; emphasis added)

Sirach clearly reflected a popularly held perception against which Jesus protested. John records the disciples' questioning of Jesus regarding a blind man: "Rabbi, who sinned, this man or his parents? Why was he born blind?" Jesus responded: "It is not that this man or his parents sinned; he was born blind so that God's power might be displayed in curing him" (John 9:2–3). Jesus rejected the notion that God had deliberately disabled this man—and, conceivably, others—on account of sin, or merely to provide an opportunity to demonstrate God's power. Indeed, Mark presents Jesus as requiring the disciples to keep silent concerning such acts lest they be regarded by the populace as merely displays of power designed to coerce a positive response to the gospel—and thus be misunderstood. Luke records that Jesus was challenged to explain the sufferings of the innocent: for example, the Galileans slaughtered by Pilate and the eighteen upon whom the tower of Siloam fell (Luke 13:1–9). An easy solution would be to say, echoing Job's friends, that the fate of the Galileans overtook them in the providence of God, a just punishment for some iniquity of which they were doubtless guilty. Although it is precisely this theory that Jesus rejects, he does not advance any alternative explanation at this point.[5] The question of the problem of suffering is unanswered, for Jesus treats the story, and another that he raises, as parables. And the whole issue of the parables is the urgency of the gospel. It is this urgency that is offered as the basis for the Johannine statement: "While daylight lasts we must carry on the work of him who sent me; night comes, when no one can work. While I am in the world I am the light of the world" (John 9:4–5).

The issue for Jesus is the primacy of the gospel. He had come into Galilee "proclaiming the Gospel of God" (Mark 1:14). What followed, whether teaching, confronting, ministering compassionately, or healing, was the manifestation of the power of God at work: "If it is by the finger of God that I drive out the devils, then be sure the kingdom of God has already come upon you" (Luke 11:20). The healing acts were entailed by the message he proclaimed. Nothing, including disease and devils, could impede the progress of the kingdom's unveiling or withstand its power. Hence, the Markan "secret": the healing acts would only be correctly perceived when people recognized them as outbreaks of the kingdom's presence. In any other context, they would appear as mere "signs and wonders," which Jesus refused to provide (Matt. 12:39; Mark 8:12; see also John 4:48).

When one turns to examine how Jesus acted when confronted by human distress arising from disease and disability, the evidence is overwhelming: Jesus responded at every opportunity to relieve such affliction. Healing was often performed in a manner indicative of confrontation with illness. The Gospels identify Jesus as engaged in two types of healing activity: the driving out of demons and the healing of the sick and physically disabled. The twelve disciples were sent out with instructions to heal the sick, raise the dead, cleanse lepers, and cast out devils (Matt. 10:8). In Capernaum, the crowds brought to him all who were ill or possessed by devils (Mark 1:3). To Pharisees who urged him to escape from Herod, he replied, "Go and tell that fox, 'Listen: today and tomorrow I shall be casting out devils and working cures' " (Luke 13:32). The separate identification of the two activities suggests two functions. In the case of demon possession, the confrontation with evil is emphasized, but such actions are viewed in the context of the struggle between the power of the evil one and the power of God. Edward Schillebeeckx notes, "As Jesus pursues his ministry and manifests himself, this in itself is regarded by the evil powers as an act of aggression (Mark 1:23–24 and parallels; 5:7ff. and parallels; 9:20–25). Against the evil and hurtful results produced by these powers Jesus sets only good actions, deeds of beneficence."[6]

The exorcisms are presented to show that God's eschatological kingdom is now present. Illness in general, however, was a sign of disorder in God's creation that ends with physical death. Although sickness and death are customarily assumed to be evidence of the activity of evil, the healing of the sick is set in the context of the announcement of the kingdom and of Jesus' compassion for those who, because of their illness, are unable to live life to its fullest. Again and again, he is represented as reaching out to people at their points of need. Acts 10:38 states that witnesses can bear testimony to all that he did in the Jewish countryside and in Jerusalem: he went about doing good and healing all who were oppressed by the devil, "actively showing pity for the sick and those who by the standards of that time were held to be possessed by 'the demon' or by 'demons,' 'the prisoners' whom the eschatological prophet was to set free (Isa. 61:1–2)."[7] The commitment of Jesus in behalf of people in distress became the basis for the early church's emphasis on the preaching of the "glad tidings of Jesus Christ" (Mark 1:1). The Gospels report that the response of Jesus to those whose lives were disordered was one of tenderness and compassion. Nothing aroused his anger more spontaneously than unfeeling and uncaring legalists who saw not the distress of a person crippled in mind or body but an opportunity to moralize on the basis of some fine point of the Torah (Mark 3:1–6; see also Matt. 23:23, 24: "You pay tithes of mint and dill and cummin; but you have overlooked the weightier demands of the Law, justice, mercy, and good faith. . . . Blind guides! You strain off a midge, yet gulp down a camel!"). Today's legalists are similarly warned against substituting rigid proscriptions for loving compassion.

The intensity of Jesus' response to human suffering is illustrated in the story of the healing of a man with a crippled hand (Mark 3:1–6). The healing is necessary on the Sabbath, because in Hebrew thought not to heal the man would leave him nearer to death—for sickness is proximity to death.[8] That is, the struggle against sickness is a struggle to save the sufferer from the power of death and the threat it poses. Because sickness opposes the Creator God's saving power, it must be righted and the creation restored. Jesus is the Redeemer in whom the mercy of God is present. What is new in his ministry is that the beneficiaries of God's mercy are not the religious authorities and legal scholars but those considered outsiders: the poor, the disabled, the sick, and the bereaved. Jesus made himself accessible to those who needed him, ignoring conventional limitations and thus according proper recognition to those who were cast out of society for whatever reason. Consistently, he met people at their particular points of need and addressed those needs. Jesus is presented as a combatant, constantly opposing with his power those forces that kept people in subjugation. Whatever held people back from experiencing the fullness of the gospel must be confronted and its power to do so destroyed. Thus, the sick were healed, the disabled returned to full activity, and the oppressed freed.

When Jesus welcomed the sick and disabled with open arms, he presented a potent model to his followers. The manner in which churches and their members respond to people with AIDS is an indication of the degree of seriousness with which they follow the example of Jesus. A response of love and compassion—an open-arms response—is demanded of God's people. It is a mandate expressly given by Jesus, as, for example, in the parable of the Judgment (Matt. 25:31–46). Further, such a response is a sign of God's gracious love, not only to people with AIDS and to their loved ones but to the wider community. It announces for all to see and hear that the kingdom is being realized, that it is taking shape in the world. If AIDS, in fact, means that the sick person has fallen into death's realm of power, loving acceptance of people with AIDS announces that God's saving power takes the field against death's destructive power.

During a recent hospitalization, a young man who knew that his struggle with numerous infections occasioned by AIDS was reaching its inevitable end drew comfort from the knowledge that his membership in a local church had led to the development of a support group for AIDS patients in the congregation. During the final days of his struggle he was visited by members of the group. His family gathered to support him. He was distressed that his family, in particular, would remember him racked with pain and broken by disease. With a supreme effort, he spent some time with each family member, leaving each with the message of how important were their support and love and how strong his love was for them. The ministry of the religious community was one of the undergirding forces in the hospital room, both for the patient and for his family. It symbolized God's gracious and reconciling love. Such compassion is a first call upon God's people in the crisis created by the AIDS epidemic.

The "Problem of Suffering"

In marked contrast to the fact that Jesus was concerned to show compassion to the afflicted rather than to establish the causes of disease and disability, Western scholars have tended to be preoccupied with the latter concern, connecting their response to issues of morality. The church's response to sickness and disability has been influenced by both emphases, which have existed side by side in Western culture. The ministry of compassion, so integral to the ministry of Jesus, is manifested, for example, in the establishment of an infirmary in Rome as early as the late fourth century, a logical development of Christian charity. The commandment to love the neighbor (Matt. 19:19; 22:39; Mark 12:31–33) was not simply a piece of advice; it was a categorical imperative. Love for the neighbor can be manifested in a variety of ways, but spiritual concern must never take precedence over immediate material or physical help for those in need, as the Letter of James bluntly states: "Religion that is pure and undefiled before God and the Father is this: to visit orphans and widows in their affliction" (1:27, RSV).

The visitation, care, and comfort of the afflicted became an obligation incumbent upon all Christians and was repeatedly stressed in early Christian literature. This duty to attend the sick and the poor conferred on them a preferential position that has lasted until now. The example of Christ was followed in the mid-third century when, during an outbreak of plague, Christians ministered to plague victims. In a letter by Dionysius written in A.D. 263, he describes how "our brethren were unsparing in their exceeding love and brotherly kindness. They held fast to each other and visited the sick fearlessly and ministered to them continually, serving them in Christ. . . . And many who cared for the sick and gave strength to others died themselves . . . so that this form of death, through the great piety and strong faith it exhibited, seemed to lack nothing of martyrdom."[9] The commitment to the outcast sick is evident in the nineteenth century exemplified by Fr. Damien on the island of Molokai, and into the twentieth century, with Mother Teresa and countless nameless people for whom the needs of the sick and dying become a call to ministry.

Yet this often sacrificial gesture of compassionate response has been accompanied by efforts to explain the existence of pain and suffering in terms of retribution. For example, Calvin identified two purposes served by suffering caused by such events as pestilence, disease, poverty, or any other suffering in body or mind. First, suffering is punishment for high crimes and misdemeanors against God, a punishment justly deserved. Calvin prayed that God's chastisements—the affliction of disease or poverty, for example—would be effective for the reformation of the sufferer's life. In this sense, suffering has an expiatory force that imparts the assurance to the believer that guilt is thereby atoned, reflecting the Talmudic statement that the one who has suffered in this life is thereby assured of rewards in the life to come. Second, suffering is perceived to have an educational purpose. Calvin directed ordained pastors who visit those afflicted by disease or "other evils" to

> console them by the word of the Lord, showing them that all which they suffer and endure comes from the hand of God, and from his good providence, who sends nothing to believers except for their good and salvation. . . . Moreover, if he sees the sickness to be dangerous, he will give them consolation, which reaches farther, according as he sees them touched by their affliction; that is to say, if he sees them overwhelmed by the fear of death, he will show them that it is no cause for dismay to believers, who having Jesus Christ for their guide and protector, will, by their affliction, be conducted to the life on which he has entered. By similar considerations he will remove the fear and terror which they may have of the judgment of God.[10]

This manner of presenting poverty and disease—and, in fact, misfortune generally—has endured into modern Western usage and remains a powerful influence on contemporary attitudes to disease and disability. During a morning television news presentation late in 1986, the parents of a promising college athlete who had died during 1986 were interviewed. Asked what meaning they attached to their son's death, his mother responded that God had made their son an example to other youth "so that millions might live." The same attribution of suffering is evident in the tracts left in hospital waiting areas or placed on bedside tables that carry such messages as: *Sickness is an opportunity to mature inwardly; the Lord does not place burdens upon us that are more than we can bear; affliction is God's test of our faith; we must pray for strength.*

It seems that either the experience of personal affliction or the awareness of suffering in another person inevitably drives humanity back to the question asked poignantly by the psalmists: Why do righteous people suffer? Attempts to answer that question seem endless. The Hebraic perception of God, which attributed all phenomena to a divine purpose, was carried over into early Christendom and remains a pervasive influence in much "folk religion." As the Renaissance paved the way ultimately for the enhancement of the sciences, however, larger and larger areas of human life were explained on the basis of a growing body of scientific data. Included in this explosion of knowledge was the matter of illness. A small group of British scientists was convened in the late 1950s to review the relationship between religion and science. The group recalled that in the Middle Ages people crowded into churches to seek deliverance from plagues, whereas twentieth-century societies dig drains and educate the public concerning matters of hygiene. Whereas primitive societies prayed for rain and abundant harvests, we invest resources in water conservation and teach developing countries the benefits of fertilizers and crop rotation. When humans were forced to account for phenomena they could not understand, the tendency was to fall back upon the age-old measure of attributing causality to some unfathomed divine purpose.

The problem arose, however, that as rational explanations emerged to account for more and more areas of human experience, the extent of experience ascribed to a purposive God began to shrink. Now that science can explain in intricate detail the manner in which viruses enter and affect the human body, and how the body's immune system defends itself against such attacks, it is tempting to divide human experience into two (or more) parts, granting science control over one while retaining the control of religion over the other. This is a mistake. To assert that some sort of hedge can be planted in the country of the mind to mark the boundary where a transfer of authority takes place is a twofold error. First, it presupposes an intolerable dichotomy of existence. Second, it invites "science" to discover new things and thence gradually take possession of that which "religion" once held.[11] Soon, God becomes no longer necessary because the gap between the explained and the unexplained is closed. If this image is applied to the science of medicine, any attempt to remove disease from the arena of medicine to that of religion assumes the same dichotomization, an untenable position. God does not reserve certain areas of life in which to dabble. In particular, AIDS was not "sent" on some divine intention to communicate a message; for example, to remind humans that God retains some areas in which to manifest initiative.

There is a second and more disturbing objection to the notion that the answer to suffering is to be found in some divine purpose. Dorothee Soelle put the issue forcefully when she objected to what she termed "theological sadism." For her, "Christian masochism" had "so many features that merit criticism: the low value it places on human strength; its veneration of one who is neither good nor logical but only extremely powerful; its viewing of suffering exclusively from the perspective of endurance; and its consequent lack of sensitivity for the suffering of others." But what bothered Soelle was not the well-meaning attempts of onlookers to comfort a disabled person; such attempts may be genuine efforts to speak in comfort and compassion. Her greatest discomfort and anger arose because "the picture changes as soon as theologians, in a kind of overly rigorous application of the masochistic approach, sketch in as a companion piece a sadistic God." Her concern was that such a God who causes affliction and suffering is presented as one who demands the impossible and then tortures people.[12]

As this chapter was being written, a father sat for three weeks at the bedside of his dying 28-year-old son. He dealt with his grief out of images derived from the Middle Ages. He stated simply that what was happening was God's will, which he had no alternative but to accept. When the chaplain asked how he would feel if he were to discover that his son's imminent death was not "willed" by God but that instead God "grieved" over the death of one of God's children, he dismissed the image without consideration. The chaplain did not return to the theological issue; at that moment such a discussion was not appropriate. The father's conviction that his son's death was at God's behest was his only source of comfort. It might have been easier to accept his perception if his consolation had been deep and genuine. But it was as if he were engaged in a never-ending struggle to hold back the waters of bitterness behind a narrow dike, with his finger plunged into a fissure through which the waters seeped, constantly threatening to become a surge that would overwhelm him. Similarly, a hospital chaplain recounted a ten-year-old patient's struggle to come to terms with his diagnosis of AIDS. Who knows the source of the child's images? Had some well-meaning relative, friend, or pastor sought to comfort him by suggesting gently that God had "chosen" him? He sat up in bed and cried out, "Why did God choose me? I did not want to be chosen!"

These images of God are derived from perceptions of God's transcendence that leave little room for immanence such as manifested in the life of Jesus of Nazareth, who sat beside a woman alienated from her community, or who crouched in a dusty village street alongside another threatened woman. These biblical pictures contrast sharply with the image of a transcendent God, far removed from human concerns except to use them as teaching opportunities. It is right to criticize radically all attempts to reconcile God with misery or, worse, to represent God as sanctioning misery. Such a God, who uses affliction merely or primarily to reprove, correct, or educate, cannot be separated from the accusation of injustice. If God "comes to a sufferer only with pedagogical intent,"[13] then God seems deaf to the anguished protest of a ten-year-old child or any other person with AIDS, on whose behalf all must cry out for justice and compassion.

To attribute suffering to an all-powerful God who uses such power to inflict pain and misery upon humanity flies in the face of the incarnation of God's love in Jesus Christ. Such love is expressed in an active goodwill toward people, moved by a genuine sensitivity to their deepest needs. This type of love includes, but is not limited to, compassionate sympathy. Sympathy indeed has received a bad press, with the contemporary emphasis by social scientists on terms such as "empathy." Sympathy involves being present with a person—weeping with the sad, rejoicing when there is cause for celebration. It is comforting for one who is sick to know that he or she is not alone and that others care. "Empathy," on the other hand, is a construct that more fully expresses a human attempt to speak of God's love. The term involves a relationship between the helper and the afflicted person in which the helper knows, or can imagine, the depth of the pain and struggle the other is experiencing. It is a relationship that opens the possibility of change or, if that is not possible, assures the struggler that the helping person has the ability to enter into the feeling of helplessness or even despair and know what it means. If these images may be applied validly to God's love, they suggest that God is in touch with our pain, that God "feels" our anguish and is affected by it. This conception is in stark contrast to the Greek notion of divine impassibility that has permeated traditional theism, a notion that sharply restricts the biblical perception of divine love that is responsive to human suffering.

The idea that God's knowledge of the world is complete and unchanging implies that God has determined every aspect of the world, down to the last detail. Nothing can happen that is not immutably known. There is little provision for creaturely freedom in such a fixed system. Process theology, on the other hand, sees God's creative activity as based upon responsiveness to the world. Because the very meaning of actuality involves internal relatedness, God as an actuality is essentially related to the world. Because actuality as such is partially self-creative, future events are not determined. Even perfect knowledge, process theologians argue, cannot know the future. Thus, God does not wholly control the world. God's power, even creative power, is persuasive, not coercive.[14]

Process thought has three immediate consequences for

this inquiry. First, it provides a theological basis for the assertion that God does not select specific diseases to punish certain human behaviors. If God's power is persuasive, not controlling, finite actualities can fail to conform to the divine aims for them. Deviations from divine aims may give rise to evil. Because deviation is possible, though not necessary, evil is not necessary. It is the *possibility* of deviation that is necessary, and that makes the *possibility* of evil necessary. The risk in all this for humanity is that a new actuality may develop that introduces a novel element into creation. It may add to the variety of existence, and so to the value that can be enjoyed. But the new reality may be a strain of virus that leads not to enjoyment but to discord.[15] Human immunodeficiency virus (HIV) surely falls into this category. If the intention had been to exclude the possibility of all discord, God would simply have abstained from creating a world altogether, and so have guaranteed the absence of all suffering. Risk is part of the created order, a price paid for freedom, God's trump card. Thus, God does not "send" AIDS for some retributive purpose (such a thought flies in the face of the New Testament witness to a loving God). Rather, God "risked" creating a world in which HIV could develop.

The second consequence of process thought centers around the question of persuasiveness vs. control. It is on just this issue that conservative Christians oppose radically any stance to the left of their own positions. "Fundamentalist" and "liberal" Christians may fight over matters of ecclesiology and biblical and historical theology, but what is at stake is the political issue of management styles and measures of control and freedom. This battle has certainly invaded areas of ethics and theology in accounting for human suffering, but it also plays a key role in the form that pastoral care takes—for example, in shaping attitudes toward people with AIDS. Care and compassion can be offered to people in need without attempting to coerce them into adopting the caregiver's religious commitments. It is appropriate for ministries to reflect religious and moral values; it is not appropriate, however, to expect the other person to adopt those values as the *condition* for the relationship and the care.[16]

Both the Hebrew scriptures and the New Testament characterize God as choosing to deal freely with humanity. God offers humanity choices. The question then is whether the choices made are trivially or morally evil or are genuine attempts at responsible living. This matter of choice is always unambiguous. It is the choice expressed by Joshua to the Israelites: "Hold the Lord in awe then, and worship him in loyalty and truth. Banish the gods whom your fathers worshipped beside the Euphrates and in Egypt, and worship the LORD. But if it does not please you to worship the LORD, choose here and now whom you will worship. . . . I and my family, we will worship the LORD" (Josh. 24:14–15). The choice is presented as sharply by Jesus to the rich young ruler: "Jesus said to him, 'If you wish to go the whole way, go, sell your possessions, and give to the poor . . . and come, follow me' " (Matt. 19:21).

The fact of freedom places the responsibility for decision and choice on the only one who can assume such responsibility, the person who must decide. The attempt to control the choices of others is a constant temptation for caregivers. One of the temptations is to reject a person who has made a decision with which one disagrees or, more pointedly, that is offensive to one's own moral judgment. It is also tempting to use the power implicit in the role of the caregiver to overwhelm the person who needs help and to make help contingent upon the adoption of an "acceptable" lifestyle.[17]

This raises the third consequence of process thought for this inquiry. It is logical to argue that if God's relationship with humanity is persuasive, that characteristic should be the model for our own interpersonal relationships. It should apply particularly to the role of caregiver. If persuasion, rather than control, is the divine mode of relation, this manner of doing things is expected of believers. These images of relationship—offer, freedom, and persuasion—are true to the gospel. The object of preaching the gospel is "full life" (John 10:10). That invitation is offered, but in large measure it is up to each of us how that full life will be appropriated. God's creative purpose for humanity is loving because God is always a completely *gracious* God. God's aim for people is existence that they experience as intrinsically good. But God is not in complete control. We are in part responsible for who we are and what we shall become. We are certainly responsible for the choices we make and for their consequences. The freedom God offers humanity is therefore risky, but it is a necessary risk if there is to be the chance for greatness. Thus, the question as to whether God is indictable for evil reduces to the question of whether the positive values enjoyed by the higher forms of life and experience are worth the risk of the negative values; namely, the sufferings. Should humans, therefore, risk possible suffering in order to have at least the possibility of intense enjoyment? Process theologians Cobb and Griffin respond affirmatively, explaining that the divine reality is an Adventurer who not only enjoys humanity's experience of the pitch of enjoyment but who also experiences sufferings.[18] God knows what it is like to taste the bitter waters of our valleys of Marah (Ex. 15:-23).

The desert plains across which lie our paths, as we press forward looking for Canaan, that land flowing with milk and honey, are broken by more than one valley of Marah. The ancient pilgrimage of the children of Israel remains a prototype for all. AIDS is but the latest tragedy to evoke from humanity the age-old question "Why, Lord? Why me?"

It has been suggested that from the most primitive of ancient cultures to the more highly developed religious forms, humanity has always struggled with the tragedy of affliction, resolving the paradox of life pockmarked by suffering by attributing disease and disability to the gods' anger at human failure and sin. Primitive Hebrew thought incorporated this concept, and much of contemporary Christian "folk religion" reflects it. Yet the biblical response is one of affirmation. It does not answer the question "Why me?" other than to remind us, through metaphor, that we are called to be children of our Father in heaven, who makes the sun rise on good and bad alike and sends the rain on the honest and dishonest (Matt. 5:45). We are assured that God makes those whom society denigrates God's people. It is salutary to remember that the first epistle of Peter was addressed to just such people: domestics, street sweepers, laborers, and Gentiles. The writer's joy is in seeing people who once were "no people" becoming "God's people." Those who had not previously received mercy were now recipients of God's mercy. Nobodies were receiving the dignity and the joy of being God's children. Is there not comfort for a patient in the theological notion that his or her God, who has rejoiced in human achievements and enjoyments, now shares in the pain and physical discomfort of his or her dying?

There is no formula for erasing the pain and anguish of people with AIDS and of their loved ones. Moreover, as sick and disabled people constantly remind those who just stand around, one who has not experienced catastrophic crisis cannot know the feelings it evokes in the sufferer. In the face of such pain, the witness of scripture is plainly and simply stated: God is a God of unfathomable love who tends people like a shepherd tends the flock. The human analogy is of a loving parent who loves to the uttermost. This affirmation moves Paul to reassure his readers that nothing can separate people from the love of God revealed in the Christ. Not persecution, hunger, nakedness, peril, or sword; not illness, disability, or AIDS.

Yet our thoughts are not God's thoughts; neither are our ways God's ways. We do not rise to Paul's level of maturity but continue to judge from our human point of view. We cannot say, with the apostle, that "worldly standards have ceased to count in our estimate of any man" (2 Cor. 5:16). So we continue to place people in categories, creating new groups of "the poor" from whom, because they do not fit our stereotypes, we distance ourselves.

As we face and acknowledge this sin in ourselves, Parker Palmer reminds us that we live under a "relentless divine calling to engage in the work of reconciliation—to God, to one another, and to ourselves."[19]

5

God and the Poor

Illness and disability are seen in scripture as opportunities for God's people to provide compassionate care and protection. The record of the church's ministries of visitation, health care, and asylum demonstrates the seriousness with which the biblical examples and admonitions have been taken. These ministries are extensions of Jesus' ministry and represent creative responses to the command to love one's neighbor.

Sick and disabled persons are only two instances within a broader category of persons toward whom the people of God are to be benevolently disposed—the poor. "The poor" is a theological metaphor representing that collection of persons in biblical society who were vulnerable to exploitation or were afforded less than an equal place because of their condition or situation in life. The poor were people who were without the necessary human or material resources to protect their welfare or to secure their place in society.

The Poor in Jewish Scripture

Within the speeches of Moses reported in Deuteronomy, Israel is told that living in covenant with God requires nothing less than total loyalty and obedience to the Holy One. Israel is to have an attitude of reverence toward God, to live according to God's instructions, to love God, and to serve God without reservation. Moses describes this God who merits and commands such service as one who "secures justice for widows and orphans, and loves the alien who lives among you, giving him food and clothing" (Deut. 10:18). Orphans, widows, and aliens in Jewish culture were potential victims of social and legal abuse. Their ally and defender is God; and Israel, in imitation of God, is to stand as God does in relation to these people.

Other biblical passages also identify the orphan, the impoverished, and the stranger as subject to God's special protection (e.g., Ex. 22:21–27; Lev. 19:33–34). "Weak" and "poor" were used by the prophets as terms for these people and others who could not maintain their own support or status in society and who, as a consequence, were particularly vulnerable to exploitation or to having their rights violated. They are those whom society tends to treat unjustly and to whom few offer comfort, defense, or care. They are people who tend to be forgotten and whose claims are ignored by those with power and prestige. They are people who are marginalized by social structures, practices, and dominant values. The witness of scripture, however, is that God is their ally (Isa. 3:15), advocate (Ex. 22:21–24), and protector (Isa. 25:4; 41:17). God's concern for the poor is so great, according to Isaiah, that the manner in which they are protected is the divine, functional measure of whether or not a society is just (Isa. 3:14–15).

The situation of the poor was seen as the result of social factors rather than as a consequence of personal failings. They were people with little power, victims of fate in need of compassion, or victims of injustice in need of justice (Isa. 10:2). The great expression of God's will for the oppressed was the liberation of Israel from slavery in Egypt. God heard the cry of the oppressed covenant people and restored them to a position of power and freedom (Ex. 2:23–24). This event became the prototype and standard by which Israel's response to oppression and injustice was to be measured. In addition, the memory of Israel's enslavement was frequently invoked by God's messengers as a motivation not to abuse the rights of the socially and legally weak. The refrain "for you were strangers in the land of Egypt" (e.g., Ex. 22:21; 23:9, RSV) beckoned the people to identify with the suffering of the weak and resist the temptation to neglect or exploit the vulnerable.

The witness in Jewish scripture is that the needs of the poor and weak must be recognized and met. The prophets especially were sensitive to the legitimate needs of individuals and groups in society. Their pronouncements were calls to righteousness as much as they were pronouncements of judgment. Isaiah, speaking for God, entreats Judah: "Wash yourselves; make yourselves clean; remove the evil of your doings from before my eyes; cease to do evil, learn to do good; seek justice, correct oppression; defend the fatherless, plead for the widow" (Isa. 1:16–17, RSV). The prophet assumes that it is possible for people to change when the contrast between what they do and the way of righteousness is made known to them. According to the prophets, power was to be used to promote the welfare and rights of others. Nevertheless, the prophets surely were realistic. They must have known that no temporal society would be perfect. But their understanding of humanity and social relationships was perceptive enough to recognize that the character of any society reflects the character of the people who shape and control it. Thus, the prophets' passion was for individuals and society to obey the will of God. In the words of Micah: "He has showed you, O man, what is good; and what does the LORD require of you but to do justice, and to love kindness, and to walk humbly with your God?" (Micah 6:8, RSV).

Central to the Bible's teachings regarding the poor is the conviction that they are subjects of divine concern and therefore worthy of just and merciful treatment. Though their positions in society were inferior, their needs and rights were to be given the same regard as the needs and rights of society's more privileged and secure members. All persons, weak or strong, were equal under God and therefore were to be treated with equal respect (Ex. 21–23). The objective of the various commands regarding orphans (e.g., Ex. 22:22; Isa. 1:17), widows (Isa. 1:23; 10:2; Deut. 14:29), and strangers (Lev. 9:33–34; Ex. 22:21; 23:9)—that is, the poor—was to empower the vulnerable, to remind the strong of the equality of the weak before God, and to provide security for the poor. Because God was the source of all justice and righteousness, the rights and needs of everyone in the land, members and nonmembers of the covenant community alike, were to be respected.

By the time of the prophets, the interests of society as a whole were too easily identified with the interests of the ruling classes in maintaining their position and privilege. The interests of the poor tended to be ignored or minimized. As a consequence, the community, common purpose, and quality of common life that God willed tended to be obscured (Isa. 5:1–7; Hos. 1:9; Amos 5:23–24). God's anger toward Israel for these failures was not "the cold anger of a judge upholding law, but the passionate anger of a master whose goodness has been flouted, of a guardian whose helpless wards have been maltreated"[1] (Isa. 1:2–3; Hos. 11:1–4, 8–9). The prophets who denounced Israel's transgressions and called the nation to repentance were "social revolutionaries" because they were "religious conservatives" articulating the essential ethics and social creativity of historic Yahwism. Yahweh was in the struggle for social justice, and Israel, God's elect, was to participate in that struggle. God was the ally of the wronged and disadvantaged, and Israel, in loyalty and obedience to God, was to be their ally as well.

Together with this knowledge of God, Israel's concern for the poor was to be motivated by the memory of their experience in Egypt (e.g., Ex. 23:9; Deut. 15:11; 16:12). Fulfilling the duty of the strong to protect and care for the weak was not considered a burden; it was a privilege

(Job 31:16–22). God did not look favorably upon indifference, abuse of the weak, or abuse of privilege. The people could not mask their corruption and failures with piety (Isa. 1:10–17). God could see through the pretense. The warning in Proverbs applied to all who ignored the cries of the poor and weak: "He who closes his ear to the cry of the poor will himself cry out and not be heard" (Prov. 21:13, RSV). God is a loving, empowering, liberating being who wills community and justice in human history, and the divine will is to be carried out by human beings, individually and corporately. Beyond all ethnic boundaries, God values justice and compassion for all.

The value of the poor to God and the importance of their place in the community are evidenced in and through the legislation and exhortations regarding their treatment. The poor were not to be maltreated and their needs were to be met. For example, a primary purpose of the law requiring a man to marry his brother's widow was to provide her with security (Deut. 25:5–10; cf. Lev. 22:13). The immigrant or resident alien was to be protected like the widows and orphans who were members of the covenant community (Ex. 22:21–22). Some grain and fruit was to be left unharvested, to be gleaned by the poor, fatherless, widow, stranger, or traveler (Lev. 19:9–10). A tenth of one's produce or income every three years was to be committed to the poor (Deut. 26:12). The specific provisions of these rules are less significant than the principle they express: the poor are valued and deserve compassion.

By being benevolent toward the poor, one honors God and is blessed by God (e.g., Prov. 14:21). But when the rulers or ordinary people fail to provide for and protect the weak, God is insulted (v. 31). God's parental anger is stirred and judgment falls on the offending authority or people (Deut. 27:19; Mal. 3:5). God's passion for the weak, vulnerable, powerless, and displaced is a recurring theme in Jewish scripture. The manner in which the strong and privileged are to meet their obligations toward the needy is variously expressed. A substantive, yet deceptively simple, compound truth emerges through these expressions of Israel's understanding of God and God's will for human relationships: God's love is not conditioned by social role or status, unless an individual is among the poor. In that case, God's alliance with that person is paramount, because other individuals and society have failed in their duties to act justly and compassionately toward them.

Jesus and the Poor

God's concern for the outcasts and the poor depicted in Jewish scripture is echoed in the New Testament, especially the Synoptic Gospels. The Evangelists demonstrate that the poor are a primary concern of Jesus, both in his teaching and in his ministry. Identifying with the prophetic tradition in Israel, Jesus recognized that people whose situation excluded them from full participation in the social, religious, and legal institutions should not be considered beyond the scope of God's love and human regard. His message and mission were explicit challenges to the prevailing notions of who was acceptable to God and for what reasons. He scandalized the official custodians of religion and morality by proclaiming an inclusive message rather than an exclusive one. His behavior was a living testimony of God's will to have fellowship with all. The fact that Jesus' opponents reviled him, calling him a glutton and drunkard, and criticized him for being a friend of tax collectors and sinners is evidence that he practiced what he preached (Matt. 11:19; Mark 2:16; Luke 7:34). Jesus' opponents were unable or unwilling to celebrate the redemptive, liberating, and inclusive activity of God, powerfully symbolized in the table fellowship of Jesus (Luke 14:15–24).

Jesus' concern for the needy reflects his radical sense of an egalitarianism of the coming end of the age. His offer to have fellowship with the outcast is an explicit repudiation of temporal norms of worth and status (Mark 2:15–

17). It also is an expression of Jesus' belief that all people are valued by God and that God's will for relationship excludes no one. Greatness, according to Jesus, had little to do with one's piety or conformity to the letter of the law. Instead, true greatness is tied to one's ability to recognize the worth and importance of people normally considered least important in society (Luke 9:46–48). In Jesus' day, for example, the least important included children, women, sinners, tax collectors, the impoverished, publicans, prostitutes, and the sick. The message and example of Jesus were that it is God's will and humanity's responsibility to find ways to enable these outcasts to participate fully in the ongoing life of the community (Luke 14:12–14). The means by which this goal is to be achieved, according to the example and teaching of Jesus, is through humility and service (Luke 14:7–11; 17:7–10; 22:24–27). Charity and care for persons, according to Jesus, are central to a life of discipleship.[2] Self-centeredness and self-righteousness are impediments to the sort of edifying, loving relationships that God wills for people.

In Jesus' time, "sinner" was a general category of persons notorious for violating the commandments of God. It also was a term for people engaged in despised occupations that were seen to lead to immorality or dishonesty, such as dice gamblers, usurers, tax collectors, and herdsmen (see Luke 18:11). Tax collectors, or publicans, especially were hated by the people. They were subtenants of wealthy toll farmers, who made the highest bid to collect the toll or tax from an area for a fixed period. They extracted the appropriate toll and an additional sum as profit (Luke 3:12–13), exploiting the public's ignorance of the toll scale for their own gain. As a consequence of their evil actions, publicans were denied civil rights and honorary offices, and were prohibited from testifying in trials. Repentance meant abandoning the profession and restoring what was unjustly taken, plus one fifth of the total. Given the scope and degree of their deception, repentance virtually was impossible. Their segregation from community life on moral grounds was practically irreversible.

Despite the moral condemnation and social ostracism directed toward publicans and others similarly situated, Jesus had fellowship with them, undeterred by their conduct or the societally mediated judgment of their actions. In addition to these despised and ostracized individuals, the company of Jesus was described by his opponents as the "little ones" (Mark 9:42), the "least" (Matt. 25:40, 45, RSV), or the "simple" (Matt. 11:25). These designations were applied to the religiously uneducated, the backward, the irreligious people in Palestinian society. Yet, as the Gospels reveal, these people were among the followers of Jesus. People whose religious ignorance or moral misdeeds were barriers to salvation, according to the prevailing views of Jesus' time, were the predominant groups among Jesus' following. Jesus called them the poor (Luke 6:20), people who "labor and are heavy laden" (Matt. 11:28, RSV).[3]

The meaning Jesus gave to the poor is based on the use of the term in Luke 4:18 and its parallel in Matthew 11:5. The setting is the synagogue in Nazareth. Jesus read a composite of Isaiah 61:1–2 and 58:6: "The Spirit of the Lord is upon me, because he has anointed me to preach good news to the poor. He has sent me to proclaim release to the captives and recovering of sight to the blind, to set at liberty those who are oppressed, to proclaim the acceptable year of the Lord" (Luke 4:18–19, RSV). Luke conspicuously omits from the reading "to proclaim . . . the day of vengeance of our God" (Isa. 61:2, RSV). Afterward Jesus announces, "Today this scripture has been fulfilled in your hearing" (Luke 4:21, RSV). The eschatological, messianic mission that Isaiah foresaw, according to Jesus, was being inaugurated in his ministry. His was a mission of salvation and inclusion, not judgment and exclusion. Unlike the Baptist, who heralded the coming kingdom and pronounced judgments (Matt. 3:1–2), Jesus announced salvation for the poor. This whole incident in the synagogue at Nazareth prefigures the ministry of Jesus and the primitive church. It is the opening scene in an unfolding drama in Luke–Acts in which fellowship and salvation are extended to all persons, regardless of cultic, national, racial, moral, or social prejudices.

Jesus' opponents criticized his fellowship with the despised and outcast, asking the disciples: "Why does your teacher eat with tax collectors and sinners?" Jesus responded, "Those who are well have no need of a physician, but those who are sick. Go and learn what this means, 'I desire mercy, and not sacrifice.' For I came not to call the righteous, but sinners" (Matt. 9:11–13, RSV). Jesus' teaching and lifestyle were clear repudiations of the view that the letter of the law was more important than the spirit of the law. The revelation of God that was intended to facilitate redemption and fellowship was being distorted to become a barrier to the fulfillment of God's purposes. As a consequence, God's invitation through Jesus was received by people who recognized their needs, rather than by those who had needs but refused to recognize them. Neither John the Baptist nor Jesus demanded in principle that toll collectors, for example, must give up their profession as a condition for fellowship. Jesus met all outcasts as they were in the midst of their situation and offered them fellowship.

The good news that Jesus brought to the poor was that they are invited to God's festive meal. Jesus dramatized the forgiveness he was offering in action, most impressively in his table fellowship with sinners. Jesus invited sinners into his house (Luke 15:2) and dined with them in festive meals (Mark 2:15–18). It was an honor to be invited to a meal. An invitation was an offer by the host of peace, trust, brotherhood, and forgiveness. Thus, by table fellowship, by lodging with a toll collector (Luke 19:5), and by calling publicans to be his disciples (Mark 2:14), Jesus demonstrated that God had accepted the despised, the outcast, and the poor.

Given this background regarding Jesus' concern for

the poor, the full meaning of the First Beatitude becomes clearer. The poor are blessed because the reign of God belongs to them alone (Luke 6:20). Salvation can be received only by people who recognize their need. Sinners, publicans, and prostitutes, according to the Gospels, will be acceptable to God, whereas the righteous who believe their place to be secure will discover that they have no place at all (e.g., Luke 18:14). In solidarity with the poor and outcast, Jesus takes upon himself their hurt from being declared outside the realm of concern. His declaration that God, too, stands in solidarity with the marginalized because of God's compassion and concern for justice was, as the Gospels reveal, intolerable to the power and status brokers concerned to preserve their privilege.

Jesus' unconditional offer to have fellowship with everyone, especially the poor, aroused the opposition of the religious establishment. Nevertheless, Jesus continued to violate official religious and social protocol in order to take the good news to people in need. Sexual, social, and cultic barriers were broken; risks were assumed in order to communicate God's inclusive message. Prejudice, regardless of its source or agency of mediation, did not inhibit the witness of God's agent. Some of Jesus' most dramatic acts of ministry—feeding, healing, casting out, forgiving—were directed toward people who had been abandoned or squeezed out according to the dominant values in society. In the language of liberation theology, Jesus made an option for the poor.

Opting for the poor means to opt for people, acting and living in a way that respects the inherent value of all to God, especially those who are not treated with respect according to prevailing social norms. Living in this manner may result in a radical change in lifestyle, approach to work, political concerns, or understanding of the faith community. Following the example of Jesus may entail a change in priorities; a higher priority for people and a suspicion of social norms that oppress and divide people (Matt. 19:16–22).

Opting for the poor also has a social component that subjects social structures or institutions to claims of justice and mutuality. People oppressed by social structures have their self-image and their lifestyle determined by the definitions, priorities, and interests of the powerful people and institutions within society. Equality, concern for others, and social change occur in such a situation when the oppressed assert their just claims for regard and when at least a few oppressors acknowledge the legitimacy of those claims. This is an implicit act of repentance by the former oppressors, who then are freed to progress from a dialogue between stronger and weaker to a solidarity of strong and weak in the struggle for total liberation.

The biblical prototypes of widow, orphan, poor, hungry, thirsty, naked, sick, and stranger are symbols of otherness. The symbols and, moreover, the actual people they represent are a call to community and solidarity, a limitation to self-interest forged on the anvil of justice. Their claim to hospitality helps to shape moral consciousness. They expose selfishness and summon us to repentance. They call others to be moral and to enter into solidarity with them. The solidarity or community that results from the answered call is not due, according to this reasoning, solely to guilt. It occurs because the value of the stranger to humanity and to God is perceived and affirmed. It occurs because each stranger accepts responsibility for all other strangers.

Solidarity with and compassion for outcast and oppressed people—the poor—constitute an implicit criticism and explicit rejection of being content with the way things are rather than striving to conform things to the way God intends them to be. Solidarity and compassion, accordingly, are key features of prophetic ministry, which is an active ministry, embracing the pain and suffering of people, reminding people with power to lessen these burdens and that oppression in any form is an affront to God (Prov. 17:5). Thus, God's people are called to be prophets, to oppose the conditions that generate and perpetuate human deprivation, indignity, and oppression (Isa. 1:17; Amos 5:14–15). By so doing, God's people respond to God's love and compassion for all revealed in the humanitarian legislation of Israel, in the oracles of Israel's prophets, and in the person and ministry of Jesus.

The Poor in Our Midst

We have seen that the poor are described in scripture as widows, orphans, the fatherless, sojourners, strangers, the impoverished, afflicted, enslaved, oppressed, sick, thirsty, hungry, and naked, sinners, prostitutes, tax collectors, or publicans. Regardless of their specific social role, the poor were people who could be placed in one or more of the following categories: (1) a person without the resources necessary to maintain his or her support or status in society; (2) a person devalued and scorned according to the dominant values and norms; (3) a person whose rights and claims tended to be easily ignored, rendering him or her vulnerable to exploitation and abuse; or (4) a person whose inferior status was socially conferred, enforced, and alleged to reflect God's estimate of that person. It is not surprising, given these conditions and estimations, that the poor were people whose anguish was overlooked, whose cries for compassion and justice were ignored, and whose divinely conferred value and dignity were disregarded.

God's revelation made several counterclaims. (1) The poor are loved by God and deserve compassion. (2) God hears poor people's cries of distress and is their hope for deliverance. (3) God's people, in loyalty and obedience to God, are to recognize the needs of the poor and meet them. Despite these pronouncements and affirmations, the poor generally remained segregated and oppressed during the biblical era because of the dominance of cultic, national, racial, moral, and social barriers that tended to serve the interests of the privileged at the expense of the poor. The intensity of the opposition that Jesus encountered indicates how threatening a ministry to the poor can be to a society's sense of security and order.

Expanding the scope of our concern to include people who are different, disadvantaged, or unfortunate entails the risk that the encounter may prompt a questioning of our privileges and the values and structures that support them. Yet this examination and the changes that could ensue ought not deter God's people from seeking the poor. An encounter with them should result in an inclusive and loving response. There is no other option for the people of God if they are to be true to their identity and faithful to their calling. The biblical witness allows no exceptions and accepts no excuses. As long as there are people who are included among the poor according to the criteria just identified, God's people are required not only to welcome them as neighbors, and to extend hospitality to them, but to identify fully with them as members of God's family.

People with AIDS, almost without exception, satisfy one or more of the criteria for being included among the biblical category of the poor. Their physical and fiscal losses often make them almost totally dependent on others, unable to provide for themselves, and ineffective advocates of their interests. They are often feared and ostracized in society because of their disease. If the person is gay, bisexual, or an IV drug user, these labels are cited as an additional justification for relegating him or her to the edges of society. The rights of marginalized people are nonexistent, because such people tend to be unable, and few others seem willing, to assert and defend those rights. Finally, the label of gay, bisexual, drug user, promiscuous, or person with AIDS is a stigma reflecting society's condemnation. Moreover, AIDS is seen by some people to validate society's censure of those whose sexual identity or lifestyle is considered unacceptable. Clearly, people with HIV/AIDS are contemporary manifestations of the poor who, despite society's judgments to the contrary, are loved by God and deserve to be treated compassionately by God's people.

The AIDS poor, however, are not only those people diagnosed with AIDS. The category includes people diagnosed with asymptomatic or symptomatic HIV disease. Both often are subject to the same disregard and disparaging treatment, which makes them functional equivalents to people with AIDS. In addition, family and friends of people in each of these classes become a component of the HIV/AIDS poor. Because of their association with people with HIV disease, they tend to experience the isolation, stigma, and hopelessness so familiar to people with an HIV-related diagnosis. The circle of the AIDS poor expands as more and more people worldwide become infected and become clinically ill as a consequence.

The challenge that the poor presented to the religious establishment during the first century confronts us today in people touched by HIV/AIDS. In both situations the people of God are called upon to affirm what the law, prophets, and Jesus proclaimed: God loves all humanity and desires to have fellowship with all humanity. Like Jesus, the church is to be involved in prophetic and servant ministries that express this truth by word and deed. The church is under scriptural warrant not to ignore or be indifferent to the suffering of any person or group, even if that person or group is judged unacceptable and unlovable by society. The admonition in Proverbs about the fate of those who ignore the distress of the poor is being realized as the epidemic of HIV infection expands ("He who closes his ear to the cry of the poor will himself cry out and not be heard," Prov. 21:13, RSV). The needs of the original "risk groups" with HIV infection tended to be dismissed during most of the first decade of HIV/AIDS. Perceived to be "outside the camp," they largely were invisible (except through stereotype) and so were their needs. Little urgency was given to the value of informing everyone about the risk of HIV infection or of educating people regarding how to reduce their risk for infection if they were unwilling or unable to abstain from behaviors by which infection may occur. As the years have passed, many people with AIDS have died alone, unattended by God's people, and without experiencing the comfort and consolation of the body of Christ. As the years have passed, it has become better known that HIV has been "inside the camp" from the beginning of the epidemic, infecting the bodies of clergy and laity, and affecting directly, as a consequence, every member of this family. As the years have passed, the harvest of active and passive resistance of some within religious as well as secular life to effective HIV risk-avoidance/reduction education is being measured in a seemingly endless increase in new infections and predictable AIDS diagnoses. As the years have passed, those who felt safe "inside the camp" from those "outside the camp" slowly are recognizing that their own children are now imperiled by an ignorance fostered by parental, clergy, ecclesiastical, and public indifference or fear to address "sensitive" subjects. The church's response to HIV/AIDS during the epidemic's first decade has been short of what it could or should have been, had it fulfilled God's mandate to be an agent of justice and mercy for the poor, especially the poor touched by HIV/AIDS.

HIV/AIDS is more than a challenge to the church. It sets before the church an opportunity to reflect on its identity and its mission. If the church fails to act compassionately, neglects the needs that cluster around people with HIV disease, fails to express itself redemptively, and abandons people who have almost no one to cry out on their behalf for mercy and justice, then the church will abdicate its responsibility and fail in its witness even longer.

6

HIV/AIDS Ministries

As churches and individual Christians consider how to respond to the opportunities for ministry presented by HIV/AIDS, care should be taken not to underestimate the complexity of the challenge, the difficulty of the task, and the level of commitment necessary to initiate an adequate response. AIDS is a complicated medical disorder that manifests itself in a variety of illnesses having varying effects on the person diagnosed and on his or her loved ones. This means that in developing ministries, flexibility and responsiveness to individual differences are important. AIDS ministries may be more difficult to design and implement because the variations between situations require personalized attention. Finally, a high level of commitment is required to begin and sustain AIDS ministries because of the impediments and frustrations that attend them. In short, AIDS ministries should be undertaken by congregations and individuals who have their eyes open to the probable burdens and blessings associated with these activities.

Similarly, as AIDS ministries are being considered, the boundaries of concern should be generously drawn. People with HIV/AIDS-related diagnoses and their loved ones are obvious and compelling subjects of concern. But HIV/AIDS has a ripple effect, touching ever more lives.

The popular media, governmental, and scientific attention given to the prevention and treatment of HIV/AIDS has made it a matter of concern to almost everyone. As such, few people have escaped the touch of HIV/AIDS. Unfortunately, some people have been or are presently caught in its destructive grasp, and ultimately few people will escape its touch entirely.

People tend to view ministry to people touched by HIV/AIDS as overwhelmingly depressing. After all, people think, HIV infection is a fatal disease. People with AIDS are dying. There can be no joy, despite the worthiness of the activity or the self-satisfaction to be gained, under these circumstances. We do not deny that there are times of loss, hurt, disappointment, and grief during the course of faithful ministry to people with AIDS. Paradoxically, perhaps, there generally are many more occasions for laughter, joy, surprise, personal and spiritual growth, celebration, and humor. As people with AIDS begin to live longer and the secondary complications of HIV infection are better managed by skillful physicians, they tend to be reasonably well and functional more than they are acutely ill or dying. The period of degeneration prior to the terminal phase may be lengthy. The dying process, however, generally is mercifully brief, relatively speaking. Long-term ministry to people touched by HIV/AIDS, accordingly, resembles ministry to people with other chronic and debilitating diseases. Thus, AIDS ministries should be open-ended as well as open-eyed.

During most of the first decade of the HIV/AIDS epidemic, many Christians who felt called to ministry in this crisis found few opportunities to do so within religious organizations. Congregations generally had not developed special ministries, and denominations were unsure regarding what forms their programs would take. As a consequence, much ministry took place apart from religious institutions. The witness of these Christians tended to be absorbed by and camouflaged within the secular agencies where felt calls to ministry found expression. This situation was unfortunate in that it appeared that the church and Christians abandoned people facing the crisis of illness and premature death. The truth, however, is that institutionally based clergy, some pastors, and some lay people have been at the forefront of ministry, even though their activities tended not to be identified as church sponsored or, even, sanctioned. It is regrettable that these pioneers generally turned to secular organizations as a venue for ministry. They deserved the sponsorship of the church, and the church deserved to be recognized as a source of compassion. The relationship of faith to acts of loving service, unfortunately, tended to be obscured under these circumstances.

All ministries are related to faith commitments in two ways.[1] First, what is believed about God, the mission of the church, and discipleship influences the selection of ministries, their interpretation, and their manner of implementation. Second, events and experiences affect our beliefs about God, ecclesiology, and discipleship. For example, the appearance of HIV/AIDS prompted a new examination of Christian teachings about illness and outcast populations. This examination had two objectives: (1) to determine how the resources of faith can incorporate HIV/AIDS into its worldview and (2) to determine how the authorities of the faith inform and fashion the response of the faithful to HIV/AIDS. Our study has led us to conclude that the faithful are obligated to act compassionately toward all people who are ill, without regard for their identity or the way they contracted the disease, and that the faithful have special obligations under God to befriend and defend those who have few others to address their needs or advocate their cause. In sum, the church's response to HIV/AIDS will reflect the extent to which it identifies itself with its Lord, follows Jesus' teaching, and imitates his conduct.

The ministries proposed in this chapter reflect the authors' experience with people touched by HIV/AIDS directly and indirectly, on the one hand, and their experience in organizing and conducting ministries to these groups on the other hand.[2] The discussion ought not be understood as a step-by-step recipe or as an exhaustive or definitive guide to HIV/AIDS ministries. Rather, it is intended to be programmatic, suggestive, and descriptive. This approach is required because of the differences in needs and resources that exist between congregations and the specific opportunities for ministry in any given community. Thus, the applicability of any or all of the following proposals ultimately will have to be determined by individuals and congregations who feel called to be a compassionate and redeeming presence in the midst of the HIV/AIDS crisis.

General Prerequisites for Ministry

Ministering to people touched by HIV/AIDS differs in several ways from ministering to people with other illnesses. The objectives in both instances may be similar, but the negative moral attitudes, prospect of serving whole families with HIV infection, poor medical prognoses, and harsh social judgments associated with AIDS set it apart from other situations of ministry. As a result, before embarking on an AIDS ministry, three general prerequisites for ministry and three organizational recommendations warrant consideration.

Individual and Corporate Self-Examination

Being involved with people touched by HIV/AIDS can be a controversial activity. The fears evoked by the disease and the negative attitudes toward people whose behaviors place them at risk can combine to become a significant barrier to ministry. This may be the case even though individuals and congregations may feel compassion for those who are suffering in this crisis. Some will hesitate to become involved, and some may refuse because of a concern not to offend people who oppose this ministry and to protect important relationships that might be jeopardized by unsympathetic friends. The risk to fellowship that an AIDS ministry may pose ought not be underestimated. The respective risks and benefits deserve consideration, but the final decision to embark upon an AIDS ministry should be guided by the imperatives of Christian discipleship. Clearly, the perspective offered here is that the Christian mission authorizes and embraces ministry to people with HIV/AIDS. Yet such an undertaking may affect the fellowship of believers, and that fellowship deserves to be protected and preserved as much as possible, while being faithful to the Christian mission.

Initiating an AIDS ministry may first of all require courage.[3] The threat does not come from people with AIDS or HIV infection. They do not represent a threat of infection as a result of casual contact—or even more intimate contact, provided that proper precautions are taken. Rather, people involved in AIDS ministries may require courage to deal with those who oppose that ministry. Criticism and withdrawal may result. Subtle and overt messages of disapproval may be encountered. The isolation and ostracism known to people with AIDS may be experienced by those who participate in hands-on ministries to these men, women, and children. Debates may develop about the type and means of ministry that are indicated by the HIV crisis—should it be supportive or evangelistic? In short, the commitment to AIDS ministries may be tested severely during the planning and implementation phases.

The possible strain on fellowship may intensify as people with HIV/AIDS remain or become part of the corporate life of the congregation. Embracing people who are generally feared and disliked may be less threatening to fellowship as long as it is an activity outside the physical structure of the church. But if an AIDS ministry is to have maximum integrity, it would seem to require a willingness to include in the multifaceted life of the congregation the people to whom ministry is offered. The church nursery and day school are areas of congregational life where a commitment to inclusion may face a strong test. Adults appropriately are protective of young children.

Children tend to be shielded from exposure to flu, measles, mumps, and other viruses, either by segregation or vaccination. Unfortunately, a vaccine against HIV is not available. Segregation, accordingly, would appear to be the remaining method to guard children against HIV infection. These steps, however, generally are not indicated with respect to the risk of HIV infection in nursery or day-care settings. The behaviors by which HIV infection occurs are not those typically engaged in by young children. There is no evidence that casual contact and routine play among children represent a threat of HIV infection to other children from an HIV+ child. Nursery and day-care personnel should practice universal precautions for infection control with all children, not only with those children known to be HIV+. Personnel should be informed when a child is HIV+ in day care in order to be alert to changes in health status and to respond quickly and appropriately. There appears to be little reason to restrict the activities of young HIV+ children in order to protect their peers. Their activities may require restriction, however, to protect them against the infections that may circulate in child care settings to which an HIV+ child may be more vulnerable. Opening the doors of the church to people touched by HIV/AIDS may involve opening the doors of the nursery and day school as well as the doors to the sanctuary, clergy offices, church school rooms, and members' homes. Living in solidarity with people touched by HIV/AIDS may require more than public proclamation and adult participation.

Restricting ministry to a home, hospital, or hospice setting is a signal that people suffering from HIV/AIDS are less valued and acceptable than people suffering from other illnesses. This sort of discrimination undercuts the proclamation of divine and human love implicit in an AIDS ministry. Redeeming love unites; it does not exclude or segregate. The discomfort or risk to fellowship that may accompany any innovative, pioneering, or controversial ministry may be intensified in the case of AIDS ministries.

The sentiments that arouse opposition to an AIDS ministry may be deeply ingrained and may not be easily surmounted. Confronting reservations in a medically educated, socially unprejudiced, and theologically informed manner will require an openness of mind and heart. Agreeing to affirm mutual respect for the differing understandings and commitments of individuals and congregations may be a means by which diverse ministries may be undertaken and a harmonious fellowship maintained.

The second consideration is an assessment of how comfortable one is with illness, wasted bodies, anguish, death, and grief. People with AIDS tend to have repeated acute illnesses that result in an ever-increasing level of dependency. Their care can be very demanding during these periods. Care providers grow weary and frustrated as one acute illness ends and another soon appears. The physical and emotional toll is even greater for the ill person. People with AIDS may experience sudden or gradual loss of control over daily activity, environment, and body functions. Whatever the speed, they generally feel trapped in a process of irreversible debilitation and degeneration. Their bodies tend to waste away. Their anguish, anger, and grief tend to modulate as they adjust to the fact that neither they nor their physicians ultimately can control events.

People who enter this world to minister would be wise to anticipate this process. Not only should they imagine sojourning with one person and his or her loved ones through this course; they should anticipate repeating the cycle again and again at short intervals. A bond frequently develops between people, ill and well, who unite to combat HIV/AIDS and its devastating effects. Investments are made in one another. Commitments of care and personal presence are made and kept. Young men and women in their prime and young children are pulled toward debilitation, dependency, indignity, and death. Being a part of this tragedy can be as exhausting as it can be rewarding.

Once acquainted with AIDS, one rarely fails to be moved by the suffering that surrounds it. Even people who are fearful of the disease or hostile toward people whose behaviors put them at risk often will respond compassionately in the face of such severe human pain and suffering. Moral condemnation and fear may remain intact, but empathy and sympathy may move people to compassion and involvement. Suffering humanity, regardless of accompanying judgments of desert, can be a compelling force that draws even reluctant people into action. Although a compassionate response, regardless of its source, is to be celebrated, it needs to be equal to the task. In practical terms, the extent and severity of disease and bodily destruction can be such that persons who wish to help can become immobilized. An inability to fulfill intentions may come from unavoidable unpleasant sights or a too intimate identification with the person. The would-be helper may turn away in horror or in fear of inflicting additional pain on a person who has suffered too much already. As AIDS ministries are contemplated, people intending a hands-on ministry ought to anticipate what surely lies ahead as a means to determine if they can bear the pain and still provide an effective ministry. An initial affirmative response ought not be considered irrevocable. Though a person's fantasy about AIDS and its effects may be worse than the reality in some cases, in other cases the reality is far worse. Withdrawing is no disgrace, especially if persevering would be counterproductive for all concerned.

A third area of self-examination is one's willingness to be exposed to settings and lifestyles that are unfamiliar or even offensive. Some features of male homosexual culture, for example, may be interesting or they may be a significant barrier to ministry for people previously unaware of them.[4] The culture of IV drug users may engender a similar range of reactions.[5] It is important to remember, however, that meeting people in their own environment certifies declarations of concern and affirms their value under God. Ministry to people with HIV/

AIDS entails entering into their experience, learning about them, loving them, and sharing their grief. In the process, friendships are forged, commitments are made, life is shared, and horizons are expanded. What was previously foreign may become familiar as a consequence of an AIDS ministry. Whether prior stereotypes or prejudices on either side are altered in the process appears, from a Christian moral point of view, less important on balance than the willingness to seek and sustain contact.

All people involved with AIDS should meet on the same level: one person loved by God meeting another person loved by God; one person of inestimable value to God meeting another person of inestimable value to God; one vulnerable and mortal person meeting another vulnerable and mortal person. This encounter of persons, not stereotypes, is essential to a valid and successful AIDS ministry. Condescension or self-righteousness on the part of God's people is contrary to the example of Jesus, and it is usually repulsive to the very people to whom ministry is offered. The object of God's people in ministries of compassion is to be a manifestation of God's love, implicitly inviting people to faith and obedience. There is no biblical warrant for abusing the weakness and vulnerability of persons. Jesus did not browbeat weakened people into declarations of faith. Even the "deathbed conversion" of the thief on the cross was a voluntary response to the love of God revealed in Jesus (Luke 23:39–43). Entering into the experience of others, as Jesus learned, may place one in uncomfortable or threatening surroundings. Nevertheless, the command to love one's neighbor contains no exceptions. And for the people of God, there are few more powerful expressions of love for God and neighbor than that of entering unconditionally into a neighbor's experience of pain and suffering.

A fourth area is one's capacity to separate compassion from condoning the conduct by which a person was infected with the AIDS virus. Some people may resist participating in supportive ministries because they do not wish their compassion to be interpreted as approving behaviors that place people at risk for HIV infection (e.g., nonmarital sexual intercourse or IV drug use). These activities are widely condemned in church declarations and by individual Christians. Giving support to people who engage in these activities but who are now ill ought not be seen as an endorsement of their conduct. Christians who sincerely oppose smoking tobacco or alcohol consumption tend not to withdraw their support from people who become ill as a consequence of these lifestyles. In addition, the incidence of disease related to eating patterns and sedentary lifestyles may be even greater than the amount of disease related to tobacco and alcohol. Yet it is rare for Christians to turn away from people suffering from illnesses related to these activities out of fear that their presence and comforting ministries will be seen as condoning tobacco, alcohol, and food addiction. It may be that these latter "evils" have become domesticated over time and are now more socially tolerable, if not fully accepted, socially and religiously. People with diseases related to diet and "soft drug" addiction are not considered beyond the scope of Christian compassion.

People with AIDS as a consequence of socially and religiously disapproved behavior ought not be seen as a separate category of ill person, unworthy of ministry because the conduct that contributed to their illness is opposed by a significant segment of the religious community. To withhold or withdraw ministry for this reason is inconsistent with the obligations to be faithful to those who are either ill or outcast.[6] Ministries of compassion are not necessarily indicative of one's moral opinion of a person or lifestyle, but such ministries are moral statements about the value of each person to God and to the community of faith. In this sense, AIDS ministries represent moral and theological understandings of duty and the value of persons. They do not, in and of themselves, constitute acceptance, tolerance, or advocacy of homosexuality, marital infidelity, or IV drug use. The behavior associated with the transmission of HIV warrants consideration apart from the task of defining and fulfilling one's duties to sick, dying, and grieving persons. Unfortunately, it appears in the case of HIV/AIDS that negative moral judgments may distort our understandings of ministry, effectively blocking ministry to persons touched by HIV/AIDS. People disposed to participate in compassionate AIDS ministries should be able to separate in their own minds compassion from moral judgment. Similarly, they ought to recognize and be prepared to respond to the confusion of the two by other people.

The question is whether moral judgment or disapproval of behaviors or persons should be a barrier to ministry.[7] Surely it should not. One reason is that despite the high confidence that is placed in religious beliefs and moral judgments derived from them, these beliefs and judgments always should be tentative. By definition, people of faith should remain open to new insights into the nature and will of God, and to new understandings of right and wrong. If God's revelation were complete and if humanity had perceived all of God that there is to understand, the ministry of the Holy Spirit would not be necessary. In addition, what we are as humans, why we are the way we are, and why we do what we do are being better understood as scientific studies provide a more complete picture of humanity. And lastly, theological and biblical studies are continuously clarifying the meanings and applications of authoritative sources with respect to God, humanity, and the relation of each to the others.

Christians are people of faith. Faith is not knowledge or certainty. What understandings of God and morality Christians hold are incomplete. They do not, at present, constitute all truth. As a confessional people, Christians have responded to the revelation of God in Jesus. The discipleship and moral vision of Christians are grounded in the witness of Jesus. As a moral norm, therefore, human agape is an obligation for Christians. For Christians, human agape supercedes all other rules of conduct.

Therefore, enabling, sustaining, and enriching ministries should be offered in obedience to the love command to all people regardless of a Christian's moral evaluation of the behaviors that contributed to the creation of need.

Christians are obliged to offer pastoral care, unconditioned by a judgment of the person's moral guilt or innocence. A person in need, however, is free to refuse an offer of care. Just as people are free to accept or reject participation in God's saving activity, so people are free to accept or reject God's caring activity mediated through the pastoral ministries of God's people. A person's weakness, vulnerability, and dependency ought not be exploited. Offers of care and support should express genuine concerns for a person's welfare and should not camouflage an evangelistic, moralistic, or political agenda. If the latter is the case, these otherwise morally laudable and theologically justified ministries become tainted by an interest other than the care, comfort, and enrichment of the person in need. What was undertaken as moral activity, an activity grounded in human agape, deteriorates into a morally questionable activity of exploitation and coercion.

Pastoral ministries and care that primarily focus on the welfare of people in need properly are grounded in a sense of Christian mission and discipleship. They are valid and good in and of themselves. No other agenda or end needs to be served in order to justify the offer or activity of care. If the care is accepted, then both the giver and recipient gain. The caregiver is permitted to do that which is essential to his or her Christian identity. The person in need freely accepts the love, affirmation, and assistance that the provider gives. Though the exchange arises from a situation of inequality, the people involved are respected and relate as equals. Pastoral care, according to this understanding, is a moral activity, characterized by a primary concern for the welfare of a person in need and a respect for that person's freedom to decide what is good for him or her.

This approach suggests that people who offer ministry

will do so with an attitude of humility and confidence. So disposed, a caregiver is freed to risk entry into different situations without feeling compelled to ridicule or disparage that which is different. The freedom of the prospective recipient of care requires that he or she be regarded as an equal. His or her moral values and commitments do not have to correspond to those of the pastoral caregiver. They deserve to be acknowledged and accepted because they represent that person's notion of the life worth living. They do not necessarily require assent, however. Given this understanding, the integrity of the provider and recipient of care is respected. The relationship between the parties is on an adult-adult level, rather than an adult-child level (care-giver and care-receiver, respectively).

Where two or more people are brought together out of mutual need and relate on a level of mutual regard, there is a risk that one or all may change as a result of the encounter. In relationships of this description, moral perspectives may be explained, analyzed, and evaluated. This sharing is an implicit invitation to change, as much as the witness of Jesus is an invitation to faith and discipleship. People are free to accept or reject both invitations. The people of God, however, are not free to reject Jesus' command to love others, even if the others are different or considered morally deviant.

The tendency of some Christians to concentrate on their differences with others can impede ministry. These differences may be doctrinal, racial, ethnic, economic, educational, cultural, sexual, or moral. Value judgments may be attached to those differences in an effort to justify failures to provide supportive, sustaining, concrete ministries to people in need. However, it is for this reason that differences ought not be considered as a condition for providing or denying ministry to people in need. The parable of the Samaritan provides an excellent object lesson.

Recall that in Luke the parable immediately follows Jesus' summary of the law. After saying that one is to love God and love one's neighbor, Jesus tells the parable in which a man was robbed, injured, and left half-dead along a road. A Samaritan passerby saw the man, recognized his need for help, and had compassion, attending to his wounds and providing for his care (Luke 10:25–37). It should be emphasized that nothing is known about the injured man other than that he was in need.[8] Everything about the victim apparently was irrelevant to Jesus except his need. His race, nationality, sexuality, and cause of distress are not known to the travelers down the road. He simply is a man in need to whom the Samaritan responded with acts of care. This parable instructs Christians about what love means and requires, and who is one's neighbor. Neither the characteristics nor the causes of a person's need are relevant conditions for ministry. A person's need, and that alone, is sufficient to require of God's people a loving response. All other considerations have no role. From a perspective of Christian discipleship and Christian morality, to be moral and to be a faithful witness to Christ, the needs of others cannot be ignored.

This unconditioned and unqualified call to care for people in need is reiterated in the Sermon on the Mount. Jesus, according to Matthew, cautions his disciples against judging others. The mercy that a believer experiences from God should be generously expressed toward all others without question.[9] Dietrich Bonhoeffer expressed powerfully the significance of Jesus' teaching regarding the danger of judgment to love: "Christian love sees the fellow-man under the cross and therefore sees with clarity. If when we judged others our real motive was to destroy evil, we should look for evil where it is to be found, and that is in our own hearts. But if we are on the lookout for evil in others, our real motive is obviously to justify ourselves, for we are seeking to escape punishment for our own sins by passing judgment on others, and are assuming by implication that the Word of God applies to ourselves in one way, and to others in another." Bonhoeffer regards such a stance as highly dangerous and misleading because it indicates that we are trying to claim for ourselves a special privilege that we deny to others. It should be clear, he argues, that Christ's disciples have no rights of their own or standards of right and wrong that they can enforce with other people; they have received nothing but Christ's fellowship. As disciples, therefore, we are not to sit in judgment over our fellows because that would wrongly usurp the jurisdiction.[10] Having experienced the reconciling love of God, Christians are to express reconciling love to all others. We are to give freely what we have received. Nothing else is acceptable.

The care provided to people with need on the basis of the need alone not only benefits the person served, but also sets an example for others to follow. It challenges people and communities who subscribe to other, perhaps less demanding, moralities to see the intrinsic worth of a love ethic that incorporates but goes beyond justice. The emphasis in pastoral care, according to the perspective offered here, should be on being a moral agent, obeying the love command, freely and without condition committing oneself to the welfare and well-being of others.

Pastoral care, therefore, is a gift of self and sustenance to others. It is a witness to faith in God. It is an act of obedience. It does not exploit a person's need or vulnerability in order to coerce that person to believe in God or accept the caregiver's notion of Christian morality.

A fifth area of self-examination before being involved in an AIDS ministry *is an assessment of the degree of commitment to the task.* The needs of each person may fluctuate greatly over short intervals of time. Ministering successfully in this situation requires individual and organizational flexibility, capacity to tolerate rapid changes, and an ability to persevere for a relatively long time. People who commit themselves to an AIDS ministry should be willing to be inconvenienced and to sacrifice personal interests for the needs of those served. The course of the disease and the level of dependency are not always predictable. Anticipating or expecting unforeseen requests for assistance may lessen the anger or frustration when they occur. Failing to respond to legitimate calls for help may intensify a person's sense of being out of control, isolated, and abandoned. Loyalty to persons and keeping promises are important components for building secure relationships with people touched by AIDS. Alternately, the trust and confidence that persons with HIV/AIDS and their loved ones have in those who minister to them provide important bases for deepened relationships and expanded opportunities for ministry. Being clear in advance about the general type and number of ministries that may be requested allows people to determine whether their commitment to AIDS ministries is equal to the task.

The sixth area of self-examination is the availability of time. People with HIV/AIDS may feel that the church and Christians generally are unconcerned about them as persons or about their welfare. They often feel rejected and despised because of their sexuality, lifestyle, or disease. They probably have not felt welcomed in the life of most Christian churches. As a result, many gay men, in particular, have come to distrust a church that condemns them and Christians who insist that they change their sexual nature. Overtures by congregations to people with HIV/AIDS may be greeted with a degree of skepticism. Both the motives and objectives may be questioned. Many outcast people feel initially that it is hypocritical of Christians to declare their love and offer comfort in situations of illness while being hostile or indifferent, at best, before the onset of a medical crisis. Overcoming this suspicion and accompanying reluctance to believe the honorable intentions of people committed to AIDS ministries requires patience, loyalty, and perseverance. An inordinate amount of time may be required both to initiate and sustain AIDS ministries. Working with the HIV/AIDS population is often an activity that cannot be predicted or scheduled. Ministries may occur at prearranged times and locations. They are equally likely to occur on request at inconvenient times and locations.

People considering AIDS ministries should realize in advance that establishing quality relationships and providing quality ministries often require many hours of preparation and activity.

The seventh area of self-examination requires an ability to maintain self-control, as is generally important for ministry to persons in crisis situations. People should anticipate that the activities undertaken will involve them in intimate, highly personal, and private situations. There must be a sufficient commitment to enable volunteers not to flee, and there must be a balancing objectivity that enables them to be effective. When this balance of commitment and objectivity is maintained, people are freed to minister, to be involved but not be immobilized, to feel but not decompensate.[11] Determining whether candidates for AIDS ministries have the necessary character and personality traits to attain this balance is largely a matter of self-examination and experience. An objective personal appraisal may be sufficient to identify people with the appropriate disposition and willingness. Actual ministry to people touched by AIDS either will confirm or invalidate this initial assessment. Undiscovered resources may emerge in the process of ministry. Similarly, the initial assessment of personal traits and skills may be found wanting when tested in actual ministry. Should this be the case, withdrawing from AIDS ministries, either from direct to indirect ministries or to total withdrawal, ought not be seen as a defeat or embarrassment. More appropriately, this finding should be interpreted to indicate that one's gifts are better suited for alternate ministries.

The final area of self-examination builds upon positive responses to the preceding seven areas. People who have the appropriate dispositions, traits, and opportunities to participate in AIDS ministries also need to be willing to be educated and trained for this specialized ministry. HIV/AIDS and its effects on people, both as a consequence of the disease itself and society's reaction to it, have created an unprecedented situation. Much is known and more is being learned. Becoming informed about the destructive forces set in motion by HIV and how to respond in a healing, consoling, constructive manner are necessary conditions for embarking upon ministries to people touched by HIV/AIDS.

Education and Training

Being properly prepared can facilitate a competent and effective AIDS ministry. Education and training can take various forms, but they are indispensable. People who participate in AIDS ministries should be *learning as much as possible about the disease.* Learning about the HIV and the means of its transmission should help to allay common fears and anxieties that surface as AIDS ministries are being planned. Distinguishing between the facts and myths about the routes of infection followed by HIV should help people feel comfortable about contact with people with HIV/AIDS and free them to minister confidently. In addition, knowledge of the common acute illnesses, treatments, and the general progression of the disease can help people know what may happen and so formulate responses and ministries in advance of the need for them.

Learning about AIDS requires more than learning about the medical and physical facts. It means learning about the psychosocial aspects of the disease itself and the epidemic. The emotional, social, economic, and relational losses associated with HIV/AIDS can be as severe and destructive to the patient and to loved ones as the physical losses. People ministering to persons with HIV/AIDS should learn of the emotional assaults, social reactions, economic costs, and individual rejections that may follow a diagnosis of HIV infection or AIDS. Being aware of these possibilities and their impact on the affected individuals should enhance a person's ability to understand the feelings of people bearing the stigma of HIV/AIDS. A better understanding, however, is not the only gain from becoming knowledgeable about the nonmedical aspects of AIDS. Although cognitive awareness may inform and equip people involved in AIDS ministries, subjective or empathic knowledge contributes to a person's capacity to *feel and understand* what and how people touched by HIV/AIDS feel. Communicating, relating, experiencing, and ministering at this level may enrich the quality of the activity and contribute to its success. This is the level of mutual personal investment that, when achieved, creates interpersonal bonds sufficient to withstand the stresses and strains that inevitably develop.

Learning about the physical and psychosocial manifestations of HIV/AIDS involves *learning about people who are at risk* for contracting the disease. It is well known that men who have sex with men, heterosexual partners of a person with HIV infection, and IV drug users are most likely to be infected by HIV and to become clinically ill as a result. The prospects for effective ministries are enhanced if the people seeking to minister become knowledgeable about male homosexuality, gay lifestyles, and the struggle of homosexual people for ecclesiastical, social, and legal equality.[12] Similarly, the phenomenon of drug abuse is complex, not easily explained or morally judged when considered comprehensively as both an individual activity and one that is culturally induced. Becoming familiar with relevant factual literature in both these areas should facilitate constructive interaction with these groups.[13] Learning about populations whose behavior puts them at risk for HIV infection can be a means by which volunteers can assess their comfort level before contact with them. Also, greater knowledge and understanding lessens the likelihood that people engaged in AIDS ministries will be surprised, shocked, or turned away by certain features or characteristics of these populations.

A third component of the preparatory phase for AIDS ministries is *securing education and training in methods of pastoral care and ministry.* These activities are pastoral in the sense that they are supportive and nurturing, not that they are performed by ordained people. They are ministries of and by congregations. The duties of support and nurture belong to the laity as well as to those who are ordained. Just as ordained clergy typically are expected to be educated and trained in their profession before embarking upon it, people willing to provide AIDS ministries should be expected to have their gifts for ministry refined by special education and training that equip them for the task.[14] Among the skills that should be mastered at this point are the ability to listen, the ability to be nonjudgmental, the capacity to keep confidences, and the ability to persevere in the midst of hurt and grief. Finally, given the probable intensity of ministries to people with HIV/AIDS and their loved ones, appropriate oversight or supervision ought to be provided.[15] Learning to minister under supervision enables an observer to spot emerging problems and to provide counsel about how to avoid or minimize them. In addition, the supervisor can provide support, nurture, and consolation to the people engaged in hands-on ministries. The stress, hurt, and grief that are typical features of AIDS ministries can be addressed by the supervisor in order to meet the needs of the people ministering and to guard against burnout.

In addition to learning how to provide emotional and spiritual care to the sick and their loved ones, people participating in hands-on AIDS ministries may need help in *learning how to perform unskilled or semiskilled nursing tasks.* These procedures may include moving a bed-bound patient, positioning a patient in bed for comfort, changing diapers on adults, oral care, and feeding, watering, cleaning, and medicating patients (orally and via IV lines). Providing these types of care may give relief to the primary caregivers. They are tangible expressions of concern. They are evidence that inhibiting fears have been overcome.

Continuing one's education is the fifth component. Knowledge about the disease and its impact is constantly growing. Participants in AIDS ministries cannot be expected to become or remain experts on the HIV/AIDS crisis or any single aspect of it. Nevertheless, they should be alert to news reports about the disease, its treatment, and societal responses to it. These subjects often are topics of discussion during visits. Staying aware of these developments indicates a high level of interest and facilitates interaction. In addition, this knowledge can be called upon to teach people the facts about HIV/AIDS, especially the means and risks of transmission of the virus. Workshops and seminars with appropriate leadership can help achieve this objective. Similar sessions focusing on increasing knowledge about ministry and gaining or improving ministering skills also would be appropriate.

These five aspects of preparatory education and training are separately and jointly intended to enhance the competence and self-confidence of participants in AIDS ministries. By establishing an effective training program, a means is provided by which new participants can be incorporated into ongoing activities. Veteran members can keep their knowledge current and their ministering skills sharply honed. With adequate preparation and opportunities for continued education, people involved in AIDS ministries should be better able to respond creatively and confidently to unexpected challenges.

Clarity of Purpose

AIDS ministries are primarily ministries of support, nurture, and consolation. They are not primarily evangelistic ministries in the sense of pressure to convert to a particular faith or morality. To view evangelism as the primary or sole objective of ministry to people with AIDS is to misunderstand ministry and probably will be counterproductive with the targeted audience.

Authentic ministry involves the free gift of self to others, echoing God's free gift of the divine self to humanity. It involves establishing knowing and sharing relationships characterized biblically as loving one's neighbor. This and only this is the formal end of ministry. People, especially in evangelical churches, often are inclined to understand all ministries to be aimed ultimately at "saving the lost." But "saving" people is not the business of human beings. It is a task beyond their power. "Saving" people, it should be remembered, is God's business.[16] Thus, the purpose for all ministry, including AIDS ministry, is to represent God's love for all humanity, without condition, and to embody and express that love in all human relationships.

Doors are likely to be closed quickly to well-meaning people who approach men and women caught in the crisis of HIV/AIDS with declarations of their sin and need for repentance. This approach seems to some people as most properly directed toward gay or bisexual men caught in the HIV/AIDS crisis. Their "sin" is said to be what they do sexually and who they discover themselves to be: homosexual. Intravenous drug users are said to be morally culpable for their actions only, not for who they are as sexual beings, provided that they are heterosexual. Sexually active heterosexual youth and adults are said to violate the moral norm of marriage. HIV-infected women who become pregnant, either within or apart from marriage, sometimes are condemned for becoming pregnant or bringing a pregnancy to term, thereby placing the newborn baby at risk for HIV infection. In these situations, however, approaches by Christians that are in reality reproaches tend to be rejected. The prospect for relationship is significantly lessened when the first priority is seen to be that of convincing people that they are evil or that their behaviors are wrong. Further, ministries to homosexual men or drug users conditioned on changed behavior are likely to be exercises in frustration, because sexual orientation appears to be a given and drug addictions tend not to be remedied by acts of will alone.

In order for AIDS ministries to be initiated and to mature, contact with affected individuals needs to be maintained. People with HIV/AIDS are more likely to allow others to sojourn with them when they feel accepted by and acceptable to people who want to help. As everyone becomes more confident that the expressed concern is genuine and masks no coercive agenda, trust develops. People with HIV/AIDS and their loved ones may begin to feel comfortable enough to initiate discussions about their spiritual concerns, to which people involved in AIDS ministries legitimately may respond. Setting the spiritual agenda in AIDS ministries is a task to be performed by the recipients of these ministries, not the people providing them. Once raised, these subjects can be addressed in a constructive, redemptive, gentle manner, affirming to all that God's invitation to fellowship is constant and that God's love excludes no one. It seems more important, in these situations, to manifest divine and human love that encourages a turning to God than to attempt to require that a person's relationship with God conform to any particular confession or morality.

The distinctive aspect of the AIDS ministries envisaged here is the loving care offered by God's people, not the tasks that are performed. Almost all services proposed in this chapter, except for sacraments and other religious rites, can be performed competently by non-Christians. It is this feature of the church's ministry in the HIV/AIDS crisis that distinguishes it from the services provided by governments and secular agencies. The church's ministry, without fanfare and without coercion, ought to be a humble act of service following the example of its servant Lord. The church's healing presence demonstrates God's compassion and concern for all people burdened as a consequence of AIDS. Thus, AIDS ministries are to be supportive, compassionate, consoling, and reconciling. They manifest God's involvement and call all segments of society to a godly response.

Organizational Recommendations

Parish-Based Care

The care of sick and suffering people is a duty of God's people. Although the institution of the church may sponsor or operate facilities and conduct programs through which care is provided, the actual ministry, in whatever form it takes, is performed by individuals. Church-related hospitals, nursing homes, hospices, and residences are laudable activities. However, these operations do not satisfy the obligation of individual Christians to address the needs of people coping with illness and the impact of death. Congregants routinely express concern and provide care for fellow congregants in crisis. The provision of similar ministries to persons outside congregational membership is less common, except through the caring institutions founded and operated by parishes and denominations. Yet in the case of HIV/AIDS, the opportunities for ministry are greater outside the confines of these church-sponsored institutions because efforts are made to maintain AIDS patients in their homes as much as possible. Hospitalization, though frequent in some cases, tends to be short-term. It is difficult to create and sustain relationships when contact is restricted to periods of institutional care. These opportunities for ministry ought not be overlooked. But with a chronic degenerative disease like AIDS, the needs of the people afflicted persist and tend to increase between times in the hospital. Therefore, the prospect for enduring and effective ministries increases if these ministries are parish-based rather than hospital-based.

As noted, ministering in a comprehensive manner to people with HIV/AIDS may require a large investment of time and energy. In addition, the needs of affected individuals can be so numerous and demanding that a single person and his or her loved ones may require the ministries of many people. This situation seems to be best addressed by ministry teams formed within single parishes.[17] A team approach can draw upon the diverse expertise within a parish, provide for efficient coordination of activities, enhance communication within the team and with the person with AIDS, make possible a division of labor, and facilitate mutual care for the team members. Matching a parish-based team with a person with AIDS also encourages enduring contact and bonding between team members and the person and between the parish and the person. The results this approach wants to achieve are relationships of deeper quality, mutual commitments of greater intensity, and deeper trust and concern.

This sort of team ministry may make it possible for a person with AIDS and loved ones to establish rapport with one or more team members. In a sense, the team becomes a surrogate and extended family to the person receiving care. Further, the affected individuals may develop a sense of belonging to a particular family of faith, frequently resulting in a congregation's becoming a surrogate "home church" for loved ones who have come a long distance to remain with a person during his or her illness. This seems most likely when the ministry team and affected people are of the same denomination. Lastly, a team ministry is advisable, because realistically only a limited number of people in a parish will feel led to participate in AIDS ministries. Each will possess certain gifts that deserve to be used efficiently and effectively. A team approach should allow for a continuing and coordinated ministry. Thus, a self-contained unit consisting of people with a common identity, mission, and parish base offers the best likelihood for a successful ministry.

Interfaith Ministries

The opportunities for ministry occasioned by HIV/AIDS in locations where there are many cases tend to be greater than any single parish or denomination can effectively provide. AIDS affects people in all religious traditions, and therefore all religious traditions have a responsibility to conduct AIDS ministries. These ministries may take many forms—for example, visitation, services of prayer and healing, support groups, housing programs, temporary shelters, food pantries, adult and child day care, bereavement groups, and more. Denominations may facilitate communications among existing congregational or agency ministries and identify an appropriate agency, office, or person to be a resource to the denomination in its many manifestations. Some denominations have created networks with a resource office to accomplish these goals. These denomination-specific activities are but one way in which ministry can be promoted and provided. On the local level, however, an interfaith AIDS ministry can provide a coordinated program through which different faith groups support and complement each other. Such a structure on a local level also enables a coordinating staff to match patients and families with a parish team of their own faith.

However, such matching is not always required. Some people needing help prefer that it come from a denomination other than their own, particularly if their denomination is known to be unsympathetic to certain groups (e.g., gay men) or to the plight of people with AIDS. In our experience, it has proved difficult to organize an AIDS ministry that is truly ecumenical, involving individuals from several denominations in a patient-directed team. Nevertheless, the appearance and spread of HIV/AIDS is creating a growing need and opportunity for ministry that transcends traditional denominational boundaries, ideally stimulating on some levels a joint response by religious bodies. Judaism and Christianity have a common concern for ill, suffering, and bereaved persons. HIV/AIDS is an area where this concern can lead to cooperation without compromising theological distinctives or violating polity. Joint educational and service projects may be possible with HIV/AIDS but perhaps not with many other issues. In addition, if parishes and church bodies sponsor some joint activities in response to HIV/AIDS, there is an opportunity for each to learn about the other: more particularly, what they share that brought them together on this issue and the differences that inhibit cooperation in other areas.

The final reason why parish-based AIDS ministries ought to be interfaith is geographic. People touched by HIV/AIDS can be found nearly everywhere. Although people with confirmed diagnoses are concentrated in metropolitan areas, they and their loved ones live in all neighborhoods. It is unrealistic to conclude that parishes in neighborhoods with a large number of people at risk are the only ones facing the problem, or that they are able to address all the needs. The people who need AIDS-related ministries are dispersed throughout the city limits and across the countryside. Parishes next to treatment institutions or in high-incidence population areas cannot effectively minister to loved ones in other areas of the city or country. Moreover, it is important that parishes conducting AIDS ministries let their work be widely known. It does little good to have a ministry that is not known to people who would benefit from it. Publicizing the parish's stand on this issue and the ministries offered is essential. Further, referral is facilitated when parishes are aware of resources available in other parishes.

Networks

Publicizing a parish's AIDS ministries is important for reasons other than interparish referral. People desiring AIDS ministries need to know where they can turn for support, nurture, and consolation. Self-referral to a parish is one means to initiate a relationship with people coping with HIV/AIDS. An equally important means is by referral relationships with health care personnel, relevant agencies, and AIDS support organizations. There ought to be a spirit of cooperation among resource agencies grounded in a common concern for how best to serve the needs of people touched by HIV/AIDS. The governmental response to HIV/AIDS means that much of the psychosocial and physical and nearly all the spiritual care of this population falls to volunteer organizations, including the church. Unnecessary competition and duplication of scarce resources ought to be avoided. If interested persons and agencies cooperate in every way possible, supplementing the resources that each provides, this network will make it more possible to provide appropriate care in an efficient and effective manner.

In our experience, people with AIDS and loved ones tend to be hesitant to ask churches and church people for help. They anticipate a hostile, condemning, or indifferent response. Secular and governmental agencies are seen as a primary hope for assistance and as forums where they will be received with some degree of respect. Whether this perception is valid depends on the agency and personnel involved. Nevertheless, because religious communities, intentionally or unintentionally, have caused people at risk to feel unwelcome when diagnosed as having AIDS or a related disorder, they do not see the church as a resource, feeling it does not care about them or their struggle to survive. If contact is to be made with these distrustful individuals, it may need to be facilitated by secular agencies. When a parish AIDS ministry team and a person with HIV disease are matched, the process of creating trust, of discrediting false perceptions with regard to that particular parish, and of providing supportive ministries may begin. Networking with secular and religious agencies, therefore, tends to be crucial in many instances. Without a reliable network, available ministries may not be performed and all concerned will be worse off.

A final possible good to be realized from networking relates to public attitudes. When ecclesiastical and secular institutions can embrace a single position and coordinate resources to address a family of needs, they can make a powerful prophetic statement. In the case of HIV/AIDS, a cooperative response signals that HIV/AIDS is a public health crisis rather than a moral issue. It is an occasion for mobilizing a coordinated, comprehensive response, not an occasion to point fingers of blame and abdicate responsibility. It is a crisis that calls for a benevolent and compassionate attitude toward suffering people from all sectors of the community. By responding in a praiseworthy manner, secular and religious institutions can model the attitude and behavior most appropriate to the needs of all concerned. By acting compassionately and responsibly, religious and secular agencies and officials can help all of society to make a reasoned, redemptive, humane response.

Sustaining Ministries

AIDS ministries are termed sustaining ministries because they inform, affirm, and support persons. They promote certain goods and values in the midst of a situation of significant loss. These ministries are multidirectional and serve a variety of ends. They are realistic, responsive to the needs arising from the crisis of HIV/AIDS, appropriate to the mission of God's people, and representative of a contemporary interpretation of the command to love one's neighbor. The types of ministries that follow have as their focus people presently touched directly by HIV/AIDS, the church's integrity, and the character of the society within which the church exists. In short, when seen as a whole and understood theologically, AIDS ministries have a prophetic, priestly, and servant character reflecting a concern for the well-being of individual persons, the church itself, and the social order.[18]

Education

Providing factual information about the extent of suffering engendered by HIV/AIDS is one way to combat fear, indifference, and hostility. There is resistance to learning about HIV/AIDS, both in society at large and within congregations. This may be related to the convergence of two taboos in the present public health crisis—sex and death.[19] Neither topic is usually discussed in polite circles. Sex and death denote powerful, awe-inspiring forces of generation and destruction. They attract and repel. They are clothed in mystery. Everyone is aware of them, but no one seems fully to understand them. They are linked in biblical myth to explain theologically the nature of the human condition. And both are associated with God's displeasure with humanity's exercise of freedom.[20]

Although sex and death are seen in scientific communities as legitimate subjects for analysis, in religious and nonscientific circles there is a tendency to regard both subjects and the phenomena related to them as off limits. Their mysterious nature is to remain intact. Because they are related to God's judgment, discussion of either except in approved ways is to be avoided. Thus, AIDS incorporates two taboos by being sexually transmitted and by being ultimately fatal, given current therapeutics. The situation currently is compounded further by its association in developed Western countries with another taboo—male-to-male sexual conduct, which tends to be more harshly judged than nonmarital heterosexual intercourse. The taboos associated with AIDS combine to form an effective barrier to educating church people and the public about the disease and the suffering it causes. The disease has been portrayed as additional evidence of God's anger over the violation of taboos and rules of conduct. Rather than being a party to these violations and risking a further outpouring of God's wrath, people tend to avoid education about AIDS. Yet education about how to prevent the spread of HIV and changed behavior based on education are presently the best hopes of limiting the destructive effect of HIV. And finally, putting a personal face on the pain and suffering caused by HIV/AIDS may be the most effective way to generate an informed, compassionate response.

The losses HIV/AIDS causes and the opportunities for ministry it creates cannot be ignored. It seems advisable to begin to face them now as the human toll mounts and is comparatively limited, rather than later when the intensity of human suffering will have increased manyfold. In fact, becoming aware of the probable magnitude of the crisis may motivate people to prepare now to meet current and projected needs. The church classroom and the pulpit are appropriate forums in which to provide facts about HIV/AIDS and summon a compassionate response. The church classroom seems better suited, however, for examining several topics in detail and developing a comprehensive understanding of HIV/AIDS and the church's role in the epidemic.

The Church Classroom. The first obvious area of education is the disease itself. Print, videotape, and personal resources increasingly are available to provide people with a factual, understandable orientation to HIV/AIDS.[21] Sessions directed toward this end should include information on the AIDS virus, means of transmission, preventive measures, physiological tests for infection, symptoms of infection, effect of the virus on the body's cellular immune system, secondary complications, and precautions to take when ministering to infected persons.

A second general subject of study is behavior that puts people at risk for HIV infection. Learning about HIV/AIDS presents an opportunity to provide accurate information about human sexuality and drug use in a nonprejudicial manner. The facts regarding the risks for infection during heterosexual and homosexual activity may be presented in a candid, unemotional, nonsensational manner. What is known about the etiology of sexual identity, sex roles, and sexual preferences could be communicated apart from moral judgments about any specific form of sexual activity. An important by-product of such a candid, factual presentation regarding the sexual transmission of the AIDS virus would be correcting the mistaken perception that HIV/AIDS is a gay disease. Similarly, the psychological and social factors that contribute to drug use, promiscuity, and infidelity could be examined.

This two-pronged study of risk behavior could result in

a better understanding of these issues and a decreased tendency to "blame the victim" of AIDS for his or her distress. In short, all the factors that have had a role in the rapid spread of the AIDS virus might be perceived. So understood, partial responsibility for the HIV/AIDS crisis rests upon society, social conditions, and its social institutions, as well as upon individuals who knowingly and needlessly have exposed themselves or others to infection. By seeing that HIV/AIDS is not the fault of any particular group of persons, perhaps people will hesitate to scapegoat a particular group for this evil. And finally, perhaps we can resist the urge to use AIDS to frighten or coerce people to deny their sexual identity or to adopt a particular lifestyle or morality. Decisions about these matters ought to be made on the merits of the relevant arguments, not because of the association of a disease with a particular sexual practice or behavior. Thus, if moral judgments are to be part of educational programs on AIDS, these judgments should be properly based and directed fairly toward relevant persons, groups, institutions, and society, as well as the populations first described with AIDS.

A third subject for inquiry and reflection is the nature of the human condition as vulnerable, finite, and mortal. The world is filled with risks. Each day people die as a result of disease, accident, war, social injustice, and homicide. Other threats may not be lethal but nonetheless are disruptive and painful. Illness, trauma, injury, hunger, and assault impair and inconvenience people every day. Although the possibility of injury or death is known, most people go about their daily affairs in a prudent manner. They are not paralyzed by the prospect of harm that might befall them. Apparently, people consciously or subconsciously calculate the relative risks and goods associated with different activities and decide to act or not to act. Most people obviously conclude that the risk of falling in the shower is outweighed by the good of having a clean body. The good of visiting with a friend outweighs the risks of the drive to the friend's residence.

The good of not developing mumps is greater than the risk associated with vaccination. People live as if the risks of daily living will never touch them. The absence of guarantees that nothing will happen does not stop most people from functioning in a productive and healthy manner.

Some people have attempted to justify their abandonment of people with HIV disease by citing the absence of a guarantee that casual contact with infected persons is totally risk-free. Reputable physicians and scientists cannot say this with absolute certainty. They can, however, assure people that, on the basis of the extensive evidence gathered to date, casual contact does not constitute a risk of infection. The question to be asked in classes on the human condition is whether the good associated with a believer's duty toward sick and suffering people is not greater than the risk to one's welfare that may be attached to fulfilling that duty. In other words, Christians should consider the costs of discipleship and their willingness to incur those costs. People ought to understand that being a Christian may subject them to human opposition or place them in situations of possible danger. Accepting vulnerability, finitude, and mortality as inescapable features of human existence is a first step toward living freely and fully. When people are unwilling or unable to cope with these facts, they tend to be enslaved by fear, incapable of entering relationships or participating in normal human activities. Yet Christian faith affirms that love casts out fear and propels people into relationships. Living lovingly does not mean ignoring risks. Rather, it means placing them in perspective and acting prudently. The needs of others must not be ignored.

Making sense of vulnerability and mortality involves a consideration of God's loving will for humanity and the manner of God's involvement in history.[22] These are important subjects that warrant careful study. They are relevant to the HIV/AIDS epidemic because of the claim that AIDS is God's punishment on gay men and the nation that tolerates them. This claim asserts that there is a connection between the circumstances or fate of a person or society and God's evaluation of that person or society. This is a disputable claim that implicitly sanctions abandoning sick and suffering people or engenders hostility toward them as an extension of God's displeasure, wrath, or judgment. If the association of a disease with a people is an indication of God's displeasure with that people, then Tay-Sachs disease is God's punishment upon Jews, sickle-cell anemia is God's punishment upon African Americans, hemophilia is God's punishment upon men, vaginal cancer is God's punishment upon women, and Legionnaires' disease is God's punishment on members of the American Legion! This sort of reasoning is logically absurd and theologically bankrupt. In addition, if this judgmental reasoning is accurate, several questions must be answered. Why did God wait so long to express anger over male-to-male sexual conduct? Why are lesbians allowed to escape punishment for their sexual misdeeds? Is God so inept as to permit some gay men to escape what they allegedly deserve? If "innocent" people suffer because of God's misdirected wrath, is God morally blameworthy, or could it be that God's aim is bad? These questions may appear humorous or ridiculous, but they represent serious questions about the nature and character of the God implied by these assertions. These images of God as vengeful and arbitrary are contradictory to the incarnational theology of Christianity that portrays God as loving humanity and suffering with humanity. The incarnational God of Christianity invites people to fellowship and reconciliation, not condemnation and estrangement. The incarnational God of Christianity shares the suffering of broken humanity. God does not delight in it, and neither should God's people.[23] If courses, lectures, or discussions about these matters are theologically instructive, they will help people understand and respond to HIV/AIDS.

A fourth topic of study is the healing ministry of Jesus and its continuation by the church. A review of the Gospels and of church history should help people to understand HIV/AIDS as simply another illness, albeit devastating, to which the people of God are obliged to respond creatively, in a compassionate and supportive manner. When seen in this perspective, HIV/AIDS ceases to be an occasion for condemnation and becomes an opportunity to represent and actualize God's love for suffering humanity. HIV/AIDS, therefore, challenges the church to claim its identity, to be faithful to its heritage, and to follow the example of its Lord. HIV/AIDS epidemic provides the people of God with an opportunity to formulate and implement ministries that are responsive to the specific needs of people touched by a new and destructive disease.

The Pulpit. Becoming educated about AIDS, placing it in theological perspective, and discerning the church's obligations to the men, women, and children who are touched by it are activities not limited to the church classroom. Education also is a function of the pulpit ministry.[24] Pastors and preachers can heighten a congregation's awareness of the suffering, needs, and opportunities for ministry that people with HIV/AIDS present by referring to them in intercessory prayers and sermons. Pastors can remind the congregation that they are called to be a servant people serving a servant Lord. Sermons can help people understand what servant ministry means and what obedience to the love command requires. In addition, sermons on the inclusive nature of God's love, God's presence in the midst of human suffering, corporate understanding of human well-being, and God as hope and refuge can influence attitudes and shape responses. Finally, pastors can proclaim that at the center of the gospel there is a divine call for reconciliation between God and humanity and between mutually estranged human beings. Such reconciliation could be exemplified in a congregation's response to HIV/AIDS. Parishioners could be reminded that in the life and death of Jesus a new way of reconciliation was established.[25]

Spiritual and Sacramental Ministries

The second type of sustaining ministry is directed more toward people struggling with HIV/AIDS than toward the church itself, as in the educational ministries just proposed. Spiritual and sacramental ministries are meaningful ways to express God's and the church's concern for people in the present crisis. Intercessory prayers and healing rites communicate a human and divine concern for the physical and emotional well-being of the sick. Rites of baptism, communion, and participation in worship signify that the person with HIV/AIDS is a member of the family of faith. Supportive and compassionate ministries (pastoral care) validate and extend what these practices symbolize: that a person with HIV disease and his or her loved ones are not abandoned by God's people in a time of crisis. Finally, funeral, burial, and memorial services provide hope to the bereaved and signify that the care and concern for the one who is dead extend beyond life. These spiritual and sacramental ministries can comfort people in distress and set an example for society to emulate.

These spiritual and sacramental services tend to occur within a single congregation; they represent the doctrine and liturgy of that denomination and are principally directed toward the congregation's membership or others who identify with the denomination. We have noted, however, that many people with HIV disease are not active in a congregation for a variety of reasons. Further, people with HIV disease who receive ministry from a congregational group or team may not be matched with the denomination of their birth or youth. Regular interfaith services conducted for the whole community touched by HIV/AIDS, people infected by HIV and those who serve them, may provide a respectful context in which people can unite and worship together comfortably. Interfaith services may have special emphases of hope, healing, and remembrance. The need and desire for spiritual nurture and expression can be quite intense among people with HIV disease, even though some may no longer identify with a particular denomination or religious tradition. Regular interfaith services can be one means to draw people together in common worship and spiritual nurture in witness to their solidarity around the HIV/AIDS crisis.

Physical Assistance

The physical needs of people with AIDS or related diagnoses can vary between people and fluctuate for an individual person. The physical and monetary losses that characterize HIV/AIDS often create needs that congregations can meet. Numerous types of assistance can be organized and provided: preparation of meals, food pantry supplies, help in performing activities of daily living (e.g., dressing, bath, toilet), housecleaning, shopping, transportation, housing, financial subsidy, unskilled nursing care, relief for primary caregiver, home hospice care, inpatient hospice, and assistance to visiting family and friends. These ministries, when performed in a sensitive and effective manner, can significantly improve a person's quality of life. They are means by which relationships with people with HIV/AIDS can be initiated and sustained. Thus, these ministries benefit people with HIV disease and enable the people of God to fulfill their calling.

Emotional Support

The physical losses that require supplementing are paralleled by emotional stresses. Feelings of abandonment, loneliness, and loss of self-esteem can be alleviated by expressions of concern and commitment through regular visits and phone calls. Separate support groups can be organized for people infected with HIV, families (including lovers), clinicians, friends, and the worried well. These groups should be led by properly trained, adequately informed, and appropriately certified professionals. Groups that are heterogeneous, open to anyone with a concern or need, also can be a valuable source of emotional support. Finally, the experience of bereavement following an AIDS death tends to be different from common bereavement, because the cause of death may be kept secret or misrepresented. The process of catharsis and healing may be frustrated as a consequence. Bereavement groups restricted to these people may provide a safe haven where their specific and special feelings can be aired and their concerns addressed.

Parish clergy may be called upon to respond to the spiritual concerns and needs of the circle of people touched by HIV/AIDS. One's personal relationship with God or the church, questions of God's role in the HIV/AIDS epidemic (i.e., theodicy), understandings of healing within the Christian tradition, family issues of embarrassment, anger, and secrecy, unresolved grief and bereavement, reconciliation of estranged family and friendship relations, and many others might be brought to the clergy. Clearly, the clergy's effectiveness in these situations will be improved by a basic understanding of the consequences of HIV infection and a compassionate attitude for all people caught in this crisis. The clergy's skills in pastoral care and counseling, as well as understanding of the theological and biblical authority for functioning in these roles,[26] may be put to the test in these situations. Considering how one, as clergy, will respond before being drawn into this circumstance would appear wise, because the increasing incidence of HIV infection suggests that few people will escape its direct touch. The spiritual and emotional care that clergy can provide may significantly affect how the people who seek their support and counsel cope with the losses that HIV generates.

Another area of emotional support that ought not be neglected is the care of the ministry team in a parish. As indicated above, AIDS ministries ought to be properly supervised. The intensity of these ministries can inflict a heavy toll on the people who provide them. An objective supervisor should be able to identify or foresee potential problems and act quickly to avoid them. Further, the emotional or spiritual needs of the team or its individual members may be addressed by a trained supervisor, perhaps a member of the clergy staff. It is important to remember that the caregivers probably will themselves require care because of the emotional assaults they sustain in the process of ministering in the HIV/AIDS crisis. The ability of team members properly to minister over the long term may depend on this type of resource's being available.

Health care personnel are another group of caregivers whose needs for emotional support present opportunities for ministry. As noted in Chapters 2 and 3, many people with HIV disease have long-term and frequent contact with the people who provide their ambulatory and hospitalized health care. Intense bonds may be established among them as each becomes well known to the other over the course of time. Patients may see their physicians and other caregivers as their link to life and defense against death. Their hopes and expectations may never be overtly expressed to caregivers, but their existence and intensity tend to be evident. Moreover, caregivers want nothing more than to fulfill these expectations, so they often work tirelessly to improve and extend life for those who have entrusted themselves to them. Caregivers know that, at present, the desired ends cannot be achieved. There may be victories of sorts, but not the victory that is most wanted. Ultimately, the reversal, loss, and disappointments will come. Grief tends to be their companion. Feelings of failure and inadequacy, however inappropriate, may burden caregivers, impairing their ability to care for the one slipping toward death and the others yet to reach death's grasp. Sensitive, compassionate caregivers, regardless of their training, experience, or professionalism, feel the sting of these losses. Their emotional needs may be great. However, they may be reluctant to make public their feelings. They are expected to be emotionally strong, dispassionate in the performance of their duties, and unaffected by physical loss and death. Even though caregivers may not have these beliefs about themselves, they tend to be reluctant to admit their needs lest such an admission be seen as a weakness. Support groups may be acceptable to individual caregivers or caregivers in certain support roles. Physicians, however, appear reluctant to participate in a support group. Emotional support ministries to health care personnel, accordingly, may need to take several forms in order to be acceptable to the person or population to be served. In addition, patience and perseverance may be required while caregivers adjust to being in the role of care-receivers.

Social and Political Leadership

The church can provide moral leadership to society by formulating and implementing a compassionate response to HIV/AIDS.[27] This prophetic ministry can provide legal assistance to patients whose rights are being denied by employers, landlords, insurers, medical institutions, or governments despite the protections in the Americans with Disabilities Act. The church through its officials can articulate, advance, and defend the claims of people touched by HIV/AIDS for social services and for personal respect.[28] Stigmatization and discrimination wherever found should be denounced. Government, at all levels, should be challenged to foster an attitude of compassion, conduct research, provide therapy, and protect the rights of patients. Political leaders should be subject to a similar encouragement. Indifference, prejudice, discrimination, and hatred should be identified and condemned. Finally, claims that people with AIDS deserve their fate should be discredited, because they are mistaken and because they undermine simple decency and compassion. In order for the prophetic voice of the church to have credibility, it must express justice and compassion in its response to HIV/AIDS. By so doing, the church is faithful to its identity and mission. And moreover, the church sets an example for other segments of society to follow.

These types of ministries and specific proposals are suggestive of what the church and God's people can do to fulfill their calling and to lessen the suffering caused by HIV/AIDS. Individually and collectively, AIDS ministries ought to be redemptive and prophetic, modeling an attitude that performs a teaching and healing function in society. More specifically, AIDS ministries serve a variety of ends consistent with the gospel. They embody the good news that all persons are valued by God and God's people. They are indications of care and concern for sick, suffering, and bereaved people. They are evidence of God's continued commitment to people abandoned or cast out in society. They represent God's will that the burden of oppression be lifted in whatever form it is found.

They are directed toward the relief of suffering and anguish. The church's healing presence in the midst of the HIV/AIDS crisis is a reminder that God is present to those who suffer. God's participation through the agency of the institutional church and of individual Christians ought to summon others to share in the work of countering the loneliness, isolation, stigma, and fear that too often are the only companions of people touched by AIDS. In short, the church's passive and active presence can sustain and heal, even in situations where physical cure is presently not available.

They are faithful to the church's identity and mission. The people of God are a servant people. By definition, they cannot neglect the needs of others. In this sense the church, in order to be true to itself and its Lord, needs people with HIV/AIDS more than people with HIV disease need the church.

They are redemptive in form and function. AIDS ministries by their existence and performance weaken the barriers of prejudice, fear, suspicion, and hatred that separate people. They are testimony to God's inclusive love. They affirm the value of all persons to God.

They promote understanding and mutual respect between estranged groups. The church and people with

AIDS are drawn into relationship because of their need for each other. Because of their respective needs to give and receive help, the church and estranged populations (such as gay men, bisexual men, and IV drug users) have an opportunity to learn about, help, and develop respect for each other.

They enrich the lives of the people who serve and who are served. AIDS ministries seem to verify the claim that one gains life by spending it on others. The investment of life moves in two directions, each person investing in the life of the other. The tragic difference with AIDS is that one person will survive and the other probably will not. Yet each person is enriched as a result of the relationship.

Finally, they heal. Participants in AIDS ministries naturally hope that a cure soon will be found, but the absence of a cure ought not suggest that all healing is beyond reach. The healing that can occur is of indifference, mistrust, anger, hatred, prejudice, ignorance, callousness, and estrangement wherever and in whomever they are found. Such healing is likely when people, regardless of their differences, are willing to affirm each other's inherent value and dignity. This sort of healing is possible when each is willing to risk loving the other.

7

The Global Impact of HIV/AIDS

It is still not possible to determine when and where HIV began to manifest itself in humans around the world, though the available evidence suggests this occurred in the 1970s. HIV spread rapidly in large urban centers where behaviors involving multiple sexual partners and sharing of needles and syringes during drug use were prevalent. The exploding number of HIV/AIDS diagnoses now being reported are due to infections that began and spread unnoticed and extensively in the late 1970s and early 1980s before the retrovirus was isolated and its pathogenesis and transmission understood.[1] Surveillance of HIV infection began in 1982 in the United States when the Centers for Disease Control (CDC) developed a case definition to collect data on the incidence of AIDS. This CDC case definition has been modified three times and may be revised again. Although the World Health Organization (WHO) adopted the CDC case definition in 1986,[2] it developed a provisional clinical case definition for use in developing countries.[3]

The attempt to apply the CDC criteria to developing countries ran into difficulties that continue to thwart international efforts to track and collate data on AIDS surveillance. Many developing countries lack adequate laboratory facilities to analyze blood or body tissues, and the financial resources to develop them on the scale necessitated by this epidemic. Consequently, reported cases of AIDS or estimates of people infected with HIV lag far behind actual incidence, thus understating the full scope of the global tragedy of HIV disease. Whereas it is estimated that case reports in the United States represent at least 80 percent of the actual number of cases, WHO estimates that perhaps only 10–20 percent of all cases have been reported in Africa.[4] Global AIDS statistics, therefore, remain distorted. Paul A. Sato noted that "where stark differences in the level of health infrastructure development exist between countries, it is not surprising that global data are biased by wide inter-country and inter-regional variations in completeness of AIDS case detection and reporting."[5] Thus, it is not surprising that as of 1989, the United States has reported 69 percent of the world's cases and 85 percent of cases reported to WHO from the Americas.

In addition to the problem of standardizing a global case definition for HIV/AIDS, difficulties in coordinating national responses to the epidemic have delayed the development of adequate measures to meet the crisis. Governments in developed and developing countries have been hesitant to acknowledge the fact or extent of the spreading epidemic and hence have resisted both public health and public education programs. This reluctance was finally overcome in the developing world in October 1985, when the first WHO Workshop on AIDS was held in Bangui, Central African Republic, and WHO was acknowledged as the coordinating agency of the global response to HIV/AIDS.

World Health Organization Estimates of HIV/AIDS, 1987–1989.

Four epidemiologic patterns of HIV infection and AIDS have been identified. Pattern I applies to developed countries (North America, Australia, New Zealand, and Western Europe), where 65–90 percent of the AIDS cases

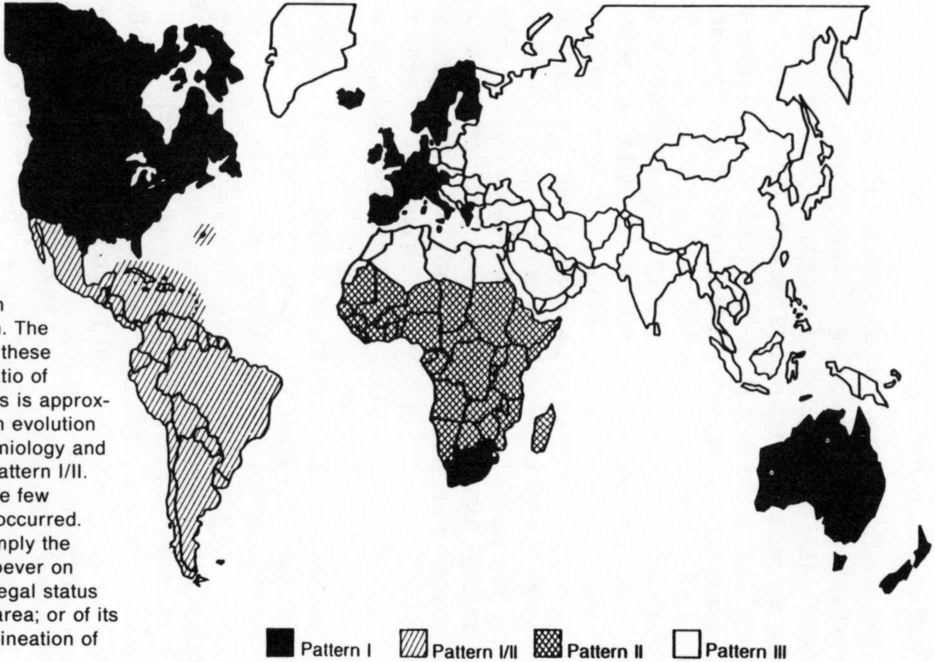

Figure 1.
Four global epidemiologic patterns of HIV infection and AIDS are apparent as of 1989. Pattern I is found in North America, western Europe, Australia, and New Zealand: about 80–90 percent of the cases in these areas are homosexual and bisexual men, or intravenous drug users. Pattern II is found in sub-Saharan Africa and parts of the Caribbean. The primary mode of transmission in these areas is heterosexual, and the ratio of infected males to infected females is approximately equal. Latin America is in evolution from Pattern I to Pattern II epidemiology and is now classified separately as Pattern I/II. Pattern III consists of areas where few cases or infections have to date occurred. Boundaries on this map do not imply the expression of any opinion whatsoever on the part of WHO concerning the legal status of any country, territory, city, or area; or of its authorities; or concerning the delineation of its frontiers or boundaries.
By courtesy of WHO/GPA.

are among men who have sex with men or among people who use intravenous drugs. Pattern II countries include sub-Saharan nations in Africa and nations in the Caribbean where transmission is primarily heterosexual, with the ratios of men and women approximately equal. WHO reports that Central and South American countries are in transition from Pattern I to Pattern II (i.e., Pattern I/II). The remaining areas (Pattern III) are those in which few HIV infections have been reported. AIDS cases have now been reported from all major areas of the world, as indicated in the WHO map reported by James Chin and Jonathan Mann.[6]

With the development of the WHO Global Program on AIDS (WHO/GPA), it became possible, even if only approximately, to assess the current situation and to estimate the probable course of the epidemic through the year 2000. Figure 2 provides a graphic image of data for the respective reporting regions through 1987.[7] The cumulative total of reported AIDS cases from 1980 through mid-1988 was 124,114 (Table 1).[8] By December 1990, the total reached the 300,000 level predicted in 1988 (Table 2).[9]

In 1987, WHO estimated that 5 to 10 million people were infected by HIV-1 or HIV-2, with approximately equal numbers in Pattern I and Pattern II countries and perhaps 100,000 in Pattern III areas. These estimates

Table 1

AIDS Cases Reported to the World Health Organization (WHO) as of October 31, 1988.

Continent	Number of Cases	Countries with One or More Cases	Countries with Zero Cases
Africa	19,141	45	6
Americas	88,233	42	2
Asia	281	22	16
Europe	15,340	28	2
Oceania	1,119	5	9
Total	124,114	142	35

were lowered to a total of 5 to 6 million in 1988 as more data were acquired and knowledge of the disease was increased (Table 2). Because HIV may have a latency period of ten or more years, the vast majority of cumulative cases of AIDS were assumed to be due to infection 5–10 years ago, and the 5 to 6 million cases expected during the next decade would occur even if no new infections occurred. "Thus, over the next decade, at least 3 million additional adult cases worldwide can be expected to develop among the more than 5 million people estimated to have *already* been infected with HIV as of 1988."[10]

It is even more difficult to estimate the number of children with HIV/AIDS than to predict the total number of cases. In 1989, WHO estimated that approximately 70,000–80,000 infants were infected by 1987 and that the total would reach 150,000 by 1990. Two factors add to the difficulty created by a shortage of accurate information. It is estimated, first, that about 30 percent of infants born to HIV-infected mothers are also infected; second, that approximately 85 percent of HIV-infected children worldwide die by age five.[11] Many of these children may not receive adequate medical care.

Jonathan Mann, former director of the WHO/GPA, observes that countries seem to progress through three stages of response to the AIDS crisis: governmental denial of the scope of the crisis, followed by reluctant

Table 2

Estimated Cumulative Total of HIV Infection and AIDS as of Mid-1988.
By Courtesy of WHO/GPA.

	Cumulative HIV Infection	Cumulative AIDS
Pattern I	1.5–1.8 million	Close to 125,000
Pattern I/II	0.8–1.0 million	Over 25,000
Pattern III	About 2.5 million	About 150,000
Pattern III	About 100,000	Less than 1,000
Global	5.0–6.0 million	About 300,000

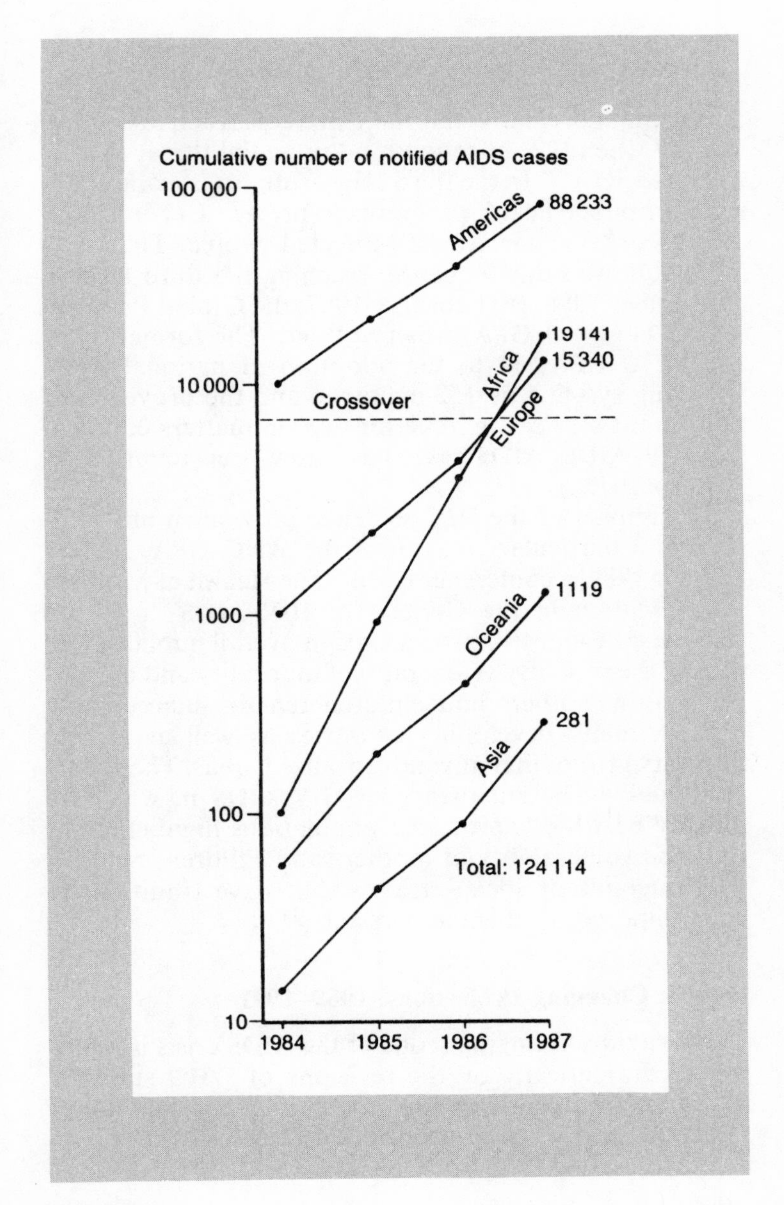

Figure 2.
Cumulative number of notified AIDS cases reported to the World Health Organization (WHO) by year from 1984 to 1987.

acknowledgment that there is an actual public health problem, and, finally, the stage of "constructive engagement," when HIV infection is a "potential threat to [the] entire society."[12] In the third stage, support is made available for public health programs to prevent HIV infection and to provide care to HIV-infected people. The WHO itself followed this sequence, reaching the third level in November 1986. By February 1987, the Global Program on AIDS (WHO/GPA) was instituted. The formation of the WHO/GPA led to the adoption of national AIDS planning systems by 152 countries and the provision of consultant services to governments on matters concerning HIV/AIDS. AIDS cases have now been reported by 176 countries.

The impact of the HIV epidemic on women and children is a particular concern of the WHO/GPA. In November 1989, a conference titled "The Health of Mothers and Children in the Context of HIV/AIDS" reported that, despite many improvements in overall public health during the past fifty years, rates of morbidity and mortality among mothers and children remain unacceptably high in many developing countries as well as among minority groups in many industrialized areas. The report continues: "The emergence of HIV/AIDS in what are already health-compromised populations highlights not only the vulnerability of mothers and children, but also the concomitant social stresses that have traditionally been imposed on them as a result."[13]

WHO's Changing Projections, 1989–1991

The rapidly changing scope of the AIDS crisis is represented dramatically by the revisions of WHO statistics and estimates regarding HIV/AIDS, maternal and infant infection, and sexually transmitted diseases (STDs).

1. November 1989

Statistics presented to the 1989 conference on maternal and child health in the context of AIDS provide a sobering picture of the potential scope of the AIDS crisis. WHO estimated that by 1990, almost 2 million women of childbearing age would be infected by HIV. About 80 percent of these women are in sub-Saharan Africa, where social, economic, and demographic factors limit the capacity of health and social services to meet the growing needs of families living with HIV/AIDS. In countries with HIV/AIDS epidemiological Pattern II, it is projected that "by the end of 1992 about a million children will have been born to HIV-infected women; about a quarter of them will be HIV-infected, and most will die of AIDS. The remaining 750,000 children will have lost, or can be expected to lose, one or both parents as a result of AIDS."[14]

2. July 1990

AIDS projections were again revised in mid-1990. Countries were warned that HIV infection was accelerating dramatically in some parts of the world. As a result, WHO updated its previous estimate of 6 to 8 million people infected with HIV around the world to 8 to 10 million. Michael H. Merson, director of WHO/GPA, stated: "It is now clear that the toll of HIV infection around the globe is worsening rapidly, especially in developing countries. Furthermore, if HIV prevalence over the next couple of years increases markedly in Asia and Latin America, and continues to expand in sub-Saharan Africa, then our projections—which are considered conservative—will need to be revised even further upward."[15]

The report reviewed AIDS estimates by region. In sub-Saharan Africa, projections of HIV infections were doubled to 5 million. Most reported cases previously were located in large urban populations; by 1990, rural areas, which contain the majority of the population on the continent, were being affected. It is estimated that one in forty adults in sub-Saharan Africa is HIV seropositive, compared to an earlier estimate of one in fifty. Recent surveillance data from Asian countries are equally disturbing—rising from nearly nil in 1988 to a 1990 estimate of 500,000, a much more rapid increase than projected even one year earlier.

3. September 1990

The most alarming report came on September 25, 1990, when further revisions included new estimates of pediatric cases. WHO offered the following conclusions:

a. An estimated 400,000 cases of HIV/AIDS in children under the age of five years occurred between 1980 and 1990. Ninety percent of these cases are in sub-Saharan Africa. They raise to 1.2 million the estimated number of AIDS cases among men, women, and children worldwide through 1990.

b. By the year 2000, WHO estimates that 10 million or more infants and children will have been infected with HIV. Thus, WHO projects that the total number of people infected with HIV by 2000 will reach 25 to 30 million. (WHO had previously lifted its projections of adult AIDS cases to 15 to 20 million by 2000.)

c. Of the 10 million or more children expected to be infected, most will develop AIDS and die by the year 2000. By that year, AIDS will be the leading cause of pediatric death.

d. A worldwide cumulative total of over 3 million women of childbearing age have been infected with HIV.[16]

4. December 1990

WHO reported a rising incidence of STDs and growing evidence that many STD infections that cause genital lesions or inflammations can greatly increase the risk of sexual transmission of HIV. An estimated 250 million or

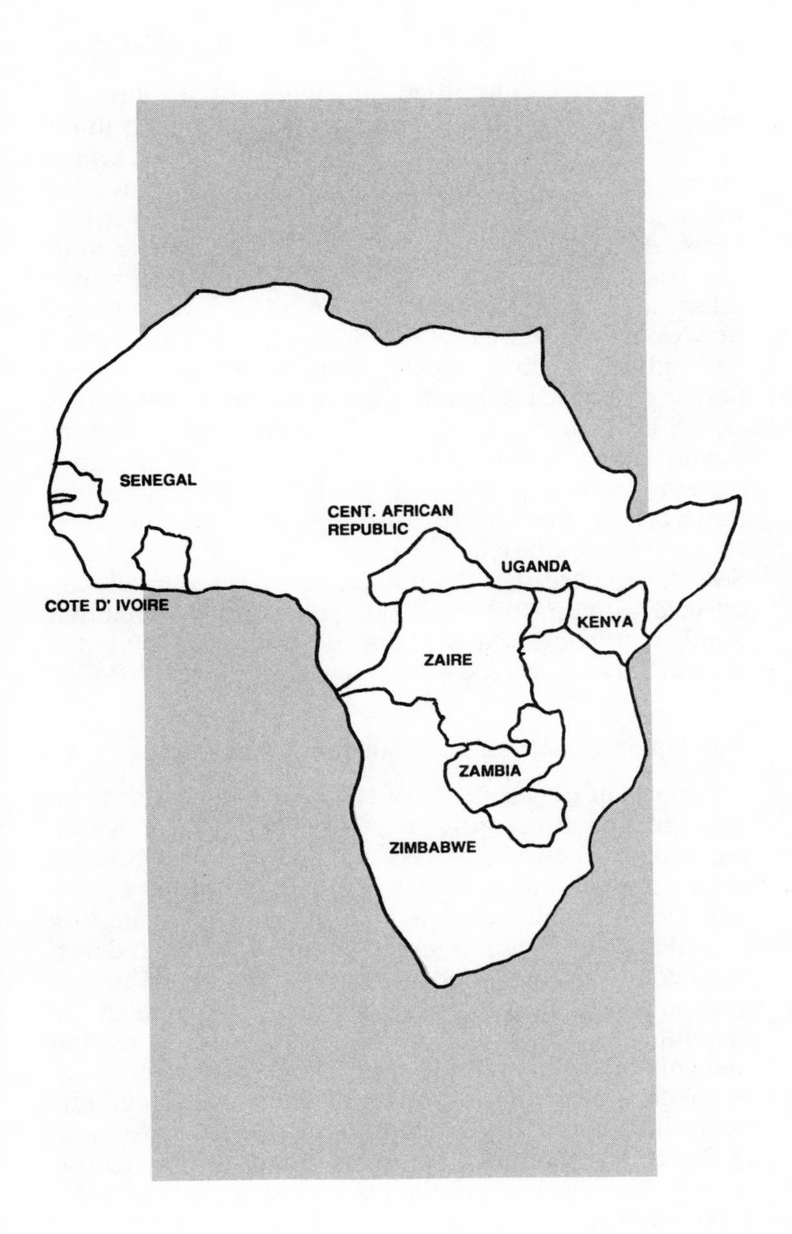
SENEGAL
CENT. AFRICAN REPUBLIC
UGANDA
COTE D' IVOIRE
KENYA
ZAIRE
ZAMBIA
ZIMBABWE

more sexually transmitted infections occur annually around the world, and the number is growing. As in the case of HIV, there are no curative treatments for genital herpes and genital papilloma virus, and resistance has developed in some areas to drugs used to treat symptoms. A WHO statement notes that "one of the most important factors in the epidemic of sexually transmitted infections is sexual behavior, in both the developed and developing world. Fear of AIDS, massive media attention and public information campaigns as well as voluntary peer group education activities are having an impact on sexual behavior . . . [but] sexually transmitted infections are not under control, and in the developing world, they remain at unacceptably high levels."[17] As an indication that STDs are not a health crisis only in developing countries, a recent study by the United States Public Health Service reported that 2.5 million teenagers annually are affected with an STD.[18] A CDC spokesperson stated that numbers of congenital syphilis infections for 1989 in the United States increased 400 percent over those for 1987.[19]

Developing Countries: Sub-Saharan Africa

Reports of the incidence of HIV/AIDS infections from individual countries grow more somber as the impact on particular societies is traced and the accounts become more personal. The attempt to provide complete authoritative data is hampered by the difficulty of collecting surveillance data in developing countries. Even in developed countries, public health services are unable to furnish accurate information regarding the number of HIV-infected people and are forced to resort to mathematical models from which approximate projections may be made. Developing countries are in an even more difficult situation as they attempt to provide the most basic health care with limited resources. Nevertheless, the following accounts capture the sense of tragedy created by HIV disease.

Côte d'Ivoire. Abidjan, a city of 1.95 million people, is the largest city in Ivory Coast, the population of which is approximately 11 million. During 1988 and 1989, 698 adult cadavers in Abidjan were examined for HIV infection. These cadavers represented 38 to 43 percent of all adult deaths in the city during the study period, and 6–7 percent of annual deaths. Forty-one percent of male and 32 percent of female cadavers were infected with HIV. Fifteen percent of adult male and 13 percent of adult female deaths annually are due to AIDS. Thus, in Abidjan, AIDS is the leading cause of death and premature mortality in males, and the second leading cause of death in women, after pregnancy and abortion.[20]

HIV-1/AIDS was recognized in Ivory Coast only in 1985. Until then, most HIV-1/AIDS cases reported from African countries had been located in Central and East Africa. Since 1985, seroprevalence studies report a dramatic increase in HIV-1 infection in Ivory Coast, where HIV-2 is more common than in other African countries. In one of the city's larger hospitals, 19 percent of medical admissions and 33 percent of deaths are attributable to AIDS.[21] The authors pointed out that their data provided only an estimate of the minimum incidence of AIDS in Abidjan and certainly greatly underestimate the impact of HIV infection. It is difficult to ascertain actual incidence, because people with AIDS are spread through many hospitals and clinics, and some die or leave the city without obtaining medical care.

Zaire. The equatorial region of Zaire is a remote rural area 2,000 km from Kinshasa, the capital city. Between 1976 and 1986, HIV prevalence in this region was stable at approximately 0.8 percent. During the same period, the HIV prevalence in the general population of Kinshasa rose from less than 1 percent to approximately 6 percent. The discrepancy in estimates draws attention to one of the most critical factors affecting an understanding of the spread of AIDS in sub-Saharan Africa; namely, its relation to the social disruption of traditional African life resulting from rural depopulation and the concentration of people in large, urban, and increasingly industrialized centers.

Social disruption owing to the flight of rural families to cities is common in almost every developing country. People whose families have lived for generations in rural villages with limited outside contact have moved in large numbers to industrialized cities like Kinshasa, Nairobi, Kampala, and Abidjan. N'Galy and colleagues note that "these individuals have suddenly been thrust into a situation characterized by considerable social disruption with a concomitant loss of the traditional fabric of African society, in which promiscuity was neither possible nor tolerated."[22] The resulting disruption of family life and social mores already had been linked to a vast increase in sexually transmitted diseases before AIDS burst on the scene. Promiscuity, which was a factor in long-neglected epidemics of veneral disease, is now one of the factors driving the HIV/AIDS epidemic.

Similarly, changing patterns of sexual practices are rooted in a migratory lifestyle that is a further disrupting factor for many families. For example, the Trans-African Highway linking Kenya, Uganda, Zaire, and central Zambia was begun in the early 1970s. It is now a heavily traveled truck route. It is also a corridor that has become a major route of HIV infection, and cities along the highway are reporting rising incidence of HIV/AIDS. Increasing HIV seroprevalence among female prostitutes (in Nairobi, Kenya, HIV seroprevalence has increased from 49 percent in 1984 to 90 percent in 1988) coincides with similar increases reported in male truck drivers who travel this route. They may be absent from home for months on end and are bringing home their earnings—and HIV infection.

The impact of HIV/AIDS upon every segment of society is as marked in Central African nations as it is in those of Western Europe and the United States. A report from Kinshasa gives some indication of how HIV/AIDS is changing the social fabric of large cities. Researchers studied the impact of HIV infection on utilization of health care in large corporations. The staff of a large bank was surveyed, revealing that increases for total medications of HIV-infected employees were 31 percent higher than those of a control group. Other factors showed more startling increases: antidiarrheals (280%), antibiotics (160%), vitamins (39%), laboratory and diagnostic tests (34%), outpatient visits (34%), days hospitalized (5200%), and work absences (710%).[23] The report noted that by law, health care benefits are provided to employees and their immediate families by all large corporations in Zaire, benefits that constitute a large proportion of labor costs and may even exceed wages. Many Zairian companies are learning that incidence of HIV infection is high (in this bank, 6.3 percent of the work force) and that AIDS has become the leading cause of death (53 percent of all deaths in 1988 and 1989 among employees in this bank).

Uganda. A Ugandan study determined that by 1986, 35 percent of male long-distance truck drivers tested in Kampala were HIV-infected. Samples of drivers along the major transportation routes who were tested indicate that 21–64 percent visit prostitutes frequently. Over half showed evidence of a variety of sexually transmitted diseases. One of the highest concentrations of infections lies in southern Uganda and areas in surrounding countries through which the Trans-African Highway runs. Whereas 12 percent of adults in rural villages have contracted AIDS, 35 percent in towns along major routes are infected. Tens of thousands of children have been orphaned.[24]

Another factor linked to the breakdown of traditional tribal structures and sexual mores is the large number of women with no urban skills who have moved to cities. Many of these women are unable to find employment. Selling sex to support themselves seems their only alternative. This factor is in turn associated with a more traditional behavior on the part of adult males in many Central African societies. Societies that tolerate an exceptionally large difference in the age of first marriage of men and women (8.4 years in Western Africa) have two related characteristics, surpluses of women of marriageable age and surpluses of young unmarried males. Consequences may include polygyny, nonremarriage of widows, and widespread acceptance that men are not expected to remain chaste. Linked also to tribal patterns of postpartum taboo and multiple wives, the result is often the transmission by males to their spouses of sexually transmitted diseases contracted either pre- or extramaritally.

Prostitution is highly correlated to areas of high HIV seroprevalence in areas of Central Africa. Studies in the United States, Europe, and Central Africa have linked higher incidence of HIV infection with the occurrence of untreated STDs (e.g., genital herpes). Heterosexual transmission of HIV infection in Central Africa may therefore be related directly to untreated STD lesions that enhance the risk of infection. That is, the rapid spread of STDs that are untreated may be a principal factor in higher levels of morbidity and mortality in this region.

Education programs designed to persuade people to change sexual behaviors that are deeply rooted in traditional societies are being given high priority, but, as in Western countries, resistance to change in areas of human sexuality is high. "You can improve their knowledge," said Dr. Warren Naamara, director of Uganda's AIDS control program, "but how many people are behaving differently at night—that is the big question."[25]

Senegal. Traders who travel regularly to Central and East African countries are returning with HIV infection and communicating the disease to their families in rural villages. A study of 258 merchants who travel throughout Central African countries found that 27 percent were HIV-1 or HIV-2 positive; that is, HIV-1 disease is spreading to rural West Africa, where HIV-2 is already endemic, from the more heavily infected Central and East African countries.[26]

Zambia. A rural hospital reports that 8 percent of pregnant women are infected with HIV. Between 30 and 40 percent of their children will be born with AIDS. In an extensive review of the impact of HIV/AIDS in Central Africa, the *New York Times* reported that "so many soldiers are dying that nurses in a military hospital, with the grim humor many Africans adopt to keep going, refer to their work-place as 'the departure lounge.' " The same article notes that in one district AIDS is called "the disease of shame": "One result of the stigma is rampant rumors as Africa's newspapers carry more and more announcements of deaths of political and military leaders, entertainers, businessmen, and others 'due to a short illness.' "[27]

Developing Countries: South America, Central America, and the Caribbean

Compared to Central African countries, most Central and South American countries have relatively high standards of health care, much of it privately funded. Although this may provide some Latin American countries with greater resources than those available to countries in Central Africa, HIV disease poses as catastrophic a threat in Central and South America as it does in other regions. Some examples will serve to illustrate the concern.

Brazil. Brazil has experienced the sharpest increase in AIDS cases among South American countries and is probably a model for the course the HIV/AIDS pandemic will take on the continent. With a population of over 141 million, the incidence in 1988 was reported at 3,000, rising to a total of 11,000 by mid-1990. The AIDS case rate is 22 per million, the highest in South America with the exception of Honduras (25 per million). This rate compares with the case rates for Malawi (Central Africa) of 360 per million, and Uganda of 196 per million.[28] (By contrast, incidence of reported cases of AIDS in U.S.

states per million of population include New Jersey [315], Florida [312], California [249], and the District of Columbia [1,211]).[29]

In contrast to the heterosexual spread of HIV in Africa, Brazil, like the United States, first reported AIDS predominantly among men who have sex with men (approximately 95 percent of total cases), but the rate among females is rising. The high proportion of married men who have sex with men and women is expected to contribute to the spread of HIV/AIDS not only in Brazil but throughout Latin America.[30] A 1990 study indicated that the mean survival in Brazilian AIDS cases is shorter than those reported in many countries, but this may be accounted for by delays in the dates of diagnosis or other medical anomalies.[31] A second study reported that pulmonary tuberculosis (TB) is a strong predictor for HIV seropositivity among hospitalized patients in Rio de Janeiro and is clearly one of the opportunistic diseases among these patients. TB is present in 25 percent of intravenous drug users with AIDS and is now included in a new AIDS surveillance case definition proposed for Brazil.[32]

As of 1989, 359 pediatric cases of AIDS have been reported in Brazil since 1980, 79 percent of which were reported from São Paulo and Rio de Janeiro (2,786 pediatric cases were reported in the United States by December 1990). Approximately 50 percent of the Brazilian cases were vertical transmission from the mothers, with 65 percent of these being born to drug-using parents, about the same rate as in the United States. This increase in incidence of pediatric HIV/AIDS is linked to an increase in HIV infection among intravenous drug users and also reflects a change in male/female ratios of reported AIDS cases from 120:1 in 1984 to 8:1 in 1989.[33]

One of the most dramatic stories comes from São Paulo State. With a population of 33 million, it is a region where development and misery live side by side. "The streets of São Paulo City are full of children [who] start early their sexual life and the use of drugs. AIDS is changing this dramatic social problem in[to] a tragedy,"[34] as HIV infection takes hold among the street children. This threat is borne out in a parallel study in which 55 street youth in Belo Horizonte, Brazil, were interviewed. Their mean age was 14.9 years, and sexual activity was reported by 80 percent of the group, and drug use by 84 percent. The level of risk behavior, researchers emphasized, calls for aggressive educational programs specifically targeted to this population.[35]

Central government expenditures on health care in Central and Latin America vary from $5.00–$35.00 per capita. Thomas Quinn and his colleagues note that "if the same type of health care is to be provided for all surviving AIDS patients, . . . there will be enormous pressure on the health services throughout the region, with cost estimates of up to 90 million dollars per year."[36] When the cost of drugs now available in the United States is included, an additional $35 million will be needed. If the presumed under-reporting of cases is factored in, costs will escalate still further. Thus, "when evaluated on the basis of proportion of median income, the cost of treating cases for HIV-1 related disease may be higher in developing countries than in the United States,"[37] so less expensive, simplified methods for managing HIV/AIDS and its complications are urgently needed to reduce the crushing economic burden of the epidemic.

Bermuda and the Bahamas. Whereas Brazil, with a population of 141 million, reports a case rate of 22 per million, the case rate in Bermuda and the Bahamas is in the range of 600–650 AIDS cases per million in a population of 500,000. There are other large discrepancies between nations in incidence of reported cases of AIDS. Five countries—the United States, Brazil, Canada, Haiti, and Mexico—contribute over 96 percent of all cases reported in the region. Excluding North America, the English-speaking Caribbean countries with only 2 percent of the population and the Latin Caribbean countries with 6 percent of the population have reported 10 percent and

21 percent, respectively, of all AIDS cases in the Caribbean and Latin America. In the Caribbean, 11 percent of AIDS cases were in persons under five years of age. The Bahamas report that 19 percent of AIDS cases were in persons under five years of age, compared to 1.7 percent in the United States.[38] Nevertheless, there is a remarkable similarity in the pattern of rates of increase throughout the Americas. "Once HIV-1 was introduced within a population, indigenous transmission soon became established, thus propelling the epidemic at a rate similar to that observed in the U.S. and other countries."[39]

Europe, Asia, and Oceania

Europe. Of nearly 300,000 cases of AIDS worldwide reported by WHO in December 1990, European countries reported 40,000 cases, with France (9,718), Italy (6,701), Spain (6,210), Germany (5,266), and the United Kingdom (3,798) accounting for almost 80 percent of the total. Exponential increases early in the course of the epidemic were similar to those reported from other countries. For example, France reported 3,073 cases of AIDS in December 1987. Two years later, the total had more than trebled.[40]

Whereas in Central Africa the epidemiological pattern of HIV infection is strongly bidirectional-heterosexual transmission (that is, the male to female ratio approaches 1), the overwhelming majority of AIDS cases in Europe reflect the pattern in the United States, where the majority of AIDS cases are men who had sex with men or are intravenous drug users. The number of HIV-infected women is still low but is rising steadily because, more and more, HIV is being spread by heterosexual intercourse, especially in urban areas with high rates of other sexually transmitted diseases and drug injecting.

Southeast Asia and the Western Pacific. Absence of reports and under-reporting mean that less is known about the spread of HIV/AIDS in this vast area than in other areas of the world. Only 2,448 cases were reported to the WHO by mid-1990, and of these 2,021 were from Australia and New Zealand, where HIV/AIDS epidemiology and patterns of transmission are almost identical with those of the United States and Europe.

The Impact of HIV/AIDS on Maternal and Infant Welfare and Family Life

Rates of HIV infection in pregnant women are often a reliable indicator of adult infections and of incidence of pediatric AIDS, because approximately one-third of infants born to infected mothers will be HIV+ after one year. Rates of infection in women of childbearing age have reached 25 percent in some Central African cities. WHO estimates that over 400,000 babies in Africa have been HIV-infected, and most have already died. By the end of 1992, another 600,000 will be born with the virus. Health officials in Zimbabwe report that the death rate in children had reached the lowest levels in the country's history prior to the AIDS epidemic. AIDS is now the leading cause of infant deaths in urban hospitals, and the mortality rate is rising.

Marked progress had been made in some developing countries to reduce infant mortality, although rates are still catastrophically higher than in developed countries. Efforts to reduce infant deaths had been successful against such common threats as diarrhea by educating mothers in preventive measures and against other childhood diseases through vaccination programs. Health, nutrition, and hygiene education programs have been extended to wide areas of rural Central Africa, but the discrepancy between services in urban and rural areas persists. Depending on the country, from 40 percent of populations in some Latin American countries to more than 80 percent in sub-Saharan countries live in medically underserved rural areas.[41] It is likely that many mothers and children with AIDS live short lives, the cause of death undiagnosed and unreported, and receive little or no medical care other than the ministrations of traditional village healers.

During this century, a reduced rate of infant mortality has been one of the most important indicators of a country's progress in health matters. This, in turn, represents a country's movement toward a level of social and economic progress taken for granted in developed countries. For the world as a whole, infant mortality rates declined by 51 percent between the 1950s and the 1980s.[42] This trend was predicted to continue, with marked progress in developing countries. Yet in the five years to 1985, 98 percent of pediatric deaths were in developing countries. Africa still leads the tragic list, with 40 percent of all deaths still occurring among infants and young children. Pediatric AIDS is expected to worsen this situation.

AIDS is drawing new and unwanted attention to another consequence of the pandemic, namely, the inequities and inadequacies in national health care systems. Jonathan Mann suggests that the world community must reexamine and reassess the impact on health care of such problems as the prostitution of men, women, and children, intravenous drug use, availability of blood for transfusion, procedures regarding use of hypodermic syringes and other invasive practices, and the way communities educate their members about health. He notes: "AIDS remorselessly highlights our most complex problems, challenges our assumptions, and shakes our complacency."[43]

The impact on extended families is equally devastating. Survivors often must assume the responsibility of caring for children whose siblings and parents have died. Healthy older children and uninfected infants born into these families will join the growing numbers of AIDS orphans. In ten countries in Central and Eastern Africa, 3 to 6 million children, 6–11 percent of all children under age fifteen, will lose one and usually both parents to AIDS in the 1990s, according to Elizabeth A. Preble,

AIDS adviser to UNICEF. In these countries, surviving family members have usually cared for orphans, but many are likely to be overwhelmed by the sheer weight of numbers resulting from HIV/AIDS.[44] It is estimated that because AIDS predominantly affects young adults, dependency ratios (the balance between economically productive adults and the dependent young and old) will rise in hard-hit areas. "AIDS may cause mortality rates among the economically and socially most productive age groups to double, triple, or rise even higher"; that is, "each surviving adult would have to support a larger number of children and elderly dependents, making economic growth less likely."[45] Most families are poor and have few resources to meet this crisis. The deaths of so many parents are creating "unusual new households with dim prospects: teen-agers heading families of siblings, elderly grandparents caring for a dozen grandchildren."[46]

The impact of HIV/AIDS on children and adolescents in developing countries is twofold. First, infected infants are stricken with a disease that still is presented as ultimately fatal, and for most, the period from infection to death is much shorter than for adults. The parent or parents of some children dying from AIDS have predeceased them or will do so. If infected children outlive their parents, they must be cared for by surviving grandparents and older siblings whose resources to provide basic services are inadequate at best.

Second, uninfected children of parents infected with HIV lose also. They are at risk of losing one or both parents. Reduced economic resources owing to the deaths of working parents means that even the most basic services (food, shelter, health care) may be inaccessible. They may be denied opportunities that otherwise may have been open to them, for example, education, employment, and general physical and psychosocial health. Yet it is these children, aged from five to fifteen years, in countries with HIV infection rates of 30–40 percent, who are the seed of future populations—the future parents, educators, politicians, administrators, workers, and caregivers, as well as unskilled workers and transport drivers.

Effect of HIV/AIDS on Population Growth

The question arises whether HIV/AIDS is capable of reversing population growth rates in some African countries. This question was analyzed by R. M. Anderson and colleagues in 1988.[47] They studied consequences of the deaths of children and adults of childbearing age for their effect on the rate of population increase in developing countries in which, prior to the AIDS crisis, growth had been explosive despite high levels of maternal and infant mortality.

The researchers concluded tentatively that AIDS is capable of reducing population growth rates significantly, perhaps to negative values; that trends might not become evident for many decades; and that changes, if they occur, will be dependent on the major demographic and epidemiological parameters prevailing in particular societies. Thus, for example, specific conclusions may apply to one country more than another, and to urban more than rural areas.

Effect of HIV/AIDS on Political, Industrial, and Economic Structures

The fact that HIV may be transmitted horizontally by sexual contact or vertically from mother to fetus, the high mortality rate of HIV/AIDS, and the extended period over which infected individuals are asymptomatic but infectious are causes for concern that the epidemic will be more disruptive to social organization and economic development and stability than first thought. Anderson and colleagues note that all the indicators suggest that the very high predicted mortality owing to a disease that requires repeated hospitalization, perhaps over periods of a few years, and that is thought to enhance morbidity because of other infections such as tuberculosis will be devastating to already overloaded health care systems in poor countries.[48]

The impact of HIV/AIDS on political, economic, and social development in developing countries may be more catastrophic than that of other diseases because it strikes men and women in the 20–40-year age-group who are in their most productive years. The consequences are not difficult to grasp. In developing countries:

- Sparse government resources must be redirected to combat this epidemic that threatens the stability of political life in countries with only short histories of self-government;
- Economic and industrial structures are threatened by loss of skilled and unskilled employees from the work force and disruption of production of food, raw materials, and finished products;
- The loss of more highly educated men and women from government, banking, law, education, and other essential services will further delay progress toward political and economic stability, and may impair critically the whole fabric of some societies;
- The creation of a potentially vast population of orphans and the absence of a generation to care for elderly people will impose additional and unprecedented stresses on communities in countries least able to bear this burden.

It is not possible to estimate the ultimate costs that these political, economic, and social consequences of HIV/AIDS will have in developing countries, but economists predict that some key industries will be jeopardized. With the deaths of truck drivers in Africa, for example, transportation of raw materials and food is threatened. The First International Conference on the Global Impact of AIDS, held in London in 1988, was informed by a Zambian official that the country's copper mines, which produce 20 percent of Zambia's gross national product, may suffer catastrophic losses owing to AIDS deaths in the labor force, because many workers are in the 20–44-year age-group. A study to determine the economic cost of HIV/AIDS in Mexico, based on years of employment lost and disability time prior to death, indicates that the total cost per patient is forty times the per capita gross national product for the same year.[49]

In developing countries, the presence of an AIDS patient exerts an overwhelming impact on a family: if the patient is an adult, sources of income are threatened, real income is lost as the severity of the disease progresses, and health care expenditures may be beyond the family's shrinking resources. These HIV-related costs compete with costs of basic needs, for example, food and shelter. In some developing countries, funeral costs expected of the family may mortgage the family's future security, creating a particularly heavy burden in families facing multiple AIDS deaths. AIDS is thus a particularly dangerous threat to family life, the existence of communities, and, perhaps, of nations. Halfdan Mahler, director-general of WHO, put the issues succinctly to the 1988 London summit of ministers of health: "With AIDS, the world's quota of misery, already so full, is even fuller."[50]

In developed countries, families living with HIV/AIDS and community-based organizations that provide support to them learned from the beginning of the crisis that HIV/AIDS is accompanied by grief, the intensity of which surpasses that of previous experiences at individual, community, and national levels.[51] Dismayed leaders are asking what the loss of large numbers of people in their prime years will do to society—economically, politically, and spiritually. "We need to start thinking about how to deal with social grief, communal grief. How do you counsel whole communities?" asked the Rev. Chad Gandiya, chairman of a small AIDS counseling group in Zimbabwe.[52]

The AIDS pandemic is affecting individuals, families, towns and villages, cities, the futures of businesses and industries, government at all levels, and global relationships among nations. Jonathan Mann, addressing the

London summit of ministers of health, presented the AIDS pandemic as a global problem requiring a global response: "AIDS has become a great and powerful symbol for a world threatened by its divisions, East and West, North and South. In a deep and remarkable way, the child with AIDS is the world's child; the man or woman dying with AIDS has become the world's image of our own mortality; AIDS is also uncertainty and the unknown. Yet we face responsibility for this day and these lives. Against AIDS we have set our common course—the global AIDS strategy."[53]

Mary Catherine Bateson and Richard Goldsby go a step further. If the nations, acting together in the face of the global AIDS crisis, can use this opportunity "to expand and apply knowledge cooperatively and humanely, we may also learn to control the dangers of the arms race and of world hunger and environmental degradation, for the imagination of AIDS is the imagination of human unity, intimately held in the interdependent web of life."[54] Visionaries have called on the world community to respond to global challenges with global strategies. Wendell Willkie's *One World* sounded this note, calling for recognition that the Second World War compelled us to act as citizens bound together in a single world society.[55] President Kennedy projected the same image in his inaugural address when he greeted his "fellow citizens of the world."[56]

This image is partially realized at best. The struggles of nations linked through the European Economic Community to forge stronger ties is hampered by reluctance to surrender national identity in the interests of European unity. The fragility of relations between nations, and particularly the distrust that often impairs relations between developed and developing countries, indicates how difficult is the task of achieving a global commitment to common actions in the face of international or global threats. Although the WHO response to the HIV/AIDS pandemic demonstrates dramatically what can be achieved through joint action, humankind still awaits a like commitment of the financial and material resources from developed to developing areas of the world that will be necessary to remedy the havoc caused by HIV disease.

Development of Education and Prevention Programs

The prolonged period over which social and demographic changes owing to the HIV/AIDS epidemic are likely to occur may provide time for educational strategies and behavior changes to develop, and for the development of more effective drugs and, possibly, a vaccine. However, vaccines, however inexpensive, do not always benefit developing countries, where the costs of vaccination programs may be prohibitive. For the foreseeable future, the main hope for checking the spread of HIV lies in the development and aggressive application of education programs aimed at changing behavior. The present course of the HIV/AIDS epidemic emphasizes the urgency of developing and implementing such programs.

The response to HIV/AIDS proceeds on two fronts; namely, the search by biomedical scientists for effective chemotherapies and for a vaccine and the efforts of social scientists to identify effective means to promote behavioral patterns that will stabilize and reduce the spread of the infection. As we enter the second decade of the pandemic, prevention remains the best and primary weapon against HIV/AIDS. In its survey of education programs, the Panos Institute found that hundreds, perhaps thousands of AIDS awareness programs are in operation around the world.[57] Researchers are learning from these programs that information may increase knowledge but not necessarily change behavior; that fears about AIDS inhibit the readiness of individuals and communities to appropriate new information in their own behaviors; and that the source of AIDS information must be trustworthy.

AIDS raises profoundly complex and difficult cultural, ethical, political, and social issues, compounded to a considerable extent by the reality that the chief modes of infection involve very sensitive forms of personal behavior. Consequently, effective responses by governments at all levels and the communities to which they are responsible must address uncomfortable choices.

Religious traditions may exercise a powerful influence upon such efforts. But because the primary global vector for the transmission of HIV/AIDS is sexual contact, and consequently the use of condoms is widely proposed as a vital step in preventing the spread of AIDS, educational efforts focused on these issues meet with considerable ambivalence from many religious institutions. The issue remains one that divides the religious community; yet it is one that bears directly on the global impact of AIDS. The second area in which ambivalence is most strongly felt is that of wholehearted commitment to human sexuality education. AIDS is forcing entire societies and their constituent parts to educate all age-groups concerning the nature and threat of HIV and the steps necessary to limit its transmission. Communities are faced with the task of providing adequate curricula in secular schools. Public health agencies are leading the way in developing advertising materials used in the print and audiovisual media. Some national religious bodies have prepared curricula materials and teacher guides for use in congregational education programs, yet many clergy are slow to provide leadership in the provision of human sexuality courses, and many congregations are hesitant to implement them.

Denominations and their congregational units have an important, perhaps decisive, part to play in human sexuality education that constitutes a responsibility that cannot be shirked. In the words of the members of the Administrative Board of the U.S. Catholic Conference: "As a society, we must develop educational and other programs to prevent the spread of [AIDS] Such programs should include an authentic understanding of human intimacy and sexuality as well as an understanding of the pluralism of values and attitudes in our society."[58]

In contrast to the ambivalence of the religious communities, the widespread distribution of condoms in some developing countries has been adopted as government policy. In Zaire, the country's national AIDS prevention program has endorsed the distribution of condoms through a method termed "social marketing." The objective is to promote the use of condoms and make them widely available at subsidized prices to low-income workers in order to reduce the spread of AIDS. The program applies the technologies of mass consumer marketing and uses the existing private sector marketing and distribution channels.[59] For example, in Zaire, total sales of condoms rose from 933,000 in 1988 to 4,140,000 in 1989; in 1990, condoms are being distributed at a rate of 9 million per year. No one knows precisely what effect the program is having on Zaire's AIDS epidemic: "In a country of 30 million, 9 million condoms a year can only do so much—but the sales figures are one of the few clear signs of progress against AIDS in Africa."[60] "There's been a revolution in perspective since 1985," according to Jonathan Mann. "African countries deserve credit for moving quickly, although none of them has had the external support and the internal commitment to do what would really be needed to stop AIDS. It would take a society willing to take on the challenge as if it were war."[61]

The Church's Role: "Joint Action for Mission"?

The religious communities linked through the World Council of Churches (WCC) developed extensive mutual support programs in the 1950s and 1960s under the rubric of such phrases as "Joint Action for Mission," demonstrating their capacity to share resources between Western societies and developing nations. More recently, leadership training and responses to natural disasters have brought together agencies of the WCC and Caritas International, a relief agency of the Roman Catholic Church. A global response will certainly depend upon such cooperative efforts if it is to be adequate in the face of HIV/AIDS.

National religious bodies and their regional and congregational expressions are feeling the impact of HIV disease. Judicatories and many individual congregations have acted to close the gaps left by the initial reluctance to confront HIV/AIDS. But many congregations have yet to demonstrate through active programs the compassion that surely is the church's only viable response to the AIDS crisis and to people living with HIV/AIDS. Some remain antagonistic to any involvement at all; inaction suggests an apathy that, in the face of this epidemic, may be fatal. One of the questions remaining is how much can—or should—be done on an interfaith basis, both within nations and at a global level. It is difficult to gauge the extent of interfaith discussion and cooperation. Certainly, little information from the world level has reached the local scene. If there is a sense of ferment, its depth and breadth is not immediately apparent to the general public. Yet a case can be made for a response to the HIV pandemic at a level comparable to the joint WCC-CORE UNUM ventures that have addressed other global crises on behalf of the Roman Catholic Church and the three hundred members of the WCC. We await a call to the churches to act together to provide prophetic and servant leadership.

Mutual Responsibility and Interdependence in the Body of Christ

The Anglican Congress that convened in 1963 selected the theme "Mutual Responsibility and Interdependence in the Body of Christ" to represent "the new Anglican version of the contemporary Christian's certificate of citizenship" in the world community.[62] It is an appropriate note to sound in the midst of the AIDS pandemic. Since 1986, at the urging of WHO, over 176 countries have pooled their efforts to meet the AIDS crisis, sharing scientific and epidemiological research, and information on AIDS therapies, public health issues, and preventive education. It is, indeed, inconceivable that AIDS could be confronted other than as a global threat requiring a global response. The WHO Global Program on AIDS provides a model to global and national religious bodies, which, with existing WCC-Caritas International programs, may serve as a basis for structuring an interfaith response to HIV/AIDS.

At this point in world history, with national and international efforts bent on safeguarding access to energy supplies, with defense budgets at their highest levels, and industrialized national economies threatened both by inflation and recession, the Christian community cannot evade its responsibility to fulfill the servant and prophetic roles to which it is called by God.

8

Conclusion

The underlying theme of this book is simple. People living with HIV/AIDS, their family members, and friends have a claim on church and synagogue simply by virtue of their plight. Perhaps there was a touch of irony in Jesus' voice as he challenged religious leaders and even his close friends regarding their public behavior. To his friends and the curious crowd he presented the case for a quality of love that supersedes mere keeping of technical rules. The forefathers were told to love their neighbors, but there is a higher order of relationship. We are to love our enemies and pray for our persecutors. *Only* by living in accordance with this "new" commandment can we be children of God. Jesus chided his listeners: If we love only those who love us, surely we would not look for any reward (for doing what is customary and expected). *Surely the tax gatherers do as much!* And if you greet only your brothers, what is extraordinary about that? Again Jesus observes, *even the heathen do as much!* The standard for relationship Jesus sets for his disciples is the example of God: "There must be no limit to your goodness, as your heavenly Father's goodness knows no bounds" (Matt. 5:48).

We may twist uncomfortably at such words. We may shrug them off as hyperbole, ideals surely not meant to be taken seriously. But Jesus does not leave us much room to wriggle. The message is hammered home at every opportunity, in stark language and with a piercing look. To the naïve, he retorts that the Son of Man has nowhere to lay his head. The person who decides to follow him had better count the cost, because the going may get rough (Matt. 5:20; Luke 14:25–35). Indeed, Luke (14:26, 33) records Jesus' warning to his followers: "If anyone comes to me and does not hate his father and mother, wife and children, brothers and sisters, even his own life, he cannot be a disciple of mine. . . . None of you can be a disciple of mine without parting with all his possessions." Then comes the thundering warning: "Salt is a good thing; but if salt itself becomes tasteless, . . . it is useless either on the land or on the dung-heap: it can only be thrown away. If you have ears to hear, then hear" (vs. 34–35). To the hesitant, he replied, "Follow me, and leave the dead to bury their dead" (Matt. 8:22) and "No one who sets his hand to the plough and then keeps looking back is fit for the kingdom of God" (Luke 9:62).

This unswerving commitment is required by the importance of the task to which Jesus' disciples are called: "You must go and announce the kingdom of God" (Luke 9:60). The apostles understood the intention of the call to announce the kingdom that would be manifested as they preached the good news and healed the sick and disabled. They knew the risk, for a follower must always be ready to take up his or her cross (e.g., Matt. 16:24) and walk in Christ's footsteps (Matt. 10:38; Luke 14:27).

The scriptures declare unambiguously that God looks with anger upon indifference to suffering, abuse of the weak, and abuse of privilege at the expense of the poor. God's feelings about these matters were expressed by the prophets. Isaiah, speaking to the nation, declared:

> Shame on you! you who make unjust laws
> and publish burdensome decrees,
> depriving the poor of justice,
> robbing the weakest of my people of their rights,

despoiling the widow and plundering the orphan.
What will you do when called to account,
when ruin from afar confronts you?
To whom will you flee for help
and where will you leave your children,
so that they do not cower before the gaoler
or fall by the executioner's hand?
For all this his anger has not turned back,
and his hand is stretched out still.

Isaiah 10:1–4

Jeremiah echoed Isaiah's words:

But your wrongdoing has upset nature's order,
and your sins have kept from you her kindly gifts.
For among my people there are wicked men,
who lay snares like a fowler's net
and set deadly traps to catch men.
Their houses are full of fraud,
as a cage is full of birds.
They grow rich and grand,
bloated and rancorous;
their thoughts are all of evil,
and they refuse to do justice,
the claims of the orphan they do not put right
nor do they grant justice to the poor.
Shall I not punish them for this?
says the LORD;
shall I not take vengeance
on such a people?

Jeremiah 5:25–29

The prophets' message (see also Hos. 4:2–3; Amos 2:6–7; 4:1–3; Micah 6:9–15) is echoed by Jesus. Because the care and nurture of the poor was mandated by Torah, Jesus' general warning clearly applies: If one sets aside "even the least of the Law's demands, and teaches others to do the same, he [or she] will have the lowest place in the kingdom of Heaven" (Matt. 5:19). But Jesus was even more specific, as seen in Matthew's record of Jesus cleansing the Temple (21:12–13). It was not merely the commercial enterprise that was under judgment; the money-changers and the dealers in pigeons customarily used their privileges to enrich themselves at the expense of the poor who came to worship. In his confrontation with the doctors of the Law and the Pharisees (Matt. 23:1–36), Jesus accuses the rulers of overlooking the "weightier" demands of the Law—justice, mercy, and good faith (v. 23). Especially in the parable of the last judgment (Matt. 25:31–46), he rebukes those who failed to exercise loving care toward the poor. The message, once again, is stark and unrelenting. We are expected to do for others what God has done for us. And, just as clearly, we will not be called into God's presence unless we show compassion to the excluded and welcome them into the community of God's people.

The Biblical Metaphors

Hospitality. Jesus did not merely greet sinners. He included them with other social groups to whom the gospel applied equally, invited them into the kingdom, and encouraged his followers to do likewise. He engaged in intimate actions that dramatized his personal concern for them. He searched for them (Luke 14:23) and welcomed both table fellowship and physical touch. The scriptural image of hospitality played an important part in Jesus' teaching. In accepting those who were "different," he declared clean what others regarded as defiled. Hospitality takes seriously the differences, the "otherness" that separates people from one another. But the metaphor invites us to supersede those differences in order to achieve a higher end: recognition and acceptance of our common humanity as children of God.

Thomas W. Ogletree draws attention to the term "hospitality" in its metaphorical sense as one that does not simply refer to literal instances of interactions with people whose societies and cultures differ from one's own. He identifies a sense of "otherness" that includes "openness to the unfamiliar and unexpected in our most intimate relationships, regard for the characteristic differences in the experiences of males and females, recognition of the role social location plays in molding perceptions and value orientations, [and] efforts to transcend barriers generated by racial oppression."[1] He reminds us that "regard for strangers in their vulnerability and delight in their novel offerings presuppose that we perceive them as equals, as persons who share our common humanity in its myriad variations,"[2] while recognizing that there is also an inequality in our relationship. Hospitality includes a moral dimension: the moral imperative for the host is to share one's own world and blessings with the stranger and thus to affirm the common humanity of host and stranger. The moral imperative for the oppressed is not to show hospitality to strangers: they are already "daily subjected to an alien world against their wills, forced to live in a society which denies them their full humanity. Their challenge is to secure social space within which an alternative world of meaning can be established and nurtured, generating resistance to oppression. It is to expose the deceit and the distortions of the dominant culture."[3]

Stanley Hauerwas also elaborates on the image of hospitality as metaphor, using the novel *Watership Down* as a starting point. The community that the rabbit Hazel and his companions build is one that always remains open to the stranger, even to welcoming a former enemy from a warren that had attempted to destroy the little band of pilgrims. Hauerwas suggests that Hazel institutes a unique community, one in which the stranger, even an alien, is welcome. For "it is one thing to accept an enemy who is like yourself, but it is quite another to help those with whom you share no kinship at all."[4]

When God's people act out their vision, hospitality becomes a "way of being." Parker Palmer, addressing the same theme as that of Ogletree and Hauerwas, notes that "the God who cares for our private lives is concerned with our public lives as well"; and this God "calls us into relationship not only with family and friends, but with strangers scattered across the face of the earth, a God who says again and again, 'We are all in this together.' "[5] Palmer presses his point that participation in the community of God's people compels us to live out what the church preaches, namely, a vision of human unity that must be lived out in the public realm. "Surely that vision applies to more than family and friends. Surely it is a vision which claims more than the commonality of those who think and act and look alike." That vision must include our reaching out to people from whom we differ, to whom we are strangers. "If so, then the church *must* incarnate its vision in public, for there and only there is the stranger to be found."[6] Palmer reminds us that we use the term "stranger" for people outside our circle of family and friends; but in Jesus' ministry, the stranger has a more specific identity: "He or she is one of those who suffer most, who is among the lowliest, . . . who is pressed to the bottom layer of our world"[7] (compare Matt. 25:40).

Jesus' inclusion of outcasts, those who are "different," is embedded in references to the poor generally. In the Beatitudes, Jesus used the words "the poor" and "those who mourn" in their original sense. They are those who expect nothing from society and thus expect everything from God. The poor do not fit into the structure of the world and therefore are rejected by it. The Beatitudes alert God's people that the weak and powerless are unable to obtain recognition from society; therefore, the people of God must act for them. The situation of people who are at the limits of human existence is not to be glorified in itself. Misery and poverty mean distress and torture, just as do blindness, lameness, leprosy—and the prospect of death from AIDS.

The message of the Jewish and Christian scriptures is that God comes near to give counsel and to reprove, but also to call people to a loving relationship. The Jewish Bible offers many images of God's initiative: to Abraham (Gen. 18:1–15); to Jacob (Gen. 28:13); to Moses (Ex. 3:2); to Samuel (1 Sam. 3:4–14); to Elijah (1 Kings 19:9–18); to Isaiah (Isa. 6:1–13); to Ezekiel (Ezek.

2:1—3:11). God not only reveals the divine presence to the commissioned representatives—kings and prophets—but, through them, continually both reassures and reprimands the entire nation. The New Testament images continue this emphasis, as the writer of the Letter to the Hebrews testifies (1:1–3). God has taken the initiative to show the divine nature and purpose to humanity and to call humanity into fellowship with God, a theme reflected, for example, in the kingdom parables relating to invitations to the king's feast (e.g., Matt. 22:1–14). The implications are clear for God's people in the midst of the HIV/AIDS crisis: There is an urgency to the task of finding the outcasts and embodying God's invitation to them. But with that task comes a warning: The despised (to Jesus' hearers, "tax-gatherers and prostitutes") are entering the kingdom of God ahead of those who expected to occupy the places of honor (Matt. 21:31). God's people are sent as servants to summon and offer hospitality to people excluded by society, inviting them to participate in the joy of God's kingdom. For in this royal priesthood, this dedicated nation, all are welcome.

The people of God are called, therefore, to be a community that welcomes "the poor" and treats them as full members of the community. When love for God is manifested through love for people, as well as for the world, which also is an object of God's love, the church becomes a sign to the world, signifying that community which is God's gift to all people. Each member of the community is to be a manifestation of that community into which other people may choose to enter. Members of God's community are called to express love to the neighbor, to welcome the stranger, to speak comfort to the poor, and all in the context of announcing the kingdom of God and manifesting its presence and activity.

Forming and sustaining God's community is an adventure that requires courage and hope. As a community of faith, the church is summoned to live by values other than those that predominate in the world. Society *beyond* the church may choose to be blind and deaf to the needs of people whom it either has, or wishes it could, cast aside—though there are many heartwarming instances of citizens who manifest concern and compassion for the outcast, including people with HIV/AIDS. But the church does not have an option to be uninvolved. It is a community that must be characterized by a compassion that seeks out the outcast as the objects of its love.

This Christian courage includes, but is not limited to, the readiness to take the next step, to become involved in ministry to people with HIV/AIDS. Health and physical risks are minimal. Courage is required to face with the patient or family the imminence of death, the wasting effects of infection, the questions about the meaning of life, and the meaning of this disease in particular. Courage also is required to sit with people whose wasted bodies and inability to manage the most intimate functions of daily life have robbed them of those aspects of life on which we rely to maintain our sense of dignity. At the deepest level, those who care for dying people must have resolved for themselves questions that arise from the realization of life's finitude. Only if we face these questions with courage can we offer care with openness and hope.

Hope, the other requirement for being part of God's adventure, assumes a special meaning when a person faces end-stage care. In the case of people with AIDS, hope can be even more elusive. Often even those resources available to other people—the support of family members and a sense of personal privacy and dignity—are absent or greatly reduced. Hope for the people with AIDS does not at present include the hope of being cured. The prayers of well-intentioned people for physical healing may seem a mockery. In the face of death, hope takes on other meanings: hope that what is left of life can be lived with dignity; hope that one will not die alone; hope that one's suffering will in some small way contribute to the resolution of the crisis.

We have noted that a crucial identifying feature of the community of God's people is that it remains open to the stranger. To remain open to the stranger with HIV/AIDS, to love this stranger, requires a special measure of courage and hope that, left to our own resources, we achieve only partially. In the face of societal prejudice and hysteria, the willingness to reach out and touch the life of a man, woman, or child with HIV/AIDS is possible only to grace-filled people empowered by a Spirit who promises always to counsel and strengthen us. For such a grace-filled people there can be no disparity between words and deeds. If the community is to be a community of integrity, the "doing" of the community must be an expression of its "being"; and that being, both for the community and for its individual members, is established by God's self-disclosure. Therein lies the rub. Jesus spoke in terms of finding life only when we are prepared to lose it in ministry to others. At least we are warned that this is a "hard saying" and that we should not attempt to follow Jesus unless we have counted the cost. Discipleship that issues in loving service to others then becomes a matter not only of how responsive we are to the servant-leader who strides ahead toward Jerusalem but of how responsible we are in manifesting that response in our ministries. Membership in God's community is not a free ride; it involves the readiness to lose our lives for Jesus' sake and for the sake of the gospel. And we should not imagine this saying to be mere hyperbole.

Servanthood. The scriptures help God's people to understand that we are called to fill a servant role. The term "servant"—or, more accurately, "slave"—was accepted by Jesus as the inner core of his person and mission, and it must become ours. Paul was not deterred from applying the title to himself. He gloried in it and urged his fellow servants to appropriate its meaning for their own lives. Jesus upbraided his friends when they pointedly rejected a servant role on entering the upper room for the Passover meal (Luke 22:24–27). It is only through sharing in Jesus' servanthood that his fellow servants become heirs with him to God's promises (Gal. 3:29; Titus 3:7; Heb. 6:17). Sharing in Jesus' servanthood means sharing in his work, the "work" of loving one another as fellow slaves and joint heirs to God's grace (1 John 4:7–12; see also John 13:34–35). In the Johannine account of the Last Supper, Jesus washed the disciples' feet. His message is explicit: "I have set you an example: you are to do as I have done for you" (John 13:15).

A Talmud story teaches the same message. Rabbi Joshua was concerned that he might not recognize the Messiah, and asked Elijah to instruct him:

"Where," R. Joshua asked, "shall I find the Messiah?"

"At the gate of the city," Elijah replied.

"How shall I recognize him?"

"He sits among the lepers."

"Among the lepers!" cried R. Joshua: "What is he doing there?"

"He changes their bandages," Elijah answered, "He changes them one by one."[8]

The New Testament identifies two facets of service: ministry to the members of the fellowship (typified, for example, in the Johannine literature: John 15:9–17; 1 John 3:18–24; 4:7–12); and ministry to the "neighbor" (Mark 12:31, 33; and Luke 10:25ff.). At first sight, the instruction to love one another may seem exclusive, even self-centered (John 13:35). But the commandment that one who loves God also should love one's brother and sister also raises the question of who is one's brother or sister. D. Moody Smith proposes: "If all men and women are brothers and sisters before God, the command to love one's brother is equivalent to the command to love all people."[9] That is, love for members of the fellowship moves inexorably to love for any "neighbor," as the need emerges. If love among the members of the community establishes its unity, it similarly establishes its unity with all outside the community. The Gospels and epistles are one in announcing that the members of the community are charged with manifesting the love of God and of one another in their ministries beyond the fellowship (Matt. 25:31ff.; Rom. 13:9–10; Gal. 5:13–14). One cannot say "I love God" while hating a brother or sister (1 John 4:19–21).

The love to which the Gospels and epistles bear witness therefore is a servant ministry directed equally to fellow members of the community of faith and to the "neighbors" whom we are called to love. Love of neighbor touches all of the disciple's life. As a consequence, for example, we share responsibility if "any of the least of these [poor]" is denied equal opportunities for education, employment, and access to health care. We are thus charged with the task of redressing such inequalities. As one of us has proposed elsewhere, "We are to share Christ's passion for justice for the oppressed . . . [because] servanthood is not an attribute that may be confined to selected corners of one's life; it is all-encompassing in its reach and application."[10] Now its reach encompasses people living with HIV/AIDS.

Prophetism. Like other images in the scriptures, the image of prophet derived from the lives of Jewish figures is rich in meaning for this discussion. The prophets cared deeply about the moral shape of society. The prophets are best understood not when seen as individuals but when seen in the context of organized society and in the performance of important social roles. The prophetic image applied to the church implies that it must either accept the values and derivative decisions of the larger society or, when its own values differ from those of society, stand and confront them. It is doubtful if keeping silent is a response that God will countenance. The prophets did not keep silent. Their presence was a destabilizing force at the king's court, the place where decisions were made.[11] The prophets consistently charged that the system was not to be equated with reality, that alternatives were thinkable, and thus the values and the claims of the system were subject to criticism.

Is there a message here for God's people in the midst of the HIV/AIDS crisis? We believe there is. If people are excluded from society, they may in fact be unable to make themselves heard above the clamor of representatives of government—national or local—debating with one another, or the hostile voices of citizens demanding that people with AIDS (including young children) be segregated from the rest of society. Just as the prophets could not remain silent in the face of oppression, the church's voice must be raised in defense of the outcast. For this cause also, Jesus' voice is raised in behalf of people who have been cast out of their communities. In this matter also, he has given an example that we are to do for one another what he has done for us (John 13:15).

Walter Brueggemann describes this process of identification with the "poor" as expressing "transformative gestures of solidarity." When Elijah is sent to the widow, "he is driven outside the normal support systems. . . . He is sent there to receive, to be given life precisely by this one whom society has defined as having no life-giving resources." And although this experience is not designed merely to test Elijah, "what the sovereign word of Yahweh does is to drive the prophet out beyond everything conventional and safe, perhaps to push him to 'faith alone.' "[12] Three elements essential to the Elijah story are also characteristic of the church's ministry in the midst of the HIV/AIDS crisis. First, because society is careless of people who are estranged from the mainstream, Elijah is sent to minister to people outside the "normal" support systems. So are we sent, if we are to be true to our calling. Second, the prophet finds there that he is sent not so much to minister but to receive nurture. As Palmer notes, Matthew 25:31ff. reminds us that, if we take the parable seriously, we will see how central is the stranger to the Christian concept of life. "The stranger is not simply one who needs us. We need the stranger."[13] Third, though the visit to the widow is not concocted to test Elijah, the episode does test the prophet. But if he is faithful, he will experience God's power and know that he will be sustained, whether in the presence of the marginalized or of the king and his four hundred prophets! Likewise, the HIV/AIDS epidemic is both test and challenge that we may meet only with the grace and strength God waits to pour upon God's people.

Not surprisingly, there are drawbacks to adopting the role of prophet. It can be a life-threatening role, as the prophets found. Elijah fled for his life from Queen Jezebel. Her ruthless response to a poor farmer had shown that there are no limits to greed when the system permits oppression. Because Elijah challenged the system, Jezebel vowed to destroy him. The challenge to God's people is that even in the face of dire threat, the establishment must be called into question by God's prophets when civil power is used to isolate and further deprive the helpless and excluded.[14] Only through such action can a way be opened so that God's love can be extended to the outcast. If the church does not speak for the outcast at that moment, the outcast may miss God's invitation to enter into the joy of the kingdom. If the people of God fail to act, Jesus warns his followers, they will be excluded from the kingdom themselves. If speaking for "the poor" places the church in situations of risk, it should come as no surprise (see Mark 8:34–38).

Interfaith Ministry as Prophetic Witness

The HIV/AIDS epidemic is thus a challenge to the church to be in the forefront, filling a servant-leader role, prophetically beckoning the larger community to follow and serving as advocate for Jesus' "little ones," and providing adequate resources (hospitality) to people whose lives are blighted by HIV/AIDS. Being God's voice is not enough, however. Whether or not society acts, the church is to do God's will by loving and serving the needs of people with HIV disease and their families. This obedient response should be an interfaith ministry for several reasons.

First, the public response to people with HIV/AIDS and their families has been so vitriolic that programs designed to serve them will be received with greater seriousness if developed and endorsed by local religious leaders acting together and speaking to the civic community with one voice. The churches should join hands with the Jewish community and other concerned groups. Such a united effort can stand as an expression of the ability of God's people to undertake joint projects that are redeeming and compassionate, aligning deeds with words. It may be added parenthetically that there is something tragic in the fact that often it takes a crisis to motivate God's people to manifest the unity that God's word indicates is expected of us. The HIV/AIDS crisis presents this opportunity. Only if the challenge is accepted can we expect the civil government to assume its own particular responsibility.

Second, the costs to people who respond to the needs of people with HIV disease are heavy. The level of nurture and support necessary to sustain such efforts can best be provided by an interfaith response. An individual rabbi or pastor may be misrepresented and denigrated if he or she expresses concern for people with HIV/AIDS. But if neighborhood clergy and laity act together, their voices will be heard more widely and can evoke a more concerted response. Such joint action also provides a stronger and broader basis for community education. In the same manner, if church and synagogue act and speak together at the civic level, their united efforts not only are more likely to receive appropriate attention; they also will be able to address community concerns related to the HIV/AIDS crisis with greater effect.

Third, the nature and scope of the epidemic makes HIV/AIDS a national concern. Although much of the response is local in nature, many aspects of the crisis are best addressed at federal legislative and executive levels. Funding for research, the protection of HIV+ people from exploitation, and access to social welfare resources are issues upon which local action will have little bearing. There is, therefore, a need for nationwide interfaith action to influence these decisions. At that level, as much as in local communities, religious bodies can exercise more influence if they speak with one voice. At that level also, the representative bodies may project a sense of unity for which there are all too few examples.

The problem of how to disseminate information regarding HIV/AIDS is one that Jews and Christians could address with a single national voice. The debate about how to discuss matters of sex and sexually transmitted diseases—and especially whether and by what means they ought to be confronted through public education—continues to be intense and bitter in the United States. It may well be that the HIV/AIDS epidemic will force disparate groups in society to arrive at mutually acceptable approaches to the underlying controversies. In any case, the emergence of HIV/AIDS confronts the religious community with the opportunity to develop study materials for all ages focused on the nature and meaning of human sexuality and sexual relationship.

There is probably even deeper ignorance and misunderstanding of the factors that contribute to the emergence of the drug culture and the entrapment of particular individuals within it. Perhaps the time has come to begin to look for answers to certain nagging questions. Does our society, as presently constituted, contribute to the very destructiveness that it publicly condemns? Does the intensity of competition, from which springs an unending drive to succeed, contribute to the use of either soft or hard drugs? Can congregations assist people to identify and explore courses of action that could prevent the very situations which, if unaddressed, may result in antisocial and self-destructive conduct? It is a fact that the local congregation is one of the most widespread forms of social organization. It suggests itself, at this moment, as a forum in which these concerns can be explored to the benefit of members and the community at large. And without in any way reducing the role of lay members in bringing effective programs into being, cultural roles place clergy in a unique position to initiate and support HIV-related educational and service projects. Thus, churches and synagogues may be agents for health and reconciliation in a society at risk and in need of leadership.

The words that demand attention in the tragic drama of HIV/AIDS are *urgency, challenge, opportunity,* and *tasks.*

Urgency. The situation of people with HIV disease is one of unprecedented and chronic grief, and demands an intense pastoral response from the religious community. HIV/AIDS has created an unparalleled crisis, a crisis that is manifested in local communities, at state and federal government levels, and globally. The urgency is most graphically apparent in the lives of each individual and family suffering because of AIDS, for to most if not all people infected by HIV, AIDS will be a fatal disease. The urgency also is felt at local levels. In some cities, health care services are already strained to provide basic services, and this aspect of the crisis worsens day by day. Nationally, the CDC estimates that about one million people are infected with HIV in the United States. The World Health Organization warns that by the year 2000, 25–30 million people worldwide will be infected, including 10 million children.

Challenge. AIDS is not only a medical crisis but a social catastrophe, not only because it remains incurable, but because of the stigma that quickly attaches to the disease and those it afflicts, and its potential to destroy lives and communities. Although there are many instances in which people living with HIV disease receive understanding and compassionate care, many others are still ostracized, in danger of losing employment if their infection becomes known to employers, and left to struggle with feelings of isolation, anger, and guilt. The situation of many people with HIV/AIDS is one of unprecedented and chronic grief, demanding an intense pastoral response from the religious community. It is a situation that cries out for a redemptive response, one from which the people of God dare not turn away.

Opportunity. In our initial article on this subject, we

stated that AIDS sets before the church an opportunity to reflect on its identity and its mission. This call was echoed in a different form as we wrote about the HIV/AIDS crisis again five years later.[15] As we conclude this book, we urge this self-examination once more. It is basic if the church is to meet the opportunities for ministry created by the HIV/AIDS epidemic. Other opportunities also confront us. They include serving as a voice for those whose voices are too weak to be heard in quarters where decisions are made that affect whether they live in dignity or survive at all. They include such simple acts as driving a person living with AIDS to a grocery or clinic, or sharing a movie. Included also are ministries of hope, comfort, and companionship in the face of despair, grief, helplessness, and isolation.

Tasks. There are both immediate and long-term tasks to be performed. The task at hand is to constitute an accepting community, concerned for the needs of HIV+ people and others affected by AIDS, and to find ministry among them. Long-term tasks and challenges relate to the obligation to understand and educate people regarding the complex factors that have contributed to AIDS and the spread of HIV. We urge congregations to develop joint neighborhood projects to ensure that their members and communities are familiar with the relevant medical and psychosocial data. It is our hope that such efforts will result in the development of joint projects of ministry to individuals and families in need of care. The church is confronted with the opportunity to make credible the New Testament image of God's people as a reconciling and redeeming community. If we fail in this endeavor, it will be a failure not only of nerve, but also of love.

Notes

Chapter 1: The Evolving HIV/AIDS Crisis

1. Earl E. Shelp, Ronald H. Sunderland, and Peter W. A. Mansell, *AIDS: Personal Stories in Pastoral Perspective* (New York: Pilgrim Press, 1986).
2. Ann M. Hardy, "AIDS Knowledge and Attitudes for October–December, 1989," *NCHS Advancedata* 186 (June 25, 1990), 4.
3. Charles E. Rosenberg, *The Cholera Years: The United States in 1832, 1849, and 1866* (Chicago: University of Chicago Press, 1962), p. 4.
4. Ibid., p. 40.
5. Ibid., pp. 118, 120–121.
6. Ibid., pp. 200–220.
7. Allan M. Brandt, *No Magic Bullet: A Social History of Venereal Disease in the United States Since 1880* (New York: Oxford University Press, 1985).
8. Quoted by Brandt, p. 180.
9. Ibid., p. 5; see Joan Ablon, "Stigmatized Health Conditions," *Social Science and Medicine* 15B (1981), 5–9. Other articles in this issue may also be of interest to the reader.
10. Brandt, pp. 132, 168.
11. Ibid., pp. 23, 157, 168.

12. Ibid., p. 159.

13. Quoted by Brandt, p. 183, from the *New York Times* (June 17, 1983).

14. Guenter B. Risse, "Epidemics and History: Ecological Perspectives and Social Responses," in *AIDS: The Burdens of History,* ed. Elizabeth Fee and Daniel M. Fox (Berkeley: University of California Press, 1988), p. 57.

15. Dennis Altman, *AIDS in the Mind of America* (Garden City, N.Y.: Doubleday & Co., Anchor Books, 1986), p. 16. See also Robert Bazell, "The History of an Epidemic," *New Republic* (August 1, 1983), 14–18.

16. James Kinsella, *Covering the Plague: AIDS and the American Media* (New Brunswick: Rutgers University Press, 1989).

17. David L. Kirp has written a penetrating and eloquent case study analysis of the encounter of children with AIDS and school systems. He provides a fascinating account of how communities confront fears and choose risks. Cf. *Learning by Heart: HIV and Schoolchildren in America's Communities* (New Brunswick: Rutgers University Press, 1989).

18. See "The New Untouchables," *Time* 126 (September 23, 1985), 24–26; "The Real Epidemic: Fear and Despair," *Time* 122 (July 4, 1983), 56–58; and "AFRAIDS," *New Republic* 193 (October 14, 1985), 7–10.

19. This incident was widely reported in Houston and across the nation. See "The Backlash Builds Against AIDS," *U.S. News & World Report* 99 (November 4, 1985), 9.

20. Quoted by Jonathan Lieberson, "The Reality of AIDS," *New York Review of Books* (January 16, 1986), 46.

21. William F. Buckley, Jr., "Crucial Steps in Combating the AIDS Epidemic," *New York Times* (March 18, 1986), 27.

22. John R. Emshwiller, "LaRouche-Supported Initiative on AIDS Policy in California Spurs Debate on Han-

dling Disease," *Wall Street Journal* (August 11, 1986), 34.

23. "The Church's Response to AIDS," *Christianity Today* 29 (November 22, 1985), 50; "Jerry Falwell: Circuit Rider to Controversy," *U.S. News & World Report* 99 (September 2, 1985), 11.

24. Jerry Falwell, "AIDS: The Judgment of God," *Liberty Report* (April 1987), 5.

25. Jerry Falwell, "How Many Roads to Heaven?" Old Time Gospel Hour-760 (audio tape).

26. Earl E. Shelp and Ronald H. Sunderland, "AIDS and the Church," *Christian Century* (September 11–18, 1985), 797–800. Additional books and articles that emphasize compassion include: Wendell W. Hoffman and Stanley J. Grenz, *AIDS Ministry in the Midst of an Epidemic* (Grand Rapids: Baker Book House, 1990); Letty M. Russell, ed., *The Church with AIDS: Renewal in the Midst of Crisis* (Louisville: Westminster/John Knox Press, 1990); William E. Amos, Jr., *When AIDS Comes to Church* (Philadelphia: Westminster Press, 1988); Bill Kirkpatrick, *AIDS: Sharing the Pain: A Guide for Caregivers* (New York: Pilgrim Press, 1990); Louis F. Kavar, *Pastoral Ministry in the AIDS Era* (Wayzata, Minn.: Woodland Publishing Co., 1988); John E. Fortunata, *AIDS: The Spiritual Dilemma* (San Francisco: Harper & Row, 1987); Ronald H. Sunderland and Earl E. Shelp, *AIDS: A Manual for Pastoral Care* (Philadelphia: Westminster Press, 1987); Ronald H. Sunderland and Earl E. Shelp, *Handle with Care: A Handbook for Care Teams Serving People with AIDS* (Nashville: Abingdon Press, 1990); Earl E. Shelp, Edwin DuBose, and Ronald H. Sunderland, "AIDS and the Church: A Status Report," *Christian Century* (December 5, 1990), 1125–1137.

27. Eileen P. Flynn, *AIDS: A Catholic Call for Compassion* (Kansas City, Mo.: Sheed & Ward, 1985). For a cleverly written, misleading, and sensationalizing examination of AIDS published by a Catholic press that contrasts with Flynn, cf. Gene Antonio, *The AIDS*

Cover-Up? The Real and Alarming Facts About AIDS (San Francisco: Ignatius Press, 1986).

28. William E. Swing, "Open Letter to the Reverend Charles Stanley," January 18, 1986, unpublished.

29. AIDS-Related Complex is a clinical designation for non–life-threatening diseases and symptoms secondary to infection with HIV. The term has been displaced by a more general designation of symptomatic HIV disease.

30. John R. Quinn, "The AIDS Crisis: A Pastoral Response," *America* (June 28, 1986), 504–506.

31. John J. O'Connor, "The Archdiocese and AIDS," *Catholic New York* (September 19, 1985), 21.

32. "Resolution on Acquired Immune Deficiency Syndrome (AIDS)," adopted by the Fourteenth General Synod, United Church of Christ, Pittsburgh, Pennsylvania, June 24–28, 1983.

33. J. Gordon Melton, "Episcopal Church: Additional Resolutions on AIDS (1988)," *The Churches Speak on: AIDS* (Detroit: Gale Research, 1989), pp. 79–81.

34. Melton, "United Methodist Church: AIDS and the Healing Ministry of the Church (1988)," pp. 148–151.

35. Melton, "Presbyterian Church (U.S.A.): Resolution on Acquired Immune Deficiency Syndrome (1986)," pp. 122–125.

36. Melton, "Southern Baptist Convention: On AIDS (1987)," pp. 129–130.

37. Melton, "Greek Orthodox Archdiocese of North and South America: AIDS and You (1988)," pp. 87–89.

38. The Administrative Board, United States Catholic Conference, *The Many Faces of AIDS* (Washington, D.C.: Office of Publishing and Promotion Services, 1987).

39. United States Catholic Conference, "Called to Compassion and Responsibility," *Origins* 19 (November 30, 1989), 421F.

40. Melton, "Evangelical Lutheran Church in America: AIDS and the Church's Ministry of Caring (1988)," pp. 86–87.

41. William H. McNeill, *Plagues and Peoples* (Garden City, N.Y.: Doubleday & Co., Anchor Books, 1976), p. 257.

Chapter 2: The HIV/AIDS Epidemic

1. Thousands of medical and scientific articles have appeared in learned journals about the AIDS viruses, HIV, their effect on the human body, clinical features of the syndrome, treatments, epidemiology, and potential vaccines. Entries in this bibliography are accessible by computer at many libraries. The facts about AIDS presented in this chapter reflect this wealth of data and our experience. Citations, however, are restricted to a few summary references that are generally available (see Selected References). The bibliographies in these materials direct the reader to more technical works.

2. Randy Shilts, *And the Band Played On* (New York: St. Martin's Press, 1987), p. 452.

3. Jean L. Marx, "AIDS Virus Has a New Name—Perhaps," *Science* 232 (May 9, 1986), 699–700; and "Human Immunodeficiency Viruses," ibid., 697.

4. Mirko D. Grmek, *History of AIDS* (Princeton: Princeton University Press, 1990), p. 76.

5. Shilts, p. 529.

6. For a summary explanation of the immunopathic process of HIV infection, see Scott Koenig and Anthony S. Fauci, "AIDS: Immunopathogenesis and Immune Response to the Human Immunodeficiency Virus," in *AIDS*, 2d ed., Vincent T. DeVita, Jr., Samuel Hellman, and Steven A. Rosenberg, eds. (Philadelphia: J. B. Lippincott Co., 1988), pp. 61–77.

7. Grmek, p. 119.

8. Grmek, pp. 119–137. Cf. Peter Rodetsky, "AIDS 1990: The First Case," *Discover* (January 1991), 74–75; Myron Essex, "Origins of AIDS," in *AIDS*, 2d ed., pp. 3–10.

9. Cf. Shilts.

10. Essex, p.6.

11. Ibid., pp. 6–9; and Grmek, pp. 142–143.

12. Grmek, p. 144.

13. Ibid., pp. 143–148; Murray B. Gardner and Paul A. Luciw, "Simian Immunodeficiency Viruses and Their Relationship to the Human Immunodeficiency Viruses," *AIDS* 2 (Supplement 1, 1988), S3–S10.

14. "PCR amplifies proviral sequences of HIV-1 within DNA for detection in infant's lymphocytes." Thomas C. Quinn, "Global Epidemiology of HIV Infections," in *The Medical Management of AIDS,* 2d ed., Merle A. Sande and Paul A. Volberding, eds. (Philadelphia: W. B. Saunders Co., 1990), p. 14.

15. Cf. Hardy, 5, 7–8.

16. Julie Louise Gerberding, "Occupational HIV Transmission: Issues for Health Care Providers," in *Medical Management of AIDS,* 2d ed., pp. 57–61; R. Marcus, K. Kay, and J. M. Mann, "Transmission of Human Immunodeficiency Virus (HIV) in Health-care Settings World Wide," *Bulletin of the World Health Organization* 67 (1989), 577–582.

17. Centers for Disease Control, "Possible Transmission of Human Immunodeficiency Virus to a Patient During an Invasive Dental Procedure," *Morbidity and Mortality Weekly Report* 39 (July 27, 1990), 490.

18. Lawrence K. Altman, "U.S. Experts Try to Estimate AIDS Infections by Doctors," *New York Times* (February 7, 1991), A10.

19. Ibid.

20. See Kathleen Nolan and Ronald Bayer, eds., "AIDS: The Responsibilities of Health Professionals," *Hastings Center Report* (April/May 1988), supplement; Richard M. Ratzan and Henry Schneiderman, "AIDS, Autopsies, and Abandonment," *Journal of the American Medical Association* 260 (December 16, 1988), 3466–3469; and Sanford C. Sharp, "The Physician's Obligation to Treat AIDS Patients," *Southern Medical Journal* 81 (October 1988), 1282–1285.

21. Jonathan M. Mann, "Global AIDS into the

1990s," *Journal of Acquired Immune Deficiency Syndrome* 3 (1990), 439.

22. John M. Karon, Timothy J. Dondero, Jr., and Workshop Group, "HIV Prevalence Estimates and AIDS Case Projections for the United States: Report Based upon a Workshop," *Morbidity and Mortality Weekly Report* 39 (November 30, 1990), 1–18.

23. Cf. Lili Penkower et al., "Behavioral, Health and Psychosocial Factors and Risk for HIV Infection Among Sexually Active Homosexual Men: The Multicenter AIDS Cohort Study," *American Journal of Public Health* 81 (February 1991), 194–196; and Heather G. Miller, Charles F. Turner, and Lincoln E. Moses, eds., *AIDS: The Second Decade* (Washington, D.C.: National Academy Press, 1990), pp. 187–201.

24. Miller, Turner, and Moses, pp. 38–80.

25. Karon, Dondero, and Workshop Group, p. 8.

26. Miller, Turner, and Moses, ch. 5, "AIDS and the Blood Supply."

27. Ibid., pp. 291–292.

28. Ibid., p. 253.

29. Lytl I. Gardner et al., "Evidence for Spread of the Human Immunodeficiency Virus Epidemic into Low Prevalence Areas of the United States," *Journal of Acquired Immune Deficiency Syndrome* 2 (1989), 531.

30. James W. Buehler et al., "Impact of the Human Immunodeficiency Virus Epidemic on Mortality Trends in Young Men, United States," *American Journal of Public Health* 90 (September 1990), 1080–1086.

31. Centers for Disease Control, "Mortality Attributable to HIV Infection/AIDS—United States, 1981–1990," *Morbidity and Mortality Weekly Report* 40 (January 25, 1991), 41–44.

32. Other blood assays that can be used to detect or confirm infection are Western blot, radioimmune assay, immune fluorescence, and polymerase chain reaction.

33. Philip P. Mortimer, "The Fallibility of HIV Western Blot," *The Lancet* 337 (February 2, 1991), 286–287.

Chapter 3: Clinical and Psychosocial Effects of HIV/AIDS

1. Centers for Disease Control, "1987 Revision of Case Definition for AIDS for Surveillance Purposes," reprinted in *Confronting AIDS: Update 1988*, Institute of Medicine, National Academy of Sciences (Washington, D.C.: National Academy Press, 1988), pp. 208–217. Cf. Judith Falloon, Janie Eddy, Maryann Roper, and Philip A. Pizzo, "AIDS in the Pediatric Population," in *AIDS*, 2d ed., Vincent DeVita, Jr., Samuel Hellman, and Steven A. Rosenberg, eds. (Philadelphia: J. B. Lippincott Co., 1988), pp. 339–351.

2. People with AIDS who have taken the antiretroviral drug AZT or Retrovir for up to three years appear to have a relatively high probability of developing non-Hodgkin lymphoma. It is not clear if this development is due to prolonged survival with CD4+ T cell depletion or is a side effect of antiretroviral therapy. Cf. James M. Pluda et al., "Development of Non-Hodgkin Lymphoma in a Cohort of Patients with Severe Human Immunodeficiency Virus (HIV) Infection in Long-Term Antiretroviral Therapy," *Annals of Internal Medicine* 113 (August 15, 1990), 276–282.

3. Cf. Merle A. Sande and Paul A. Volberding, eds., *The Medical Management of AIDS*, 2d ed. (Philadelphia: W. B. Saunders Co., 1990), secs. 3 and 4.

4. George F. Lemp et al., "Survival Trends for Patients with AIDS," *Journal of the American Medical Association* 263 (January 19, 1990), 402–406. Cf. Jeffrey E. Harris, "Improved Short-term Survival of AIDS Patients Initially Diagnosed with *Pneumocystis carinii* Pneumonia, 1984–1987," *Journal of the American Medical Association* 263 (January 19, 1990), 397–401.

5. Gerald H. Friedland et al., "Survival Differences in Patients with AIDS," *Journal of Acquired Immune Deficiency Syndrome* 4 (1991), 144–153.

6. Richard E. Chaisson, "Living with AIDS," *Journal of the American Medical Association* 263 (January 19,

1990), 435. Cf. Roy M. Anderson and Graham F. Medley, "Epidemiology of HIV Infection and AIDS: Incubation and Infectious Periods, Survival and Vertical Transmission," *AIDS* 2 (Supplement 1, 1988), S57–S63.

7. George F. Lemp et al., "Projections of AIDS Morbidity and Mortality in San Francisco," *Journal of the American Medical Association* 263 (March 16, 1990), 1497–1501.

8. Martin T. Schechter et al., "Susceptibility to AIDS Progression Appears Early in HIV Infection," *AIDS* 4 (1990), 185–190; Mirko D. Grmek, *History of AIDS* (Princeton: Princeton University Press, 1990), p. 93; and "Cofactor Question Divides Codiscoverers of HIV," *Journal of the American Medical Association* 264 (December 26, 1990), 3111–3112.

9. Andrew R. Moss et al., "Seropositivity for HIV and the Developments of AIDS or AIDS Related Complex: Three Year Follow up of the San Francisco General Hospital Cohort," *British Medical Journal* 296 (March 1988), 745–750; and "General Guidelines for Initiation of ZDV Therapy in Early HIV Disease," in *The Medical Management of AIDS,* 2d ed., p. xv; A. N. Phillips et al., "Serial CD4 Lymphocyte Counts and Development of AIDS," *The Lancet* 337 (February 16, 1991), 389–392.

10. Judith Falloon et al., "Human Immunodeficiency Virus Infection in Children," *Journal of Pediatrics* 114 (January 1989), 1–30.

11. Gwendolyn B. Scott et al., "Survival in Children with Perinatally Acquired Human Immunodeficiency Virus Type 1 Infection," *New England Journal of Medicine* 321 (December 28, 1989), 1791–1796.

12. Richard W. Price and Bruce Brew, "Management of the Neurologic Complications of HIV-1 Infection and AIDS," in *The Medical Management of AIDS,* 2d ed., pp. 161–181; Marinas Dalakas, Alison Wickham, and John Sever, "AIDS and the Nervous System," *Journal of the American Medical Association* 261 (April 28, 1989), 2396–2399; Bruce Brew, Marc Rosenblum, and Richard W. Price, "Central and Peripheral Nervous System Com-

plications of HIV Infection and AIDS," in *AIDS,* 2d ed., pp. 185–197.

13. There have been several interdisciplinary collections of essays published in special issues of scholarly journals. These publications help us appreciate the fact that epidemics are social events with potential to affect every sector of society. See *Daedalus* (Spring 1989 and Summer 1989); *The Milbank Quarterly* 64 (Supplement 1, 1986), 68 (Supplements 1 and 2, 1990); and *Social Research* 55 (Autumn 1988).

14. With the passage of the Americans with Disabilities Act in 1990, people with HIV infection will have legal protection with respect to employment, public services, public accommodations, transportation, and telecommunications. Effective enforcement of the protections in the Act for people with HIV disease remains to be seen.

15. Ann M. Hardy, "AIDS Knowledge and Attitudes for October–December, 1989," *NCHS Advancedata* 186 (June 25, 1990), 9.

16. Risk avoidance and risk reduction programs have proliferated in recent years. Campaigns have been specially designed to reach people who engage in HIV risk behaviors, for example, gay men, IV drug users, sexually active heterosexual people, adolescents, and others. Analysis of prevention programs aimed at youth showed that the successful ones had several common features: one-on-one individual attention, involvement of parents, focus on schools, and communitywide multiagency approaches. Cf. Jay G. Dryfoos, "Preventing High-Risk Behavior," *American Journal of Public Health* 81 (February 1991), 157–158.

17. For a compelling mother's account of her son's struggle with AIDS, see Barbara Peabody, *The Screaming Room* (San Diego: Oak Tree Publications, 1986).

18. For a wide-ranging discussion of psychosocial issues among children and families with HIV/AIDS, see Gary Anderson, ed., *Courage to Care: Responding to the Crisis of Children with AIDS* (Washington, D.C.: Child Welfare League of America, 1990). Ines Rieder and Pa-

tricia Ruppelt have edited a collection of pieces that give voice to women touched by AIDS; see *AIDS: The Women* (San Francisco: Cleis Press, 1988). Issues related to the reproductive decisions of HIV+ women are discussed by Carol Levine and Nancy N. Dubler, "Uncertain Risks and Bitter Realities: The Reproductive Choices of HIV Infected Women," and John D. Arras, "AIDS and Reproductive Choices: Having Children in Fear and Trembling," *The Milbank Quarterly* 68 (1990), 321–351 and 353–382, respectively.

19. For discussions of some of these issues among health care providers, see Molly Cooke and Merle A. Sande, "The HIV Epidemic and Training in Internal Medicine," *New England Journal of Medicine* 321 (November 9, 1989), 1334–1338; Charles L. Bosk and Joel E. Frader, "AIDS and Its Impact on Medical Work: The Culture and Politics of the Shop Floor," *The Milbank Quarterly* 68 (Supplement 2, 1990), 257–279; E. Stephen Scarle, "Knowledge, Attitudes, and Behavior of Health Professionals in Relation to AIDS," *The Lancet* (January 3, 1987), 26–28; and Lawrence O. Gostin, ed., *AIDS and the Health Care System* (New Haven: Yale University Press, 1990).

20. See references in note 18.

21. "Developing National Partnerships for HIV and AIDS Education," *CDC HIV/AIDS Prevention Newsletter* 1 (December 1990), 10–11, 14.

22. Ann M. Hardy et al., "The Economic Impact of the First 10,000 Cases of Acquired Immunodeficiency Syndrome in the United States," *Journal of the American Medical Association* 255 (January 10, 1986), 209–211.

23. Fred J. Hellinger, "Updated Forecasts of the Costs of Medical Care for Persons with HIV, 1989–93," *Public Health Reports* 105 (January/February, 1990), 1–12.

24. Ibid.

25. Public policy and ethical issues related to HIV/AIDS began to be discussed on a broad scale and an interdisciplinary basis midway in the decade of the 1980s. The specific issues or questions have changed over time,

but the interest and vigor of the debates have been constant. Cf. Ronald Bayer, *Private Acts, Social Consequences* (New York: Free Press, 1989); the periodical *AIDS and Public Policy Journal;* American Medical Association, Council on Ethical and Judicial Affairs, "Ethical Issues Involved in the Growing AIDS Crisis," *Journal of the American Medical Association* 259 (March 4, 1988), 1360–1361; Carol Levine, "Has AIDS Changed the Ethics of Human Subjects Research?" *Law, Medicine & Health Care* 16 (Winter 1988), 167–173; Ronald Bayer, "Ethical and Social Policy Issues Raised by HIV Screening," *AIDS* 3 (1989), 119–124; Wendy E. Parmet, "Legal Rights and Communicable Disease: AIDS, the Police Power, and Individual Liberty," *Journal of Health Politics, Policy and Law* 14 (Winter 1989), 741–771; Bernard J. Turnock and Chester J. Kelly, "Mandatory Premarital Testing for Human Immunodeficiency Virus: The Illinois Experience," *Journal of the American Medical Association* 261 (June 16, 1989), 3415–3418; National Academy of Sciences, Institute of Medicine, *Confronting AIDS: Update 1988* (Washington, D.C.: National Academy Press, 1988); "Special Issue on AIDS," *New England Journal of Public Policy* 4 (Winter/Spring, 1988).

26. Cf. Bruce Nussbaum, *Good Intentions: How Big Business and the Medical Establishment Are Corrupting the Fight Against AIDS* (New York: Atlantic Monthly Press, 1990); Sandra Panem, *The AIDS Bureaucracy: Why Society Failed to Meet the AIDS Crisis and How We Might Improve Our Response* (Cambridge: Harvard University Press, 1988); Sylvan B. Green et al., "Issues in the Design of Drug Trials for AIDS," *Controlled Clinical Trials* 11 (1990), 80–87; George J. Annas, "FDA's Compassion for Desperate Drug Companies," *Hastings Center Report* (January/February 1990), 35–37; and Harold Edgar and David J. Rothman, "New Rules for New Drugs: The Challenge of AIDS to the Regulatory Process," *The Milbank Quarterly* 68 (Supplement 2, 1990), 111–142.

27. Peter J. Fischinger, "Strategies for the Develop-

ment of Vaccines to Prevent AIDS," in *AIDS*, 2d ed., pp. 87–104; Dani P. Bolognesi, "Progress in Vaccine Development Against SIV and HIV," *Journal of Acquired Immune Deficiency Syndrome* 3 (1990), 390–394.

Chapter 4: Illness in Christian Perspective

1. For an elaboration of this theme, see Earl E. Shelp and Ronald H. Sunderland, eds., *The Pastor as Theologian* (New York: Pilgrim Press, 1988).

2. Paul S. Minear, *The Gospel According to Mark,* vol. 17 of the Layman's Bible Commentary, Balmer H. Kelly, ed. (Atlanta: John Knox Press, 1960), p. 109.

3. Ibid.

4. This was the case, for example, with respect to leprosy. In this respect, it is important to recognize that the term to which reference is made in the Jewish scriptures and in the New Testament carried a different connotation from that of the disease known commonly as leprosy in the twentieth century. The leprosy of the ancient Near East actually encompassed a range of dermatological disorders that seldom approached the seriousness or evoked the level of fear with which today's leprosy (Hansen's disease) is associated. Such common skin diseases as psoriasis, eczema, and other common rashes and lesions were probably included under the general heading of "leprosy."

The real suffering of lepers was not so much due to physical discomfort as to the isolation and ostracism that sufferers met in the general community. It is a similar isolation and ostracism experienced by people with AIDS that links the two. More important, given this association, the response of Jesus to people with leprosy suggests the model for the response of God's people to people with AIDS.

5. T. W. Manson, *The Sayings of Jesus* (London: SCM Press, 1954), p. 273.

6. Edward Schillebeeckx, *Jesus: An Experiment in Christology* (New York: Crossroad, 1985), p. 184.

7. Ibid., p. 180.

8. For a development of the concept that illness and affliction place the sick person "nearer to death," see Klaus Seybold and Ulrich B. Mueller, *Sickness and Healing* (Nashville: Abingdon Press, 1981). They state, "The sick person as such has fallen into death's realm of power, not only because sickness possibly brings death . . . but because sickness *eo ipso* belongs to death's domain" (p. 123).

9. *Nicene and Post-Nicene Fathers,* Series 2, Philip Schaff and Henry Wace, eds., vol. 1, *Eusebius* (Grand Rapids: Wm. B. Eerdmans, 1979), p. 307.

10. John Calvin, *Tracts and Treatises on the Doctrine and Worship of the Church,* vol. 2 (Grand Rapids: Wm. B. Eerdmans, 1958), p. 127.

11. Charles A. Coulson, *Science and Christian Belief* (Chapel Hill, N.C.: University of North Carolina Press, 1955), p. 19.

12. Dorothee Soelle, *Suffering* (Philadelphia: Fortress Press, 1975), p. 22.

13. Ibid., p. 26.

14. John B. Cobb, Jr., and David Ray Griffin, *Process Theology: An Introductory Exposition* (Philadelphia: Westminster Press, 1976), pp. 51–52.

15. The philosopher Alfred North Whitehead suggests that, to the extent that conformity to the divine aims is incomplete, there is evil in the world. New actualities or realities (such as AIDS) may lead not to enjoyment but to discord, a term Whitehead uses to refer to physical or mental suffering that is simply evil in itself, whenever it occurs. See Alfred North Whitehead, *Religion in the Making* (New York: Macmillan Co., 1926), p. 60, and *Adventures of Ideas* (New York: Macmillan Co., 1933), pp. 329–330, 342.

16. See James A. Wharton, "Theology and Ministry in the Hebrew Scriptures," in Earl E. Shelp and Ronald H. Sunderland, eds., *A Biblical Basis for Ministry* (Philadelphia: Westminster Press, 1981), pp. 62–69.

17. See Alan Keith-Lucas, *Giving and Taking Help* (Chapel Hill, N.C.: University of North Carolina Press, 1972), p. 9.

18. Cobb and Griffin, p. 74.

19. Parker J. Palmer, *The Company of Strangers* (New York: Crossroad, 1983), p. 26.

Chapter 5: God and the Poor

1. R. B. Y. Scott, *The Relevance of the Prophets,* rev. ed. (New York: Macmillan Co., 1969), p. 119.

2. Robert J. Karris, "Poor and Rich: The Lukan *Sitz im Leben,"* in *Perspectives on Luke-Acts,* ed. Charles H. Talbert (Danville, Va.: Association of Baptist Professors of Religion, 1978), p. 117.

3. Joachim Jeremias, *New Testament Theology: The Proclamation of Jesus* (New York: Charles Scribner's Sons, 1971), pp. 109–113. Jeremias understands the literal use of poor in Luke 6:20 to be the original rather than the religious interpretation given in Matthew 5:3.

Chapter 6: HIV/AIDS Ministries

1. For discussions of the mutual influence of religious thought and social life, see Ernst Troeltsch, *The Social Teaching of the Christian Churches,* vol. 1 (New York: Harper & Row, 1960), pp. 23–37; H. Richard Niebuhr, *Christ and Culture* (New York: Harper & Row, Harper Torchbooks, 1956), and *The Kingdom of God in America* (New York: Harper & Row, Harper Torchbooks, 1959); Ernest R. Sandeen, ed., *The Bible and Social Reform* (Philadelphia: Fortress Press, 1982); and William A. Clebsch, *From Sacred to Profane America: The Role of Religion in American History* (New York: Harper & Row, 1968).

2. We have reported the hands-on or AIDS Care Team component of our program in handbook form. Cf. Ron-

ald H. Sunderland and Earl E. Shelp, *Handle with Care: A Handbook for Care Teams Serving People with AIDS* (Nashville: Abingdon Press, 1990).

3. The virtue of courage is examined in theological perspective by Peter Geach, *The Virtues* (Cambridge, Mass.: Cambridge University Press, 1977), pp. 150–170, and by Josef Pieper, *The Four Cardinal Virtues: Prudence, Justice, Fortitude, Temperance* (Notre Dame, Ind.: University of Notre Dame Press, 1966), pp. 115–141. For an analysis of the role of courage in medical contexts, see Earl E. Shelp, "Courage: A Neglected Virtue in the Patient-Physician Relationship," *Social Science and Medicine* 18 (1984), 351–360, and "Courage and Tragedy in Clinical Medicine," *Journal of Medicine and Philosophy* 8 (November 1983), 417–429.

4. Among the sociological literature on male homosexuality, the following may be helpful to people seeking an understanding of gay lifestyles and culture: Bell and Weinberg, *Homosexualities;* Tripp, *The Homosexual Matrix;* G. Weinberg, *Society and the Healthy Homosexual;* M. S. Weinberg and C. J. Williams, *Male Homosexuals;* Altman, *Homosexual* and *The Homosexualization of America;* and J. D'Emilio, *Sexual Politics, Sexual Communities.* See David E. Greenberg, *The Constitution of Homosexuality* (Chicago: University of Chicago Press, 1988); Alen P. Bell, Martin S. Weinberg, and Sue Kiefer Hammersmith, *Sexual Preference* (Bloomington: Indiana University Press, 1981); Richard A. Isay, *Being Homosexual* (New York: Farrar, Straus & Giroux, 1989). Also see *Journal of Homosexuality* for articles on a full range of relevant subjects. Several thematic issues of this journal on bisexuality are valuable resources; see 9 (Winter 1983/Spring 1984), 9 (Summer 1984), 10 (Winter 1984), 11 (Spring 1985).

5. The literature is extensive providing insight into the contributing factors of drug abuse and the difficulty of altering behavior. See Shiffman and Wills, *Coping and Substance Abuse;* Lidz and Walker, *Heroin, Deviance, and Morality;* Arie Cohen, "A Psychosocial Typology . . .";

George Serban, ed., *Social and Medical Aspects of Drug Abuse;* Bernard Segal, "Intervention and Prevention . . . "; Brunswick and Messeri, "Drugs, Lifestyle, and Health"; and Newcomb and Bentler, "Substance Use and Ethnicity." See also Joel H. Henderson, "Substance Use/Abuse Conceptualization, Etiology and Treatment," *Journal of Drug Issues* 12 (Fall 1982), 317–332; Lloyd D. Johnston, "The Etiology and Prevention of Substance Use: What Can We Learn from Recent Historical Changes," *Etiology of Drug Abuse* (Washington, D.C.: NIDA Research Monograph Series, No. 56, 1985), pp. 155–177; and Alan G. Marlatl et al., "Addictive Behaviors: Etiology and Treatment," *Annual Review of Psychology* 39 (1988), 223–252.

6. See Chapters 4 and 5.

7. This portion of the chapter originally appeared as part of a journal article. Cf. Earl E. Shelp, "AIDS, High Risk Behaviors and Moral Judgments," *Journal of Pastoral Care* 43 (Winter 1989), 329–333 passim. Reprinted with permission of the *Journal of Pastoral Care.*

8. Jay Jones helped us appreciate the significance of this feature of the parable.

9. Archibald M. Hunter, *A Pattern for Life* (Philadelphia: Westminster Press, 1965), p. 86.

10. Dietrich Bonhoeffer, *The Cost of Discipleship* (New York: Macmillan Co., 1959), p. 206.

11. The role of freedom in ministry is expertly analyzed by James A. Wharton in "Theology and Ministry in the Hebrew Scriptures," in *A Biblical Basis for Ministry,* ed. Earl E. Shelp and Ronald H. Sunderland (Philadelphia: Westminster Press, 1981), pp. 17–71.

12. The discussion of homosexuality by moral theologians has been active in recent years. Several authors have rejected or questioned biblical and theological condemnations of homosexual people. See George Edwards, *Gay-Lesbian Liberation;* Robert Nugent, ed., *A Challenge to Love;* James Nelson, *Embodiment;* John Boswell, *Christianity, Social Tolerance, and Homosexuality;* Scanzoni and Mollenkott, *Is the Homosexual My Neighbor?;*

and Earl Shelp, "Pastor, I Think I'm Gay." See also John J. McNeil, *Taking a Chance on God* (Boston: Beacon Press, 1988); Robin Scruggs, *The New Testament and Homosexuality* (Philadelphia: Fortess Press, 1983); John S. Spong, *Living in Sin?* (San Francisco: Harper & Row, 1988), chs. 9 and 14; Hugh Montefiore, "Homosexuality," in Jack Dominian and Hugh Montefiore, eds., *God, Sex & Love* (Philadelphia: Trinity Press International, 1989), ch. 4; and Peter Coleman, *Gay Christians: A Moral Dilemma* (Philadelphia: Trinity Press International, 1989). For a response, see Jeannene Gramick and Pat Furey, eds., *The Vatican and Homosexuality* (New York: Crossroad, 1988). A contrary, disapproving, and unaccepting argument is contained in the Roman Catholic Doctrinal Congregation's Letter to Bishops, "The Pastoral Care of Homosexual Persons," *Origins: NC Documentary Service* 16 (November 13, 1986), 378–382.

13. See literature cited in notes 4 and 5 of this chapter.

14. The following is suggestive of the literature on ministry as a duty of ordained and lay people: Hendrik Kraemer, *Theology of the Laity* (Philadelphia: Westminster Press, 1958); Mark Gibbs and Ralph Morton, *God's Frozen People* (Philadelphia: Westminster Press, 1965); Marie Joseph Congar, *Lay People in the Church* (London: Geoffrey Chapman, 1959); Karl Barth, *Dogmatics* IV/3 (Edinburgh: T. & T. Clark, 1962); Leslie Newbigin, *The Household of God* (London: SCM Press, 1953); C. W. Brister, *Pastoral Care in the Church* (New York: Harper & Row, 1964); John T. McNeill, *History of the Cure of Souls* (New York: Harper & Brothers, 1951); James Fenhagen, *Mutual Ministry: New Vitality for the Local Church* (New York: Seabury Press, 1977), and *Ministry and Solitude* (New York: Seabury Press, 1981); Edward Schillebeeckx, *Ministry* (New York: Crossroad, 1981); and Ronald H. Sunderland, "Lay Pastoral Care," in *Primary Pastoral Care* (Atlanta: Journal of Pastoral Care Publications, 1990).

15. Ronald H. Sunderland, "Sustaining Lay Ministry Through Supervision," *The Christian Ministry* 16 (No-

vember 1985), 15–17; Gregg D. Wood, "Hospital-based Lay Pastoral Visitation Program," *Journal of Pastoral Care* 40 (September 9, 1986), 163.

16. Wharton, p. 69 n. 6.

17. We recommend teams of twenty people per patient. Visitation can be conducted in pairs once every week, thus utilizing fourteen people. The remaining six are substitutes or can be part of a rotation.

18. Prophetic, servant, and priestly ministries are analyzed in the following books edited by the authors: *The Pastor as Prophet* (New York: Pilgrim Press, 1985), *The Pastor as Servant* (New York: Pilgrim Press, 1986), and *The Pastor as Priest* (New York: Pilgrim Press, 1987).

19. For a general discussion of the religious use of taboo, see Mary Douglas, *Purity and Danger* (London: Routledge & Kegan Paul, 1966), chs. 1, 3, and 7–10.

20. Cf. Gerhard von Rad, *Genesis* (Philadelphia: Westminster Press, 1961). Von Rad suggests that the opening chapters of Genesis are etiologic narratives attempting to provide a theological sanction for human observations of the natural and social orders.

21. Public and private agencies have produced excellent educational material. Readers are directed to the local offices of the American Red Cross to obtain written and video resources. The personal stories of patients, families, lovers, and clinicians are told in pastoral perspective in another volume written by the authors; see Earl E. Shelp, Ronald H. Sunderland, and Peter W. A. Mansell, *AIDS: Personal Stories in Pastoral Perspective* (New York: Pilgrim Press, 1986). See also Daniel Berrigan, *Sorrow Built a Bridge: Friendship and AIDS* (Baltimore: Fortkamp Publishing Co., 1989); Letty M. Russell, ed., *The Church with AIDS: Renewal in the Midst of Crisis* (Louisville: Westminster/John Knox Press, 1990).

22. Chapters 3 and 4 in this volume offer a brief examination of these matters, especially as they bear upon the HIV/AIDS crisis.

23. This text originally appeared in Shelp, "AIDS, High Risk Behaviors and Moral Judgments," pp. 334–335.

24. Cf. Earl E. Shelp and Ronald H. Sunderland, eds., *The Pastor as Teacher* (New York: Pilgrim Press, 1990).

25. Cf. Earl E. Shelp and Ronald H. Sunderland, eds., *The Pastor as Theologian* (New York: Pilgrim Press, 1988).

26. Cf. Earl E. Shelp and Ronald H. Sunderland, eds., *The Pastor as Counselor* (New York: Pilgrim Press, 1991).

27. Dennis Altman has analyzed the social, political, and psychological impact of AIDS on American society. See *AIDS in the Mind of America* (Garden City, N.Y.: Doubleday & Co., Anchor Books, 1986). See also David Black, *The Plague Years: A Chronicle of AIDS, the Epidemic of Our Times* (New York: Simon & Schuster, 1985); Monroe E. Price, *Shattered Mirrors: Our Search for Identity and Community in the AIDS Era* (Cambridge: Harvard University Press, 1989); and Elizabeth Fee and Daniel M. Fox, eds., *AIDS: The Burdens of History* (Berkeley: University of California Press, 1988).

28. Most major denominations have spoken officially about the HIV/AIDS crisis. Portions of some of these pronouncements, declarations, resolutions, and statements were cited in Chapter 1. Other interfaith and interdenominational statements have been made by the National Council of Churches, World Council of Churches (cf. Melton), AIDS National Interfaith Network, Binational (Canada/United States) Consultation on AIDS (cf. David G. Hallman, ed., *AIDS Issues: Confronting the Challenge* [New York: Pilgrim Press, 1989], pp. 98–101, 157–159, 248–250).

Chapter 7: The Global Impact of HIV/AIDS

1. James Chin and Jonathan Mann, "The Global Patterns and Prevalence of AIDS and HIV Infection," *AIDS* 2 (Supplement 1, 1989), 247–252.

2. World Health Organization, Workshop on AIDS in Central Africa, Bangui, Central African Republic, October 1985.

3. James J. Goedert and William A. Blattner, "The Epidemiology and Natural History of Human Immunodeficiency Virus," in *AIDS,* 2d ed., Vincent T. DeVita, Jr., Samuel Hellman, and Steven A. Rosenberg, eds. (Philadelphia: J. B. Lippincott Co., 1988), pp. 35–36.

4. Chin and Mann, p. 249.

5. Paul A. Sato, James Chin, and Jonathan Mann, "Review of AIDS and HIV Infection: Global Epidemiology and Statistics," *AIDS* 2 (Supplement 1, 1989), 302.

6. Sato, Chin, and Mann, pp. 301–307.

7. Chin and Mann, p. 249.

8. Ibid.

9. Sato, Chin, and Mann, p. 305; see also "In Point of Fact," WHO Press Release 72 (November 1990), p. 1.

10. Sato, Chin, and Mann, p. 305.

11. Ibid.

12. Jonathan Mann, "Introduction, AIDS and HIV Infection: The Wider Perspective," *British Medical Bulletin* 44 (January 1988), i–ii.

13. Introduction, "The Health of Mothers and Children in the Context of HIV/AIDS" (Geneva: Global Program on AIDS, November 1989), p. 1.

14. Ibid.

15. "WHO Revises Global Estimates of HIV Infection," WHO Press Release 38 (July 31, 1990), p. 1.

16. WHO Press Release 49 (September 25, 1990), pp. 1–2. See also "In Point of Fact," WHO Press Release 72 (November 1990), p. 1.

17. World Health Organization, "Sexually Transmitted Infections Increasing," *WHO Features* 152 (December 1990), 2.

18. U.S. Department of Health and Human Services, Division of STD/HIV Prevention, *1989 Annual Report,* p. 4.

19. "Syphilis Cases Rise," *Houston Chronicle* (January 11, 1991), 21.

20. Kevin M. DeCock et al., "AIDS—The Leading Cause of Adult Death in the West African City of Abidjan, Ivory Coast," *Science* 249 (August 17, 1990), 793.

21. Kevin M. DeCock, Koudou Oderhouri, et al., "Rapid Emergence of AIDS in Abidjan, Ivory Coast," *The Lancet* (August 19, 1989), 408.

22. B. N'Galy, S. Bertozzi, and R. W. Ryder, "Obstacles to the Optimal Management of HIV Infection/AIDS in Africa," *Journal of Acquired Immune Deficiency Syndrome* 3 (April 1990), 431–432.

23. N. Mposo et al., "Large Increase in Health Care Utilization by HIV Infected Employees at a Commercial Bank in Kinshasa, Zaire," *Abstracts* 1 (San Francisco: Sixth International Conference on AIDS, 1990), 172.

24. "AIDS in Africa: A Killer Rages On," *New York Times* (September 16, 1990), A11.

25. Ibid., A10.

26. Fadel Kane, "Penetration of HIV-1 in a Rural Area of Senegal," *Abstracts* 2 (San Francisco: Sixth International Conference on AIDS, 1990), 231.

27. *New York Times* (November 16, 1990), A10.

28. "Statistics from the World Health Organization and the Centers for Disease Control," *AIDS* 4 (August 1990), 825.

29. U.S. Department of Health and Human Services, *HIV/AIDS Surveillance Report* (December 1990), 3.

30. Panos Dosier 1, *AIDS and the Third World* (London: The Panos Institute, 1988), p. 136.

31. Pedro Chequer et al. "Survival in Adults AIDS Cases, Brazil, 1980–1989," *Abstracts* 1 (San Francisco: Sixth International Conference on AIDS, 1990), 143.

32. C. A. Moraís de Sá, et al. "Comparison of Tuberculosis in HIV-Positive and HIV-Negative Inpatients in Rio de Janiero, Brazil," *Abstracts* 1 (San Francisco: Sixth International Conference on AIDS, 1990), 245.

33. D. Bergamaschi et al., "Epidemiological Approach to Pediatric AIDS Cases in Brazil, 1985–1989," *Abstracts* 1 (San Francisco: Sixth International Conference on

AIDS, 1990), 303; see also E. Moreira et al., "Clinical Manifestations of AIDS in Salvador, Brazil," *Abstracts* 2 (San Francisco: Sixth International Conference on AIDS, 1990), 187.

34. C. A. Carvalho et al., "Evaluation of the Educational Training Programme to Professionals That Work with Street Kids in São Paulo, Brazil," *Abstracts* 3 (San Francisco: Sixth International Conference on AIDS, 1990), 110.

35. W. Ude et al., "Risk Behavior for HIV Infection Among Street Youth in Brazil," *Abstracts* 3 (San Francisco: Sixth International Conference on AIDS, 1990), 106.

36. Thomas C. Quinn, Jai P. Narain, and Fernando R. K. Zacarias, "AIDS in the Americas: A Public Health Priority for the Region," *AIDS* 4 (August 1990), 709.

37. Ibid., 719.

38. Ibid.

39. Ibid., 709.

40. "Statistics from the World Health Organization and Centers for Disease Control," *AIDS* 4 (December 1990), 1305; see also Alain Pompidou, "National AIDS Information Programme in France," in *AIDS Prevention and Control,* World Health Organization (Oxford: Pergamon Press, 1988), p. 28.

41. Allan Rosenfield, "Maternal Mortality in Developing Countries: An Ongoing but Neglected 'Epidemic,' " *Journal of the American Medical Association* 26 (July 21, 1989), 376–379.

42. Panos Dossier 1, p. 81.

43. Jonathan Mann, "Global AIDS: Epidemiology, Impact, Projections, Global Strategy," in *AIDS Prevention and Control,* World Health Organization (Oxford: Pergamon Press, 1988), p. 7.

44. "AIDS in Africa: A Killer Rages On," *New York Times* (September 16, 1990), A10.

45. Panos Dossier 1, p. 81.

46. "AIDS in Africa: A Killer Rages On," A10.

47. R. M. Anderson, R. M. May, and A. R. McLean, "Possible Demographic Consequences of AIDS in Developing Countries," *Nature* 332 (March 17, 1988), 228.

48. Ibid., 233.

49. R. Tapia-Conyer, "The Economic Impact of AIDS in Mexico," *Abstracts* 2 (San Francisco: Sixth International Conference on AIDS, 1990), 120.

50. Halfdan Mahler, Opening Address, World Summit of Ministers of Health on Programs for AIDS Prevention, January 26–28, 1988, in *AIDS Prevention and Control* (Geneva: World Health Organization, 1988), xix.

51. See, for example, the editorial and three theme articles in *Journal of Pastoral Care* 63 (Winter 1989), 293–335.

52. "AIDS in Africa: A Killer Rages On," A10.

53. Mann, "AIDS—A Global Challenge," *AIDS: Prevention and Control,* p. 1.

54. Mary Catherine Bateson and Richard Goldsby, *Thinking AIDS* (Reading, Mass.: Addison-Wesley Publishing Co., 1988), p. 10.

55. Wendell L. Willkie, *One World* (New York: Simon & Schuster, 1943).

56. See, for example, "Citizen of the World," an editorial in the *Washington Post* (November 26, 1963).

57. Panos Dossier 1, p. 56.

58. The Administrative Board, United States Catholic Conference, *The Many Faces of AIDS* (Washington, D.C.: Office of Publishing and Promotion Services, 1987), p. 2.

59. Carlos Ferreros et al., "Social Marketing of Condoms for AIDS Prevention in Developing Countries: The Zaire Experience," *Abstracts* 3 (San Francisco: Sixth International Conference on AIDS, 1990), 263.

60. " 'Social Marketing' of Condoms Helps Combat AIDS in Zaire," *New York Times* (September 18, 1990), A6.

61. Ibid.

62. A. Theodore Eastman, *Christian Responsibility in One World* (New York: Seabury Press, 1965), p. 84.

Chapter 8: Conclusion

1. Thomas W. Ogletree, *Hospitality to the Stranger* (Philadelphia: Fortress Press, 1975), p. 3.
2. Ibid.
3. Ibid., p. 5.
4. Stanley Hauerwas, *A Community of Character* (London: University of Notre Dame Press, 1981), pp. 26–27.
5. Parker J. Palmer, *The Company of Strangers* (New York: Crossroad, 1983), pp. 22–23.
6. Ibid., p. 23.
7. Ibid., p. 64.
8. Babylonian Talmud, Sanhedrin, 98a.
9. D. Moody Smith, "Theology and Ministry in John," in *A Biblical Basis for Ministry,* ed. Earl E. Shelp and Ronald H. Sunderland (Philadelphia: Westminster Press, 1981), p. 226.
10. Ronald H. Sunderland, "The Character of Servanthood," in *The Pastor as Servant,* ed. Earl E. Shelp and Ronald H. Sunderland (New York: Pilgrim Press, 1986), p. 41.
11. Walter Brueggemann, "The Prophet as Destabilizing Presence," in *The Pastor as Prophet,* ed. Earl E. Shelp and Ronald H. Sunderland (New York: Pilgrim Press, 1985), p. 49.
12. Ibid., p. 57.
13. Palmer, p. 65. Cf. Heb. 13:2, RSV: "Do not neglect to show hospitality to strangers."
14. Brueggemann, p. 58.
15. Earl E. Shelp and Ronald H. Sunderland, "AIDS and the Church," *Christian Century* (September 11–18, 1985), 797–800. See also Earl E. Shelp, Edwin DuBose, and Ronald H. Sunderland, "AIDS and the Church: A Status Report," *Christian Century* (December 5, 1990), 1135–1137.

Selected References

Chapter 1: The Evolving HIV/AIDS Crisis

"AIDS Center Run by Archdiocese." *New York Times,* October 28, 1985, p. B3.

"AIDS Crisis Action." *Christian Century,* November 20, 1985, p. 1056.

Berger, Joseph. "Working with AIDS Patients Tests Clerics Nationwide in Difficult Ways." *New York Times,* January 10, 1986, p. 11.

"The Church's Response to AIDS." *Christianity Today,* November 22, 1985, pp. 50–52.

Godges, John. "Religious Groups Meet the San Francisco AIDS Challenge." *Christian Century,* September 10–17, 1986, pp. 771–775.

Goldman, Ari L. "Clerics Offering Support on AIDS." *New York Times,* February 24, 1985, p. 32.

"Help for AIDS Victims." *Christian Century,* February 26, 1986, pp. 201–202.

Rohter, Larry. "Pastor Scolds Parish for Rejecting an AIDS Shelter." *New York Times,* September 2, 1985, pp. 1, 25.

Shelp, Earl E., and Ronald H. Sunderland. "Houston's Clergy Consultation on AIDS: Uniting for a Compassionate Reconciliation." *Christianity and Crisis,* March 2, 1987, pp. 64–66.

Chapter 2: The HIV/AIDS Epidemic

Bayer, Ronald, Daniel M. Fox, and David P. Willis, eds. "AIDS: The Public Control of an Epidemic." *Milbank Quarterly,* vol. 64 (Supplement 1, 1986).

Cassens, Brett J. "Social Consequences for the Acquired Immunodeficiency Syndrome." *Annals of Internal Medicine,* vol. 103 (November 1986), pp. 768–771.

Cohen, Mary Ann, and Henry W. Weisman. "A Biopsychosocial Approach to AIDS." *Psychosomatics,* vol. 27 (April 1986), pp. 245–249.

DeVita, Vincent T., Jr., Samuel Hellman, and Steven A. Rosenberg, eds. *AIDS: Etiology, Diagnosis, Treatment, and Prevention.* Philadelphia: J. B. Lippincott Co., 1985.

Dilley, James W., Earl E. Shelp, and Steven L. Batki. "Psychiatric and Ethical Issues in the Care of Patients with AIDS." *Psychosomatics,* vol. 27 (August 1986), pp. 562–566.

Flavin, Daniel K., John E. Franklin, and Richard J. Frances. "The Acquired Immune Deficiency Syndrome (AIDS) and Suicidal Behavior in Alcohol-Dependent Homosexual Men." *American Journal of Psychiatry,* vol. 143 (November 1986), pp. 1440–1442.

Gallo, Robert C. "The AIDS Virus." *Scientific American,* January 1987, pp. 46–56.

———. "The First Human Retrovirus." *Scientific American,* December 1986, pp. 88–98.

Gartner, Suzanne, et al. "Virus Isolation from and Identification of HTLV-III/LAV-Producing Cells in Brain Tissue from a Patient with AIDS." *Journal of the American Medical Association,* vol. 256 (November 7, 1986), pp. 2365–2371.

Holland, Jimmie C., and Susan Tross. "The Psychosocial

and Neuropsychiatric Sequelae of the Acquired Immunodeficiency Syndrome and Related Disorders." *Annals of Internal Medicine,* vol. 103 (November 1985), pp. 760–764.

Institute of Medicine and National Academy of Sciences. *Confronting AIDS: Directives for Public Health, Health Care, and Research.* Washington, D.C.: National Academy Press, 1986.

———. *Mobilizing Against AIDS: The Unfinished Story of a Virus.* Cambridge, Mass.: Harvard University Press, 1986.

Jaret, Peter. "Our Immune System: The Wars Within." *National Geographic,* vol. 169 (June 1986), pp. 706–734.

Laurence, Jeffrey. "The Immune System in AIDS." *Scientific American,* December 1985, pp. 84–93.

Levine, Carol, and Joyce Bermel, eds. "AIDS: The Emerging Ethical Dilemmas." *Hastings Center Report,* August 1985, Special Supplement.

———. "AIDS: Public Health and Civil Liberties." *Hastings Center Report,* December 1986, Special Supplement.

Levy, Robert M., Dale E. Bredesen, and Mark L. Rosenblum. "Review Article: Neurological Manifestations of the Acquired Immunodeficiency Syndrome (AIDS): Experience at UCSF and Review of the Literature." *Journal of Neurosurgery,* vol. 62 (April 1985), pp. 475–493.

Mills, Michael, Constance B. Wofsy, and John Mills. "The Acquired Immunodeficiency Syndrome: Infection Control and Public Health Law." *New England Journal of Medicine,* vol. 314 (April 3, 1986), pp. 931–936.

Morin, Stephen F., Kenneth A. Charles, and Alan K. Malyon. "The Psychosocial Impact of AIDS on Gay Men." *American Psychologist,* vol. 39 (November 1984), pp. 1288–1293.

Nichols, Stuart E. "Psychosocial Reactions of Persons

with the Acquired Immunodeficiency Syndrome." *Annals of Internal Medicine,* vol. 103 (November 1985), pp. 765–767.

Purtilo, Ruth, Joseph Sonnabend, and David T. Purtilo. "Confidentiality, Informed Consent, and Untoward Social Consequences in Research on a 'New Killer Disease' (AIDS)." *Clinical Research,* vol. 31 (1983), pp. 462–472.

Quinn, Thomas C., Jonathan M. Mann, James W. Curran, and Peter Piot. "AIDS in Africa: An Epidemiologic Paradigm." *Science,* vol. 234 (November 1986), pp. 955–963.

Steinbrook, Robert, et al. "Ethical Dilemmas in Caring for Patients with the Acquired Immunodeficiency Syndrome." *Annals of Internal Medicine,* vol. 103 (November 1985), pp. 787–790.

Stoler, Mark H., et al. "Human T-Cell Lymphotropic Virus Type III Infection of the Central Nervous System." *Journal of the American Medical Association,* vol. 256 (November 7, 1986), pp. 2360–2364.

Thomas, Christopher S., et al. "HTLV-III and Psychiatric Disturbance." *Lancet,* August 17, 1985, pp. 395–396.

Chapter 6: HIV/AIDS Ministries

Altman, Dennis. *Homosexual: Oppression and Liberation.* New York: Avon Books, 1973.

———. *The Homosexualization of America: The Americanization of the Homosexual.* New York: St. Martin's Press, 1982.

Bell, Alan P., and Martin S. Weinberg. *Homosexualities: A Study of Diversities Among Men and Women.* New York: Simon & Schuster, 1978.

Boswell, John. *Christianity, Social Tolerance, and Homosexuality.* Chicago: University of Chicago Press, 1980.

Brunswick, Ann F., and Peter Messeri. "Drugs, Lifestyle, and Health: A Longitudinal Study of Urban

Black Youth." *American Journal of Public Health,* vol. 76 (January 1986), pp. 52–57.

Cohen, Arie. "A Psychosocial Typology of Drug Addicts and Implications for Treatment." *International Journal of the Addictions,* vol. 21 (1986), pp. 147–154.

D'Emilio, John. *Sexual Politics, Sexual Communities: The Making of a Homosexual Minority in the United States, 1940–1970.* Chicago: University of Chicago Press, 1983.

Edwards, George R. *Gay-Lesbian Liberation: A Biblical Perspective.* New York: Pilgrim Press, 1984.

Lidz, Charles W., and Andrew L. Walker. *Heroin, Deviance, and Morality.* Beverly Hills, Calif.: Sage Publications, 1980.

Nelson, James B. *Embodiment: An Approach to Sexuality and Christian Theology.* Minneapolis: Augsburg Publishing House, 1978.

Newcomb, Michael D., and P. M. Bentler. "Substance Use and Ethnicity: Differential Impact of Peer and Adult Models." *Journal of Psychology,* vol. 120 (January 1986), pp. 83–95.

Nugent, Robert, ed. *A Challenge to Love: Gay and Lesbian Catholics in the Church.* New York: Crossroad Publishing Co., 1983.

Scanzoni, Letha, and Virginia Ramey Mollenkott. *Is the Homosexual My Neighbor?* San Francisco: Harper & Row, 1978.

Segal, Bernard. "Intervention and Prevention of Drug-Taking Behavior: A Need for Divergent Approaches." *International Journal of the Addictions,* vol. 21 (1986), pp. 165–173.

Serban, George, ed. *Social and Medical Aspects of Drug Abuse.* Jamaica, N.Y.: SP Medical and Scientific Books, 1984.

Shelp, Earl E. "Pastor, I Think I'm Gay." *Christian Ministry,* vol. 10 (March 1979), pp. 18–19.

Shiffman, Saul, and Thomas A. Wills. *Coping and Substance Abuse.* Orlando, Fla.: Academic Press, 1985.

Tripp, C. A. *The Homosexual Matrix.* New York: New American Library, 1976.

Weinberg, George. *Society and the Healthy Homosexual.* Garden City, N.Y.: Doubleday & Co., Anchor Books, 1973.

Weinberg, Martin S., and Colin J. Williams. *Male Homosexuals: Their Problems and Adaptations.* New York: Penguin Books, 1975.